Cultural Studies
as Critical Theory

Cultural Studies as Critical Theory

Ben Agger

The Falmer Press

(A member of the Taylor & Francis Group)
London • Washington, DC

UK   The Falmer Press, 4 John St., London WC1N 2ET
USA   The Falmer Press, Taylor & Francis Inc., 1900 Frost Road, Suite 101, Bristol, PA 19007

© 1992 Ben Agger

First published 1992

A catalogue record for this book is available from the British Library

Library of Congress Cataloging in Publication Data are available on request

ISBN 1 85000 964 3
ISBN 1 85000 965 1 (pbk)

Typeset in 9.5/11 pt Bembo
by Graphicraft Typesetters Ltd., Hong Kong

Printed and bound in Hong Kong

Contents

For Sarah Rose Agger-Shelton
(born August 3, 1991)

Acknowledgments

I am indebted to a number of people for their assistance with this project. Doug Kellner and Tim Luke read the whole manuscript. Their own work has helped me better understand the possibilities of cultural studies. Ray Morrow shared some of his work on cultural studies, informing this project with his sense of the priorities for an applied critical theory. John O'Neill's work, from which I have learned a great deal, is an important contribution to cultural studies *avant la lettre*.

Jacinta Evans and Ivor Goodson at Falmer helped immensely with this project, as they always do. Margaret Christie did a great job of copyediting. Kate Hausbeck, a graduate student in Sociology at SUNY-Buffalo, did timely legwork and careful checking on this project. She also helped me prepare the special issue of *Current Perspectives in Social Theory* on cultural studies – an activity that paralleled and informed the writing of this book.

Beth Anne Shelton offered her support of this project, both as colleague and partner. She patiently indulged me when I read the best parts of this manuscript aloud to her! Our ongoing discussions and writing about the Marxism/feminism relationship are an important anchor of my version of critical theory.

Ben Agger
Buffalo, NY
July 24, 1991

Chapter 1

What is Cultural Studies?

American and British university campuses are alive with new forms of interdisciplinary research. Although these activities are diverse and have multiple foci, they can broadly be grouped under the general heading of *cultural studies*. A recent *Chronicle of Higher Education* article ('Cultural Studies: Eclectic and Controversial Mix of Research Sparks a New Movement', January 31, 1990) trumpets this increasingly high-profile interdisciplinary project, depicting it as an important trend in scholarship that will probably leave its mark for many years to come. A later article in the *Chronicle* ('Protest at Cultural-Studies Meeting Sparked by Debate over New Field', May 2, 1990) reports heated controversies aired at a major cultural studies conference. Whether carried out in English departments or sociology departments, cultural studies challenges traditional assumptions of disciplinary scholars who plow the fields of cultural research in relative isolation from one another. This book is about cultural studies, both describing its multiple valences and arguing for a version of it that fits a certain intellectual and political agenda.

I devote the first two chapters to a discussion of the multiple forms of cultural studies as well as of the historical and sociological reasons for the ascendance of cultural studies. In the next five chapters I examine various theoretical approaches to cultural studies including Marxist theories of culture, the Frankfurt School, the Birmingham School, poststructuralism and postmodernism, and feminism. My three concluding chapters address the bifurcation between an essentially apolitical cultural studies and a cultural studies that is more directly engaged in the political contest over meaning and interpretive perspective. In arguing for the latter version of cultural studies, I integrate a variety of the aforementioned theoretical approaches that together comprise an interdisciplinary approach to culture.

Throughout this book I resist the tendency for 'cultural studies' to become another thoughtless slogan, even a whole new academic discipline. Although the institutionalization of critical insights and practices can often protect them, it also has the potential for defusing them. Although I consider myself to be a student of cultural studies, and my work in its various formulations contributes to a broad-gauged and politically relevant version of cultural studies, I am frustrated by the mounting tendency to turn cultural studies into a vacuous methodology for reading cultural texts that has no real political grounding. This is very much the fate of the poststructuralism methodologized into deconstruction in American literary departments. Indeed, the methodical version of cultural studies that I eschew owes a good deal to just this sort of Americanized poststructuralism. My frustration with this approach to cultural studies is intended to be nuanced enough that I can develop a more politically substantial approach to culture in my concluding chapter.

One of the central insights of cultural studies is that there is no single or singular version of it. In a certain sense, cultural studies resists programmatism – a definitive methodology and a discrete list of critical topics. Culture is found in every corner of late-capitalist society, undercutting the high-culture/popular-culture distinction. Thus, cultural studies resists a canonization of cultural products on which it focuses its attention. There is no canon, only a heterogeneity of cultural gestures, from science to science fiction. This is one of its great strengths, helping to reverse the tendency for cultural studies to become a discipline cut off from all the others. Given its interdisciplinary nature as well as its resistance to canons, cultural studies work is found all over the publishing terrain – in books cited throughout this study as well as in cross-disciplinary journals like *Cultural Studies, Cultural Critique, Social Text, Canadian Journal of Political and Social Theory, Current Perspectives in Social Theory, Representations, Discourse, Telos, New German Critique, Critical Studies in Mass Communication, Salmagundi, Media, Culture and Society, Signs, Feminist Studies* and many others.

If cultural studies is to be treated as a generic approach, one can talk about at least eleven common features, recognizing that this commonality contrasts with the diversity of ways in which actual cultural studies are carried out. It is also clear that there is no pregiven methodology of cultural studies; I reconstruct these eleven common assumptions from the interpretive practices in which writers actually engage. Indeed, it is somewhat foreign to the decentered, theoretically eclectic tradition of cultural studies to stipulate either underlying assumptions or a political agenda (see Denzin, 1991). That is a weakness this book attempts to remedy. I would argue emphatically that cultural studies should be explicit about its implicit theoretical, political and methodological investments, thus anticipating the charge that cultural studies is but a hybrid version of cultural interpretation with no rigorous justification. In some measure, then, my attempt to codify cultural studies is an attempt to provide it with intellectual legitimacy in the university, acknowledging that academization can fatally deflect cultural studies from political engagements.

An Expanded Notion of Culture

Proponents and practitioners of cultural studies imply or suggest explicitly that 'culture' is not equivalent to the received high culture of various literary and philosophical canons. Rather, culture in the broad anthropological sense is any expressive activity contributing to social learning. The expansion of the notion of culture by students of cultural studies affects the ways in which popular culture is now conceptualized as a broad ensemble of everyday discursive practices that may well fall outside the traditional parameters of official culture, narrowly defined, and the ways that science is conceptualized as cultural discourse itself. Cultural studies both renders science self-reflexively discursive in post-positivist fashion and at the same time engages in a kind of meta-canonization (or, better, a deconstruction of canon) that opens cultural analysis to all sorts of interpretive possibilities, all the way from conversation analysis (see Mehan and Wood, 1975) to film and television criticism (e.g., Ryan and Kellner, 1988; Miller, 1988; Kellner, 1990).

A good deal of the momentum of cultural studies is provided by the poststructural turn in anthropology (e.g., Marcus and Fischer, 1986; Marcus, 1988), with its reflexive attention to the impact of anthropological discourse on the topics and people studied by anthropologists as well as to the ways in which culture is constituted from the ground up. Within sociology, this tendency, albeit not fertilized by poststructuralism, stems from Harold Garfinkel's (1967) ethnomethodological version of social phenomenology, with his stress on the communicative constitution of meaning in everyday life. Since the American translation of poststructuralism, sociology has also begun to metabolize poststructural insights into the ways that science itself both frames and reflects sociological data, thus leading to a deeper, more methodical self-reflection (e.g., Lemert, 1979; Brown, 1987, 1989; Agger, 1989b) than the kind originally recommended by Gouldner (1970) and Friedrichs (1970).

It is also clear that much of the impetus behind the expansion of the notion of culture, and thus the enhancement of the relevance of culture, comes from the sweeping transformations in information technology after World War Two especially as these have influenced the huge baby-boom generation, both as cultural producers and consumers. The television generation received its cultural formation from situation comedies, variety shows and the coverage of political disasters, as I pursue further in Chapter 9. The ascendance of television, movies and rock music as formative influences is in contrast to the decline of the influence of the traditional patriarchal family on children's values and behavior (for better and worse). Popular culture matters like never before (see Ross, 1989). Vestiges of traditional high culture like classical music are either dying out because people under 40 do not regularly attend or are being turned into 'pops' programs.

More things 'count' as culture than ever before because electronic media have turned the globe into McLuhan's (1989) putative 'global village'. Although the technological-determinist and modernist implications of this line of argument must be resisted (and they usually are not, whether in McLuhan (1967, 1968) or Bell (1973)), the televisionization of public life (Luke, 1989) cannot be ignored as a crucial political factor in late capitalism. The sheer explosion of culture (e.g., 50,000 books published per year in the US) is matched by what Habermas (1984, 1987b) calls its increasing colonization of the lifeworld as well as psyche of global citizens. Elite culture is being undermined not least by the 'mechanical reproduction' that Walter Benjamin (1969) hoped could function to promote political education and hence liberation. I believe that Benjamin was wrong to conflate the mechanical reproduction of culture in general with the liberating potential of particular types of culture – whether *The Communist Manifesto* or the painting *Guernica*. Nevertheless, we cannot somehow bypass the extensive terrain of electrified popular culture in theorizing about and intervening to change the present social world.

The Legitimacy of Popular Culture

As I just noted, poststructural reflexivity is responsible for a good deal of the broadening of cultural analysis to include topics and approaches heretofore ignored by more traditional aesthetic theorists. Another factor in the broadening of cultural analysis is the growing legitimacy of popular culture itself as a venue of critical activity and intervention. Of course, this is a chicken-and-egg phenomenon: the growing legitimacy of popular culture as a thematic topic is redoubled by the influences of cultural analysts willing to entertain a broad critical agenda. The rise of journalistic television criticism is only one relevant example here. Pauline Kael's film criticism in *The New Yorker* has singularly expanded the cultural canon and elevated the status of the film critic herself.

The decanonization of bourgeois high culture might well be viewed as a kind of deconstruction, the inevitable result of a certain tendency for high culture, by virtue of its very 'height', to come unhinged from the lifeworlds by comparison to which it has historically been seen as an elevation. It might well be argued that earlier Romantic concepts of high culture were bound to erode under siege by the tendencies of what Walter Benjamin called mechanical reproduction in the realm of culture. And these tendencies (which Benjamin, unlike Adorno, lauded for their emancipatory potential) had to do with the rise of the 'culture industry', as Horkheimer and Adorno (1972) called it (see Chapter 4). According to them, the rise of popular culture both reflects and reproduces the rise of capitalism; the popularization of culture sedates large groups of people against their own alienation and at the same time helps check the tendencies of the rate of profit to fall by priming cultural production and consumption. The television, video and movie businesses are massive in their own right (Schiller, 1989).

Unlike some of the members of the original Frankfurt School like Horkheimer and Adorno, most proponents of cultural studies refuse to devalue the realm of popular culture as inherently inferior by comparison to earlier forms of high culture, notably modernism (see Huyssen, 1986). They insist that popular culture is a legitimate subject of academic inquiry because *culture matters*; it is serious business (see Chapter 2) and thus should be taken seriously. There is a certain populism in this insistence, a refusal to vouchsafe mandarin high culture in the fashion of the original Frankfurt School. One of the recurring themes in this book is the interplay between the cultural criticism offered by Frankfurt School theorists like Adorno and Marcuse, on the one hand, and the cultural studies approaches of post-Frankfurt theorists and students of culture, on the other. The Frankfurt sociology of culture is enormously relevant in that it represents the first significant revision of the Marxist theory of culture, via Lukács. One can periodize left-wing cultural theories this way: first, Marx, and his more or less derivative model of culture as an epiphenomenon of the economic system; second, the Frankfurt School theorists (through Lukács) who accorded culture a kind of relative autonomy largely unforeseen by Marx; third, the current generation of proponents of cultural studies who push the Frankfurt theory of culture one step further in order to encompass a larger terrain, and thus tolerance, of popular culture as a legitimate area of scholarly inquiry as well as political intervention.

To some extent this periodization oversimplifies a blurry past. Marx held a more dialectical theory of culture than is commonly presumed by both orthodox economistic Marxists and post-Marxist poststructuralists (e.g., see Horkheimer and Adorno, 1972). As well, the Frankfurt thinkers, especially Marcuse (1968, 1969), were less impervious to the redemptive possibilities of popular culture than meets the eye. Adorno's modernist perspective in his *Philosophy of Modern Music* (1973c) is somewhat offset by his brilliant essays on radio (1945), television (1954) and journalism (1974b) composed during and after World War Two. Finally, certain approaches to cultural studies retain the sense of continuity between modernism and postmodernism, refusing to jettison Marxism altogether (e.g., Eagleton, 1976, 1983, 1984, 1986, 1990a, 1990b; Huyssen, 1986; Ryan, 1989). As always, periodization simplifies a nuanced reality in order to generalize conveniently.

My main argument in this book is that cultural studies today splits into a conformist, comfortable version notable for its methodological approach to cultural reading (see Chapter 8) and a more critical version that can be traced directly to the inspiration of the Frankfurt School, albeit fertilized with insights from less mandarin perspectives on culture, especially that of the Birmingham School (see Chapters 9 and 10). A conformist cultural studies remains atheoretical and apolitical. The more critical version recognizes that cultural reception, including cultural studies itself, must become a form of dehierarchized cultural production in a new society. I argue for a cultural studies that locates its analytical activity in an everyday life structured by the dominant discourses of the quotidian preaching adjustment, acquiescence, accommodation (see Lefebvre, 1971; Brown, 1973). I conceive of cultural studies in its best sense as an activity of critical theory that directly decodes the hegemonizing messages of the culture industry permeating every nook and cranny of lived experience, from entertainment to education. In this sense, like Jacoby (1987) in different terms, I want to deacademize cultural studies, refusing its disciplining into yet another set of courses, methodologies, journals and conferences utterly cut off from the political reality that they purport to address.

In this sense, then, the stress on the legitimacy of popular culture as a relevant realm of academic investigation helps legitimate a peculiarly apolitical version of cultural studies. That is no surprise where we recognize that popular culture is notable for its apolitical character – its transcendence of the old-fashioned modernist 'isms' (e.g., Bell, 1960) allegedly characteristic of a stage of capitalism during which high and low culture were more sharply divided. Much of the cultural studies movement is an effort to professionalize an atheoretical, apolitical approach to the analysis of popular culture. *Cultural studies* is the technical term people often use in order to legitimize their fascination with mass culture; it gives them a certain academic authority and seems to avoid the more radical connotations of terms like the 'critique of ideology', which is what Marxists view as the proper project of cultural analysis and intervention.

Perhaps it is harsh to suggest that baby-boom academics raised on popular culture now cultivate 'cultural studies' as a way to get tenure while continuing to watch lots of television. Yet there are numerous cultural studies scholars who hoard vast video libraries that constitute their data bases (but see Ryan and Kellner, 1988, for a strongly politicized film critique). They haunt theaters, video stores and concerts in order to translate their own preoccupation with pop-culture into a respectable academic exercise. By the same token, perhaps it is overly self-congratulatory for those of us who imagine ourselves to be radical theorists of culture to imagine that we are made of more virtuous stuff. After all, I, too, am interested in the *Camera Obscura* article on the television show *thirty-something* (Torres, 1989). How the study of popular culture can become a mode of political practice is a topic I reserve for my last chapter. Like all dualities, the dichotomy of conformist-versus-radical cultural studies deconstructs upon close inspection. It is not exactly a matter of 'us' against 'them'. Both sides of the cultural studies divide meet around certain issues of common concern, like these eleven features of cultural studies theory that I am in the midst of outlining.

Cultural studies is extremely seductive for those of us who grew up with television and mass movies and recognize their powers of distortion, deception and suggestion. To some extent, we succumb to those temptations precisely because culture matters today more than ever, both deepening servitude (advertising is a modal example here, of course; see Williamson, 1978) and suggesting the promise of liberation. What Habermas (1981b) has called 'new social movements' all pivot around cultural politics, of women and people of color especially. But cultural studies has its downside: the world is not simply a performance or text, although all performances and texts, including cultural studies, are worlds in their own right. It is important to retain the distinction between cultural critique and cultural performance, even recognizing that cultural critique is an intervention in its own right.

Culture is Us

As I noted, we baby-boomers are immensely attracted to cultural studies because we learned our identities from culture. Although we may distance ourselves from the television shows, movies and magazines that distinctively mark our generational experiences, shrugging them off in a cynical postmodern way, at some level we recognize that our experience has been constituted by media. As such, media politics cannot be ignored or denied, as Gitlin (1980) has shown in his analyses of the televisionization of the New Left. But this is not merely a strategic matter. At a deeper level, we *are* popular culture – we identify ourselves not only with the generational events that are enormously signifying for us but also with the production and reception of those events through cultural forms like television. Indeed, these blur together: as I develop in Chapter 9, the generational experience of the Kennedy assassination is defined by how we watched the jarring events on television. Cultural studies would examine the cultural politics of the Kennedy assassination in terms of how viewers both constituted and were constituted by the events unfolding before our very eyes, marking us forever.

In this sense, cultural studies brings the world home, much as it is brought home through its visual and literary reception. The global village, like all villages, is a familiar place, with a well-known backdrop of habits, norms, facades and people. The CBS eye is as familiar to many of us as the Statue of Liberty was to earlier generations of European immigrants to America. We all recognize the White House or 10 Downing Street in the backgrounds of national news reports on their front steps. The craggy visage of Reagan and the cosmeticized visage of Michael Jackson are commonplace to billions. Cultural studies addresses familiar scenes, taken-for-granted knowledge, the quotidian. It is virtually a study of everyday life, albeit frequently the everyday lives of the rich and famous. (As of this writing, though, one of the most popular American television shows screens home videos taken by average citizens!)

The first generation raised on television is 'us', baby-boomers born between about 1947 and 1960. The height of the baby boom was 1957, when the largest number of children-per-woman was born in the US. Although cultural studies in the English-speaking world officially began with Richard Hoggart's (1957) *The Uses of Literacy* and the subsequent formation of the Birmingham Centre for Contemporary Cultural Studies in 1964 (run by Stuart Hall after 1968), it is clear that cultural studies is a baby-boom phenomenon, both engaged in by and addressed to the unique experiences of the television generation. Although cultural studies is not only about television, the sorts of social and personal changes inaugurated by mass television are the points of departure for this new approach to the study of culture.

People are fascinated by themselves, especially in this psychologistic age. We who do cultural studies watch ourselves watching the electronic media. We refuse the passive, unreflexive roles scripted for us by those who produce this culture. Instead, we attempt to monitor the changes subtly brought about by our own exposure to these epochal media. When I remember the early days of the US space program, I recall not only the events themselves – John Glenn's orbital flight, the beginning of the Apollo phase of the program, the first moon landing – but the ways I watched these events on television. In grade school we were gathered around classroom television sets as we watched the first lift-offs and participated in the emerging culture of the 'space race'. As with the Kennedy assassination, perhaps the most notable thing about these developments was the way we watched them together – our collective experience framing our participation in these media-ted events.

Cultural studies systematizes this attitude of reflexivity, attempting to learn from our own experience of watching history. In a sense, the practice of watching television serves as a useful metaphor here: baby-boomers watch ourselves watching by examining our own reflection in the screen. We then put these insights to work in cultural studies, as we make this experience of watching-ourselves-watch a substantive as well as methodological basis of our research program. I would argue emphatically that the major constitutional experience of the 1960s, for those of us who were baby-boomers, was not that we watched history through television and movies but that *we recognized this about ourselves*; we understood how history as what Baudrillard (1983) calls a simulation could be manipulated by those who wanted to change it.

Culture as Practice

This is the other side of the generational equation. We who watched history unfold televisually understood that reception (in the technical sense of screen theory) leads to cultural production – even to political transformation writ large. *Watchers are also potential cultural creators and historical subjects.* For example, people who organized and engaged in the various actions surrounding the Chicago Democratic Convention in 1968 (see Gitlin, 1980) understood clearly how 'the whole world is watching' – would be watching, on television and in the print media. The New Left staged its politics on the screen of popular culture. Its members recognized the formative and thus transformative power of the media, of culture generally, having grown up with those media. The New Left recognized that *culture is practice*, affording an opening to history heretofore denied mere 'receivers' of cultural stimuli.

A good deal of Birmingham cultural studies, as we shall see (Chapter 5), challenges traditional communication theory for its stimulus-response model of communication. Instead, reception is recognized to be a very powerful force of semiotic constitution in its own right, especially where it is theorized (in the way I just alluded to, above, with regard to the impact of the televisualized space program). Poststructuralism (Chapter 6) makes much the same point, indicating some of the common roots of Birmingham cultural studies, on the one hand, and postmodern and poststructural approaches to culture in the work of the *Tel Quel* group and Barthes, on the other. Although, ironically, television renders cultural consumers passive as never before, the reflexivity that television provokes – watchers-watching-themselves-watch – also leads to transformative cultural interventions.

One of the strongest insights of cultural studies is that culture is transacted between consumers and producers (via distributors). It is not simply laid on people from above, although typically in capitalism culture is differentially controlled and disseminated by elites. Cultural studies recognizes that receivers are inherently empowered in the sense that they inevitably participate in the constitution of cultural meanings; culture is never simply provided from without, to use Lenin's telling phrase in a different context. To this extent, then, culture can be remade, even where it is controlled at the epicenter of global capitalism's global village. There are varying emphases within cultural studies on the extent to which consumers help constitute cultural meanings and messages. The more traditionally Marxist cultural studies is, the less emphasis is placed on the active role of consumers in determining cultural meaning.

In this sense, cultural studies may contrast with the culture-critical themes of the original Frankfurt School and fall much more in line with certain poststructural insights stemming variously from Lacan, Derrida, Barthes and Althusser, who suggested in his important essay on ideological state apparatuses (1971) that ideology is 'lived practice' and not simply imposed from the outside. Although the modernist Frankfurt thinkers contended that certain cultural interventions could have political impact, notably modernism (e.g., Beckett, Kafka, Schoenberg for Adorno), they gave little attention to the self-deconstructing, self-transvaluing possibilities in mass culture itself. Their (e.g., Horkheimer and Adorno, 1972) analysis of the culture industry suggested few opportunities for practical, popular resistance to the dominant cultural ethos imposed from Hollywood and New York. This contrast between the Frankfurt and poststructural perspectives on cultural studies looms large where the interpretation of popular culture is concerned. The Frankfurt perspective suggests a somewhat resigned cultural politics, where poststructuralism promises a more engaged version of cultural studies as cultural intervention itself (although poststructuralist cultural studies splits into methodological and political versions, as I discuss in Chapter 9).

The notion that *culture is practice* has strong implications for what cultural analysts study (and for what is legitimated as official culture), a theme I touched on above in my discussion of the expansion of culture. Cultural studies has helped *detextualize* culture, opening cultural analysis to approaches of cultural constitution that may not result in traditional literary outcomes, notably the so-called Great Books. The concept of culture is expanded by students of cultural studies to include all sorts of oral, vocal and visual expressions that lie outside of 'literature' as defined in the Leavis tradition. This allows postmodernists to consider architecture as a 'text' of sorts (e.g., Barthes: 'The city is a discourse'), and feminists to attend to the media-ted representations of women by men (see Roman and Christian-Smith, 1988). Against the intolerance of mainstream cultural analysis that delegitimates non-literary culture, this approach allows film and television to become important critical topics (see Miller, 1988). More than anything else, perhaps, this expansion of the concept of cultural meaning and practice has revolutionized the approaches of cultural studies proponents in lasting ways. It is no longer possible for serious English departments to ignore film and media studies as important venues of meaning (although some still try!). The whole notion of textuality has been transvalued by cultural studies. Or, better, textuality has broadened under the influences of the entertainment and news industries in ways that make it impossible to ignore them in the halls of academe (see Altheide and Snow, 1979; Altheide, 1985).

Culture is Conflict (over Meaning)

Cultural studies proponents of all sorts, stemming from Hoggart's (1957) original analysis of working-class discourse, Raymond Williams' (1958) culture-and-society perspective, neo-Marxist theories of culture and feminist approaches to culture, contend that culture is not an undifferentiated system that serves to integrate society (e.g., Parsons, 1951, following Durkheim) but instead is a region of serious contest and conflict over meaning. For this reason, cultural studies proponents do not talk about a single culture but rather about many, often cross-cutting cultures – cultures of class, race, gender and nation, amongst others. Indeed, cultural politics is considered an important auxiliary of traditional class politics, more narrowly defined in economic terms.

Much of the inspiration for this line of analytical reasoning is owed to Gramsci (1971), who Hall (Hall and Whannel, 1965; Hall and Jefferson, 1976; Hall, 1978, 1980a, 1982, 1985, 1986, 1988) and the Birmingham School make central in their own versions of cultural studies. Gramsci's writings on hegemony and counter-hegemony remain central for most cultural studies perspectives, as do his comments about the transformational role of intellectuals. Going beyond Marx's more mechanical understanding of ideology, Gramsci, like subsequent western Marxists (see Lichtheim, 1961; Agger, 1979), understands culture or 'hegemony' to be a relatively autonomous region of experience and practice with respect to the capitalist economy proper. Indeed, as the Frankfurt thinkers demonstrate (e.g., Horkheimer, 1972), a dialectical Marxism quickly jettisons unidirectional causal understandings of the relationship between culture and economics in favor of a more unified perspective that they call critical theory. Hegemony for Gramsci and later western Marxists refers to the ways in which domination is not only produced from outside everyday life, through the huge structures of capital, but also from within everyday life by people more or less resigned to their fates as eternal subordinates – even cheerful about the 'goods' society.

One of the crucial differences between the Frankfurt perspective on cultural hegemony and the Gramsci perspective more characteristic of the Birmingham School (as well as the poststructural perspective) is that neo-Gramscians stress the dialectical properties of culture, notably the tendencies for cultural conflict to issue in real political change (see Morrow, 1991). Unlike the Frankfurt theorists who talked about culture as a monolith (e.g., the terms 'culture industry' and 'domination'), the neo-Gramscians of Birmingham cultural studies as well as poststructuralists stress the potential for cultural conflict to result in enlightening, even transformative outcomes. The Frankfurt theorists tended to deemphasize the conflicts within culture itself, wedded as they were to a historical model of capitalism that stressed its totalizing, totalitarian features (e.g., see Adorno, 1974a).

The inflections here are crucial: I do not believe that issues of culture can be dealt with a priori; they are empirical matters and must be addressed as such. Where Adorno, Horkheimer and Marcuse talked about cultural 'total administration' or 'one-dimensionality', they were making empirical claims about the imperviousness of capitalism to radical challenges and not engaging in speculative metaphysics. Whether or not capitalism today is equally monolithic is an open question, and one that I address in the course of this book. Some of my earlier (e.g., 1990) writing stresses the potentials within culture for conflicts to lead to aesthetic and political resistance and thus overall social change. But I have carefully tried to document this, refusing to decide this issue speculatively. Even then, of course, data do not speak for themselves. They have to be both constructed and interpreted.

Cultural studies emphasizes that culture is conflict over meaning – over how to assign value to human existence, expression, experience. Hegemonic culture attempts to define culture from the top down, in terms of the system's own needs for legitimation, productivism and consumerism. Counter-hegemonic culture resists these definitions and instead proposes alternative formulations of the good life. Conformist concepts of culture (e.g., the kind purveyed by Parsonian structural-functionalist sociology; see Alexander, 1982, 1985; Alexander and Seidman, 1990) stress the common sharing of values and meanings. Cultural studies proponents tend to emphasize the lack of consensus about common values, stressing the conflictual nature of values and meanings in capitalist, sexist and racist societies. They add that these conflicts are powerful initiators as well as symptoms of social change, not to be dispelled or suppressed.

Further, cultural studies proponents seek cultural conflict in surprising places. Ryan and Kellner (1988) in their book on the politics of mainstream film in the US stress the oppositional intent and effects behind a number of popular films, addressing the surfacing discontent experienced by many movie-goers. Against the Frankfurt School, it is not simply assumed that culture is total administration (or in Althusser's (1970) terms a 'structure in dominance'); rather, culture in its heterogeneity and multiplicity is irreducible to official narratives about it. Those fond of talking about singular values and meanings overlook or ignore oppositional cultures that spring up in surprising places and take heterodox forms. Feminist cultural studies has been especially helpful in pointing out the hegemonizing implications of official cultural approaches that equate male culture with the totality of culture, hence ignoring vital women's cultures that challenge male supremacy in effective ways (e.g., de Lauretis, 1984, 1987; Mulvey, 1988). As I discuss in Chapter 7, one of the most important political contributions of feminism to cultural studies lies in its thematization of cultural practices and traditions suppressed by dominant male culture, including the cultures of gay people.

In this sense, cultural studies challenges accounts of mainstream culture that ignore cultural alternatives. A good deal of this work is descriptive and narrational in nature: women's studies scholars and black studies scholars, for example, bring to light extant oppositional cultures of women, gays and people of color ignored by the mainstream canonization of legitimate cultural artifacts and practices. This frequently takes the form of oral histories through which women and people of color give voice to the cultural traditions, practices and meanings experienced by members of those groups (but occluded by the dominant culture). In this sense, these minority approaches to cultural studies deconstruct the culturally legitimating discourse of traditional literary studies, opening it to voices and versions that lie outside of canonized white literature proper but that are wholly legitimate and important in their own terms. This valorization of oral history and narration has a political downside, as well, where it renounces 'hard' (male) theorizing about social structures of oppression, an issue I pursue in Chapter 7.

Making Space: The Decentering and Decanonizing of Culture

Just as an expanded concept of culture forces cultural studies to expand commensurately, addressing non- or meta-textual forms of expression and experience, so cultural studies helps *decenter* cultural meaning and practice. In a sense, these are two sides of the same coin: where cultural studies addresses non-traditional forms of cultural expression (e.g., film), so we must also decenter cultural legitimacy in a way that fundamentally challenges elitism. This is a directly political project, as I noted in a somewhat different way in my earlier discussion of culture as conflict. Where cultural studies takes account of non-traditional modes and venues of cultural expression, from film to fiction, it implicitly places value on these expressions, denying the monolithic claims of traditional culture on moral legitimacy and thus critical attention. The decentering of culture is a political act that contributes significantly to the decentering of power and wealth. It is a fundamental challenge to the dominant order.

As we will see in Chapters 8 and 9, not all programs of cultural studies view themselves as political intervention. The decentering and decanonization of dominant culture are not the intents of a variety of approaches to cultural studies that view themselves mainly as academic contributions within an expanded repertoire of literary-critical scholarly activities and mass communication studies. There is a real struggle going on between proponents of a more politicized cultural studies (e.g., Ryan and Kellner, 1988; Luke, 1989; Ryan, 1989; Agger, 1990; Denzin, 1991), on the one hand, and more methodological proponents of cultural studies who view cultural studies as simply an expansion of the traditional scholarly agenda of the sociology of culture, literary criticism and communication studies, on the other (e.g., Wuthnow, 1976, 1987, 1989; Bellah *et al.*, 1985; Griswold, 1986; Lamont, 1987). The first group wants cultural decentering to have overtly political aims, empowering the culturally disenfranchised into both expressive and political action; the second group wants cultural decentering simply to expand the cultural canon so as to give academics a larger range of critical topics within the general model of value-free cultural interpretation (e.g., the so-called Yale School of American deconstruction is perhaps the most prominent example of this depoliticized, methodological approach to cultural studies). For the former group, cultural decentering serves political ends, whereas for the latter group cultural decentering makes available new interpretive techniques like deconstruction with which to read texts and cultural practices in value-free ways. I will argue later that deconstruction, once methodologized into yet another approach to literary criticism, defeats its own purpose by succumbing to the same objectivism it so deplores in the New Criticism (Ransom, 1941). Deconstruction, following Derrida, shows convincingly that all readings are 'interested' in Weber's sense. One might best ask: decentering for whom? and for what?

As in everything political, the lines between these two seemingly opposite versions of cultural decentering are clearer in theory than they are in practice. Even the methodologized deconstructive version of cultural studies that simply wants to expand the horizon of cultural and critical experience beyond official Great Books per se makes a political contribution of sorts, notably in *decanonizing* official culture. Even to suggest that certain non-mainstream figures and works have been left out of the literary and analytic canon is heretical, as Bloom's (1987) book evidences. The neoconservative assault on hairy, hip, leftish holdovers from the 1960s, who, it is argued, have single-handedly destroyed the traditional liberal arts curriculum, continues to gather momentum: colleges and universities are 'going back to basics', led by administrators and faculty armed with Bloom (1987) and Hirsch (1987) among others. But this neoconservative onslaught on the campus left (and center) is being contested vigorously by faculty, students and administrators who refuse to return to the good old days when the liberal arts canon consisted only of old-white-male authors and artists. They argue that the liberal arts should be broader than in the past, including works, authors and creators from among women and people of color – the subterranean or counter-classics.

The attempt to expand the canon per se, regardless of the degree of theoretical self-consciousness involved, is political action. At least, it challenges the preponderance of the dominant canon and the educational institution that administers it. *It makes curriculum a contested terrain*, one of the central contributions of the version of cultural studies advocated in this book. Indeed, as I will show below, the point of production of cultural studies is largely the university. Proponents of cultural studies attempt to challenge both traditional curricula and modes of scholarly evaluation in order to make space for alternative voices and versions. This activity of *making space* helps open the university to people heretofore closed out of it. In itself, this activity of making space is political work of the kind supported by many working in cultural studies today.

Differences arise over how extensive this academic deconstruction ought to be. As I discuss below, some proponents of cultural studies would not rest only with decentering and decanonizing curricula; they would argue for the wholesale dedisciplining of academic departments and specialties. They contend that the rebuilding of curricula outside of more extensive changes in the structure of academe matters little; it is only a beginning. Indeed, they argue that it is relatively easy for universities to coopt non-mainstream voices by including them in the prevailing curriculum, expanded to accommodate women and people of color. More radical cultural studies people argue that cultural studies' impact on the university ought to involve more than the politics of curricula – debates over reading lists, in effect. Cultural studies could become the basis of a new interdisciplinary critical theory that raises it to a higher, more politically self-conscious level (see Klein, 1990). But that is the argument of my concluding chapter. I am getting ahead of myself.

Production, Distribution, Consumption

Just as English department curricula have begun to change in light of the decanonization of literature and detextualization of culture generally, so the social sciences have begun to have an impact on an emerging cultural studies. This impact has mainly involved the analysis of interlocking, interdependent cultural institutions comprising the production, distribution and consumption of cultural commodities (e.g., see Schiller, 1989). My (1990) earlier book on literary political economy suggests the direction of this sort of work; in that study I considered how the political economies of trade publishing and academic writing have significant impact on what I call the 'decline of discourse'. Cultural studies, in its emphasis on culture as practice, helps us situate the creation of cultural artifacts in complex social and economic spaces within which creative activity is conditioned, even determined.

Some of this new empirical and theoretical activity has affected the way academics view themselves. Brodkey (1987) and I (1989b, 1989c, 1990) have done studies of what Brodkey calls 'academic writing as social practice', employing a variety of cultural studies insights and methods in order to examine the rhetorical features of academic discourse. A good deal of this reflexive approach to our own writing (also see Richardson, 1988, 1990a, 1990b, 1990c, 1991) stems from the major influence of poststructuralism on the analysis of discourse. As I remarked earlier, this sort of reflexivity is being carried out within and across disciplines (e.g., McCloskey, 1985; Marcus and Fischer, 1986; Agger, 1989a; Klein, 1990). All of this work together suggests that one of the crucial contributions of cultural studies lies in its heightening of the literary self-awareness of academics trained for years to view their prose and research writing as hollowly ritualistic. Instead, we learn, academic writing is a peculiar language game (Wittgenstein, 1953) that participates in the transaction of power, notably in the way in which authorial self-consciousness is either repressed or marginalized in science writing.

This is only one of the many ways that the sociological, political-economic and deconstructive examination of various cultural rhetorics helps differentiate cultural studies from more traditional approaches to the interpretation of culture (e.g., Leavis, the New Criticism; see Eagleton, 1983). It is hopeless to decontextualize cultural expression, especially where the culture industry is big business. Moreover, deconstruction instructs us that language itself is a con-text of sorts, imposing a particularly determinate meaning on those who attempt to 'use' language (but who end up being used in turn). Cultural studies broadens interpretive focus to include extra-textual aspects of a work's context (or, as I call it throughout this book, con-text). It does so dialectically, eschewing both the objectivism of the New Criticism and other pristine methodologies of close reading, on the one hand, and an economistic reductionism, on the other.

In this sense, much of the best work in cultural studies is heavily influenced by neo-Marxist and western-Marxist innovations in the traditional Marxist analysis of culture. Gramsci and the Frankfurt critics are examples of this. All of these people believed that culture is so dialectically intertwined with the economic functions of capitalism that the two spheres blur to the point of virtual indistinguishability. This is in contrast to the Althusserian emphasis on the 'relative autonomy' of culture, which, on the surface at least, appears to converge with this western-Marxist approach to culture. As I develop further in Chapter 3, the western-Marxist theory of culture refuses to separate culture from political economy, making it impossible even to talk about their relative autonomy or independence from each other. Instead – no small task – neo-Marxists want to analyze the complex conjuncture of culture and political economy in a way that refuses to decide causally between their respective contributions to domination (e.g., see Wright, 1985). Indeed, that multivariate approach to Marxism is rejected by most neo-Marxists as inherently dualist. Culture is not a realm apart, a separate variable.

All theoretical investments aside, even a bourgeois sociology of culture necessarily faces new challenges in this McLuhan era. It is simply impossible to ignore the corporate character of culture, including the circuitries of its distribution. Any analysis of the decline of discourse focuses on the impact of the displacement of small, independent bookstores by the massive chains like Waldenbooks and Folletts on publishers that gamble on the huge block-buster, jettisoning the midlist books that used to constitute publishers' source of regular income (Curtis, 1989). Television and film studios necessarily make distribution thematic, as well as the way this impacts on authorial vision and execution. These are not wild Marxist notions, although Marxism understood them first. They underwrite most approaches to cultural studies today, especially those heavily influenced by a left political agenda.

Popular Culture and Populism

Cultural studies proponents are not embarrassed by their new agenda of culture-critical topics, all the way from television soap operas to mass-market movies. Decanonization (e.g., see Nelson and Grossberg, 1988) is an absolutely central aim of all varieties of cultural studies discussed in this book. Decanonization can be phrased positively, where cultural studies not only addresses popular culture for its debasement and manipulated character but treats popular culture as a wellspring of emancipatory impulses (see Ross, 1989). There is a powerful populism about cultural studies that resists elitism in all fashions, sometimes against its own self-interest. It is somehow assumed that decanonization will liberate forgotten and suppressed voices to speak the truth in a way that is impossible from within the coordinates of classist, sexist, racist high culture (see Ryan, 1989). In other words, certain approaches to cultural studies refuse to equate the popular with cultural debasement and ideological enslavement. These strains of cultural studies point to the redemption of the popular (see Grossberg, 1986).

Much of cultural studies, especially in its Birmingham and feminist versions, is a reaction against the mandarinism of the Frankfurt School, with its high-cultural elitism and modernism (see Kellner, 1989a; Adorno, 1984). The popular is equivalent to the populist, a central positive value in both Derridean and ex-New-Left circles (e.g., see Fiske and Hartley, 1978; Fiske, 1987, 1989a, 1989b, 1990). One cannot overstate the constitutional importance of populism and populist standards of cultural evaluation in the cultural studies movement. Of course, it is easy to see how Adorno could be such a ready target: his disdain for the excesses and extravagances of 1960s youth culture is legend, as is his casual dismissal of jazz as 'fascist marching music'. I am no defender of Adorno's (1973c, 1984) sometimes arbitrary aesthetic judgments. But it is crucial not to paper over the real differences between different styles of cultural studies around this issue of the popular: the Frankfurt School's cultural studies had much less patience with the redemptive possibilities of popular culture than do Birmingham, Derridean and feminist approaches. This is not to say that the Frankfurt theorists lacked an analysis of the popular; it is their own analysis of the culture industry (Horkheimer and Adorno, 1972) that makes what we know as cultural studies possible. Rather, they refused to endorse the popular in an episodic exuberance. In short, they were not populists.

Populism is not the only issue here, as we shall see in Chapter 6 on postmodernism and poststructuralism. Derrida is hardly a populist, either. Yet he shares the rejection of Archimedean standards of aesthetic judgment typified by more Teutonic approaches to cultural evaluation, such as that of the Frankfurt School. Derrida's (e.g., 1976, 1978, 1981, 1987) radical relativism shares important features with American populism in its stress on the undecidable, irreducible nature of aesthetic evaluation. Derrida is Americanized in this sense in the work of certain poststructural feminists who harness his counter-metaphysical program to the interests of the women's movement (see Fraser, 1989). Cultural absolutism is the common enemy, whether the absolutisms of classicism, the liberal arts movement (e.g., Robert Hutchins) or the Frankfurt School. These absolutisms are rejected for their insensitivity to the heterogeneity of possible cultural subject positions in postmodern society (see Laclau and Mouffe, 1985).

Indeed, postmodernism is the cultural application of certain poststructural insights, as I (1990) have argued elsewhere. Populism and postmodernism both underwrite powerful versions of cultural studies, countering the putative elitism and mandarinism of the original Frankfurt School. In this sense, the theorists of the Frankfurt School are pivotal for subsequent cultural studies: they both initiate cultural studies in their extraordinarily wide-ranging and incisive studies of the culture industry (e.g., Horkheimer and Adorno, 1972; Adorno, 1945, 1954, 1974b) and they provide a critical foil for many post-Frankfurt cultural studies approaches, notably in the way their critique of mass culture invites a more populist approach to the study of the popular (see Zaret, 1992).

It is fair to say that cultural studies pivots around the Frankfurt version of it, if only in implicit ways. To be sure, the Birmingham School (e.g., Willis, 1977; Hall, 1980a, 1980b) rarely engaged the Frankfurt tradition directly; they were much more closely aligned with Gramsci (who, as Boggs [1976; also see Piccone, 1983] suggests, can readily be assimilated to the tradition of critical theory). Nevertheless, the Frankfurt theorists offered the most sustained challenge to the bourgeois sociology of culture as well as to Leavis-era literary theory since Marx, yet without endorsing the Zhdanovist reductionism and authoritarianism of the orthodox Marxist approach to cultural analysis and interpretation. Cultural studies, however hostile to alleged Frankfurt mandarinism, cannot ignore Frankfurt.

The central issue of dispute between populists and Derrideans, on the one hand, and Frankfurt theorists, on the other, is whether popular culture contains certain deconstructive and hence politically progressive tendencies (see Jameson, 1972, 1976–1977, 1981, 1984a, 1984b, 1991). Where Horkheimer and Adorno condemned the culture industry as the apex of late-capitalist total administration, cultural studies proponents by and large resist this blanket condemnation as lacking nuance. Instead, they argue that regular people not only see through the hegemonic haze of consumerism and positivism but that some actively struggle to create a new cultural world in the exemplary contexts of their own everyday lives. For the most part, the Frankfurt theorists paid no attention to *la vie quotidienne* except to notice that it was remarkably manipulated by external and internal imperatives. That is the whole drift of Marcuse's Freudianized Marxism: he analyzes the 'introjection' of self-neutralizing, self-defeating tendencies via the circuitries of what he (1955) called 'surplus repression' – addressing the way late capitalism mobilizes people in their own domination. His (1955) Freud book prepares the way for his (1964) later analysis of one-dimensionality, probably the sharpest and most accessible statement of the Frankfurt position on cultural hegemony.

As I explore in Chapter 4, Marcuse's Freudianization of Marxism allowed him (1969) to engage with, even momentarily to embrace, the 'new sensibilities' of the 1960s as prefigurative agents of a new world. Marcuse refuses to separate revolutionary product and process, arguing that real socialism must begin in the here and now, in the everyday lifeworlds of people committed to creating a better world embryonically in their own intimate lives. Habermas later (1984, 1987b) contrasts the colonizing imperatives of 'system' (encoded in money and power) with the self-reproducing and authentic realm of the 'lifeworld', from which consensus-building symbolically-mediated interaction is to flow in a decolonized world (also see Piccone, 1971; O'Neill, 1972; Agger, 1991a).

But Marcuse's patience with the otherwise anti-intellectual thrust of the American New Left, especially its counter-culture department, was short-lived. By 1972 he had largely recanted his optimism about the transformative impact of the New Left's attempt to create a new everyday life that could stand up to the challenges of rational administration as well as liberal democracy (see Marcuse, 1972). For his part, Habermas has never had much use for populist or Derridean everyday-life themes (see, e.g., Habermas' (1987a) response to poststructuralism); the concept of the lifeworld functions in his work less as a cultural resource than as a conceptual counterpoint to 'system'.

I will reserve a full discussion of the Frankfurt version of cultural studies until Chapter 4. Let me only acknowledge here the fault line of sorts separating Frankfurt cultural studies from Birmingham, postmodern and feminist versions. To decide in favor of one or another may well play into the very dualities so effectively deconstructed by Derrida as illusory. In fact, I will argue that we can have our cake and eat it, too: as a person closely affiliated to the general motif of the Frankfurt analysis of late capitalism, I want to be able to analyze and intervene in popular culture in a politically useful way. Indeed, one of the hallmarks of cultural studies is its theoretical eclecticism. Whether I can make this case stick depends in large measure on whether I can contextualize the Frankfurt antipathy to popular culture in a way that preserves the basic analytical logic of their position, which I regard as powerful. I also favor a populist, poststructural version of critical theory. I would like to believe that this is not a contradiction in terms.

Dedisciplining

Cultural studies is inherently interdisciplinary. It has to be interdisciplinary because traditional disciplines do not address phenomena of popular culture in a way that blends critical theory, literary theory, discourse analysis, women's studies, sociology and political economy. The traditional academic disciplines are simply too confining for people to pursue the diverse issues addressed by cultural studies scholars, all the way from film theory to the political economy of book publishing. Of course, interdisciplinarity is a fad, and has been for at least the last decade. Interdisciplinary centers, journals and courses proliferate. Much of this only reconfigures a stagnant academic world in trivial, cooptable ways. But that is no reason to reject the interdisciplinary effort of cultural studies, which is among the most fruitful interdisciplinary projects afoot today.

Cultural studies' interdisciplinary focus stems not simply from the fact that traditional specialized disciplines do not afford a sufficiently broad perspective on a complexly interrelated cultural life. It is also because, at some level, cultural studies shares the critique of the disciplinary society offered by Foucault and some of the Frankfurt thinkers (see Foucault, 1977; O'Neill, 1986; Poster, 1989, 1990; Agger, 1989b). This critique holds specialized academic disciplines responsible for contributing to overall domination by refusing a view of totality desperately needed in this stage of world capitalism, sexism and racism. Intellectual specialization, it is argued, makes its own special contribution to hegemony by falsely separating topics and methodologies that are fundamentally complementary.

This is especially true in the realm of culture. Where sociologists study some of the institutional mechanisms of popular culture, literary theorists view culture from a textual point of view. Their lack of common articulation frustrates efforts to examine culture from the simultaneous viewpoints of production, distribution and consumption. Indeed, few sociologists of culture make use of the latest continental developments in discourse theory that could help them move beyond, or beneath, the institutional analysis of culture in an important way (e.g., DiMaggio, 1986). For their part, the literary theory crowd too often eschew matters of political economy simply because they have been trained to view the text as a self-enclosed, self-sufficient world. These blind spots are less a matter of willful intellectual incompetence than of a trained incapacity to see the world in a totalizing way.

And even this talk of totality makes postmodernists uneasy (e.g., Lyotard, 1984; Kroker and Cook, 1986). Poststructuralism and postmodernism reject the subject-centered view of a universe that, according to the Enlightenment *philosophes*, could be rationally and completely understood through subjective reason – the project of the natural sciences, originally, and later the empirical social sciences. Totality is seen as a code word for tyranny (e.g., Poster, 1989). Hence there has been some significant resistance to interdisciplinarity among postmodernists who, ironically, accept Foucault's critique of the disciplinary society. Perhaps this is to say that there are different kinds of interdisciplinarity: a totalizing kind that, in Habermas' terms, aims at an interdisciplinary materialism sufficiently comprehensive so as to explain everything *versus* an interdisciplinarity fundamentally congruent with academic specialization and disciplinary identity. For the most part, left cultural studies proponents favor totalizing interdisciplinary scholarship. Yet there are those who view cultural studies not as a new metadiscipline but as a subfield within their own disciplines that can be pursued within the fundamental substantive and methodological assumptions of the disciplines in question. Some of these people reject the totalizing claims of cultural studies precisely because they share a postmodernist mistrust of any and all totalization. In a peculiar way, the hyperspecialization of academic disciplines fits the detotalizing agenda of postmodernism.

In general, most cultural studies proponents oppose the disciplinary society in Foucault's sense. They recognize that the fragmentation and specialization of knowledge lead to its hierarchization; as such, very much in Foucault's spirit, they try to check the contribution of academic disciplines to the reproduction of historical domination (e.g., as in Foucault's (1977) landmark study of the rise of the social category of criminality in his *Discipline and Punish*). More recent examples of disciplinary critique and self-critique are directed at the reigning positivism in American social science (e.g., Agger, 1989c). But, as I just indicated, there are different versions of this critique of disciplinarity. Some cultural studies people argue for more disciplinary flexibility and cross-fertilization; for these people, cultural studies tends to be an enclave within disciplines. More radical cultural studies people reject disciplinary boundaries as counterproductive and hegemonizing; for them, cultural studies is an example of what Habermas sweepingly calls interdisciplinary materialism.

This more radical version of disciplinary critique raises a host of practical as well as intellectual questions. Should academic disciplines/departments be abolished or recombined? How would this affect the institutional structure of the university, including publication, graduate training and teaching? Should we launch cultural studies programs, after the Birmingham model? Should marginal departments and programs like women's studies, black studies and American studies be the hosts of cultural studies? Does the recombination of disciplines and scholars only shuffle the deck but not change the institutional game? Could cultural studies departments make much difference within the bureaucratic university? What would be the unifying theories and methodologies behind cultural studies *qua* discipline?

My answers to these questions are necessarily personal. I want to defer them until my last chapter largely because I do not believe that the radical critique of discipline can productively ignore the various contributions of cultural studies approaches, however fragmented they may be. I am skeptical about whether creating cultural studies programs or departments will make much difference; indeed, I will argue for a version of cultural studies that extends far beyond the academy in order to become a mode of everyday life itself. This does not mean that we – academics – can dispense with the practical as well as theoretical and methodological implications of our disciplinary critiques. After all, the university plays a significant role in the reproduction of cultural hegemony as well as in the scientific–technical accumulation of power and wealth. Both the reformist and radical versions of disciplinary critique have been somewhat misfocused – the reformist version where it implants cultural studies as a subfield within disciplines, and the radical version where it entrenches cultural studies as a bona fide discipline (or counterdiscipline) in itself.

The most politically effective cultural studies work would deconstruct disciplines from within, questioning their very rights to exist *apart from* other disciplines. This burrowing from within could take a cultural studies perspective especially in the arts, humanities and human sciences, challenging a variety of dominant but differential assumptions all the way from textual objectivity to the positivist philosophy of science. Again, this sort of agenda–setting will have to await the last chapter. A note of caution here: cultural studies refuses to become a rigid program; its diversity and flexibility are its epistemological hallmarks. Thus, there is no single or static version of cultural studies, applicable across, or from within, each and every discipline. But that is precisely the power of the movement that has coalesced around the term 'cultural studies', as well as one of its shortcomings.

Cultural Studies and the Archimedean Problem

Most versions of cultural studies that diverge from the Frankfurt legacy oppose high-cultural mandarinism and elitism (e.g., Levine, 1988; Miller, 1988). This often takes the form of a poststructural aversion to the privileging of the role of the critic; it is emphatically maintained that critique is necessarily a vantage point from which to read and write about cultural products. Again, the fault line between a reformist and radicalized cultural studies, to be amplified in Chapters 8 and 9, reveals itself here: versions of cultural studies more indebted to the Frankfurt School are somewhat less relativist than cultural studies that flow from poststructuralism, postmodernism and poststructural feminism (via Lacan, Derrida, Barthes, Foucault and the French feminists).

Let me phrase the difference this way: the Frankfurt critics believed that *critique is a necessary vantage point* from which to evaluate cultural artifacts and the practices underlying them. By some contrast, the poststructural version of cultural studies suggests that *critique is not a privileged vantage point*, thus reducing some of the more universalist claims of mandarin cultural critics. Although there is a good deal of dense and important argumentation underlying these two contrasting positions, we can boil it down to the debate about false needs (see, e.g., Marcuse, 1964). The Frankfurt position holds that cultural critics can judge that certain cultural products and practices are inherently 'false', that is, they reproduce domination. Poststructuralists maintain that cultural critics have no reliable ground from which to make these assessments, given the undecidability of their own critical languages and given the 'difference/differance' that characterizes the world itself.

At some level, this debate is less important than the common assumption, made by both sides of this cultural studies divide, that cultural critique is necessarily a vantage point (if, for Frankfurt, a necessary and theoretically privileged one). All versions of cultural studies reject the objectivism of the New Criticism

– the notion that one can treat a cultural text or artifact strictly on its own terms, outside of the con-text that makes it a social text in the first place. Cultural studies in the UK arose out of Hoggart's (1957) work on the rhetorical codes of class; he refused to decontextualize working-class language. Neither Hoggart nor Stuart Hall and his cohorts at the Birmingham Centre pretended that they were free of political and social 'bias'. Indeed, Hall and his group are self-consciously devoted to a politically partisan version of cultural analysis and critique that debunks the false objectivity of traditional literary criticism and cultural inter-pretation.

By false objectivity I mean the assumption of Leavis-era critics as well as the New Critics that the reader can somehow bracket out his or her own critical interest altogether. Poststructuralism's strongest insight is that every reading is also a writing; that is, the reader brings a great deal to bear constitutionally on the sense of the text in question. There are no texts or works 'as such' any more than there are things-in-themselves, Kant's noumena. And every reading does its 'writing' in the service of certain critical, interpretive and political interests. For example, a feminist reading of *The Great Gatsby* interrogates Fitzgerald's gen-dered world from the vantage point of a certain feminist political interest that asks why Long Island men and women behave the way they do. For cultural studies scholars and feminist literary theorists that much seems obvious by now. But it flies in the face of decades of objectivist readings that suppose that *one* (a degendered, desubjectified Transcendental Reader) can simply exhume the mean-ing of Fitzgerald's work independent of the readerly or writerly interests at play in the practice of reading and writing.

Cultural studies denies the possibility of desubjectified readings, arguing that every reading necessarily takes a stand. Beyond this, poststructuralists argue that critique is not a privileged vantage, whereas Frankfurt critical theory argues that it is necessary for critique to take a stand, in spite of the imponderables of absolute judgment. In a sense, this disagreement is more a matter of emphasis than of substance. Poststructuralists and Frankfurters agree that every reading is interested; poststructuralists tend to deny the privilege of specialist readings, even those (like Frankfurt's) that derive this privilege not from transcendental qualities of interpretive privilege but from the methodical reflexivity that makes for heightened political self-consciousness – from the reader's true needs, it might be said.

I will reengage this issue in my concluding two chapters, where I address the emergent split in cultural studies between a methodologized, academized cultural studies and a more politicized, dehegemonizing version. Interestingly, the former version of cultural studies is owed to the poststructural critique of absolutism and Archimedeanism; the latter is owed to the Frankfurt neo-Marxism that privileges critique without ignoring the inherent limitations to the all-knowingness of critique itself. At issue here is the complex intermingling of epistemological relativism and critical practice. When one denies the privilege of readings, one may end up promoting endless readings ungrounded in more substantial notions of truth and justice. Although Nietzsche (1956) would seem irrelevant to a cultural studies book, this whole discussion raises what I (1990) have called the Nietzsche question – the ways in which readings of Nietzsche legitimate epistem-ological relativism (e.g., Lyotard's (1984) rejection of the grand 'metanarratives' of Marxism and the like), on the one hand, and a totalizing critique of the

Enlightenment, on the other (e.g., the original Frankfurt School). Although a rigorous exercise in Nietzscheology will not decide the issue in itself, it is important to trace the break between poststructuralism and Frankfurt critical theory to serious philosophical differences largely refracted in the reception of Nietzsche. The one significant point of contact between the otherwise hermetically separated French and German traditions of recent theorizing is the centrality of Nietzsche. The Germans turn Nietzsche into a sort of Marxist culture critic, following the lead of Horkheimer and Adorno (1972), while the French read Nietzsche as the harbinger of the postmodern – an era in which political judgments lose their grounding in any claim to absolute values.

The Rejection of Absolute Values

Having said this, I will seem to contradict myself when I suggest that all versions of cultural studies are fundamentally pluralist about what 'counts' as legitimate cultural expression and evaluation. It is tempting to read Frankfurt critical theory as absolute-idealist in the fashion of Hegel. That reading is virtually inescapable if we conduct that reading on the banks of the Seine, suffused by the French reception of Nietzsche and its concomitant post-Marxism. But the Frankfurt theorists, in their (Marxist) veneration of Reason, appear absolutist only with reference to French poststructuralism, whether in Derrida or Lacan. In fact, the original Frankfurt theorists recognized that the region of what Adorno (1973b) called the 'non-identical' guaranteed the political undecidability – democracy – insisted on by the French Derrideans. This is the argument suggested by Ryan (1982), where he shows the secret convergence of Adorno and Derrida. Horkheimer's and Adorno's (1972) critique of the Enlightenment opposes the false absolutism and objectivism of positivist science, demonstrating the dialectical alternation of myth and enlightenment under a regime of positivist certitude. As they argue, science is the most totalizing mythology where it installs itself as the only thought system somehow impervious to subjective interest and perspective.

The Frankfurt critique of science is the center of their critical theory. It enables them to explain the surprising resilience of late capitalism, surprising at least from the vantage of Marx's millennial mid-nineteenth-century optimism. The power of the scientific-technical apparatus of late capitalism flows from both its direct contribution to capitalist accumulation and its ideologizing function, legitimating a regime of technical expertise fundamentally unchallengeable by populist reason. The Frankfurt School opposes the absolutism of Enlightenment-era science in the name of perspectivity, undecidability and difference/differance – all central Derridean themes. But, unlike poststructuralists, the Frankfurt theorists refuse to abandon the generic project of enlightenment. The Frankfurt Nietzsche authorizes the possibility of a 'new' or 'gay' science (see Agger, 1976) not beholden to capitalist and disciplinary interests. The French Nietzsche has little place for this version of science. Indeed, Lyotard's Nietzsche rejects the project of science, except in terms of the bizarre new 'chaos' theory that Lyotard (1984) attempts to promote as a viable option for the human sciences.

Only a dialectical reading of Frankfurt critical theory will reveal their own dialectical perspective on the relationship between subjective and objective reason, the particular and the general. They tempered the totalizing claims of a universal reason with the aporetic understandings of non-identity theory, in this countering the identity theory of Hegel and later authoritarian Marxists. One of the reasons why French theorists cannot appreciate this nuance in German critical theory (where they even read it) is that they accept a monolithic notion of Marxism as both an identity theory and a totality theory. This has a great deal to do with the erstwhile intellectual hegemony of the French Communist Party and the ways in which this tradition intersected with the theoretical tendencies of the 1968 May Movement, such as they were. French theorists who, if they lived in Germany, might well have been critical theorists fashioned their peculiar versions of postmodern theory in response to the stultifying Stalinism of the French Communist Party. Foucault is a case in point. As such, their exuberant participation in the May Movement was more a revolution against (orthodox) Marxism than an extension of it in a new, dialectical direction. Meanwhile, their symptomatic avoidance of German critical theory only compounded their theoretical isolation. It further prevented them from resisting the neoconservative equation of Marxism with the Gulag Archipelago.

This failure to decouple the possibilities of a democratic, deconstructive Marxism from the Gulag is even more troubling in this era of *perestroika*. At a time when Soviets are queuing up for Bolshoi Maks at the opening of a Moscow outlet of McDonald's, it is virtually impossible for people in the west, including the media, to avoid celebrating the 'end of Marxism'. Triumphal democracy is epitomized in cultural imagery of the crumbling Berlin Wall, the Chinese students standing up to tanks in Peking, the electoral defeat of the Sandanistas in Nicaragua and the overthrow of Communist rule in Poland, Romania and East Germany. Cultural studies can do useful work in deconstructing these media campaigns as the ideological strategies they really are: any even half-sensate Marxist recognizes that the putative 'collapse' of Communism says much less about the theoretical viability of Marxism than about the irrationality of statism and central planning in the context of a suicidal and economically-draining arms race. *Perestroika* evidences the failure of state capitalism, not socialism. Of course, pure capitalism itself failed long ago, in the 1920s, when the state's regulatory functions had to expand exponentially in order for the 'democratic' state to keep (undemocratic) capitalism off the rocks of dangerous crises triggered by the illogic of capital, thoroughly documented by Marx in *Capital*.

It is far-fetched to blame the French theorists for western media hegemony. For all I know, Derrida is busily deconstructing the same media campaigns I have alluded to above. But in a climate of hysterical hostility to Marxism, it is no wonder that the French theorists have failed to overcome their own resistances to Marxism, whether as 'grand narrative' (Lyotard) or as yet another 'discourse/ practice' (Foucault). Anti-Marxism (sometimes couched as post-Marxism; see Dandaneau, 1992) is increasingly fashionable; to wear its symbol epitomizes postmodernism, the trendiest of social philosophies today. But German critical theory alone resists the demonization of Marxism, even in the architectonic reconstruction of historical materialism as communication theory attempted by Habermas (1984, 1987b). Alone among modern social philosophers, Habermas holds onto the totalizing ideals of Reason while decentering the arrogant subject philosophies so characteristic of the Enlightenment (albeit ending up with the equally unsatisfactory metaphysic of intersubjectivity that lies at the core of his redemptive notion of communicative practice, e.g., the 'ideal speech situation').

I want to decouple a particular Frankfurt-inspired version of cultural studies from the postulate of absolute values that has millennially wreaked havoc in western societies. All of us who do cultural studies, including neo-Frankfurters, reject the arrogance of the Enlightenment's subject philosophy. But that does not mean that we can thus dispense with a concept and practice of subjectivity or intersubjectivity; the subject's decentering by poststructuralists offers neither axiological nor strategic guidance. The Frankfurt version of cultural studies does not bypass the problematic of Promethean subjectivity. With Derrida and others, Adorno and Horkheimer acknowledge that the Promethean subject of western philosophy lies behind many of the greatest catastrophes visited upon people by people. At the same time, the rejection of absolute values ought not to imply the rejection of all values, especially those necessary to guide the task of social reconstruction. In this book, I work toward a version of cultural studies that avoids postmodern relativism and nihilism, on the one hand, and absolutism, on the other. This will involve me in an adjudication of the true/false needs debate that I mentioned above. But I will have to postpone that discussion until Chapter 8.

In my next chapter, I address four serious objections to the whole project of cultural studies, both left and non-left. Following that, I devote the next five chapters to discussions of five distinctive and sometimes over-lapping brands of cultural studies, including traditional Marxism, the Frankfurt School, the Birmingham School, poststructuralism/postmodernism and feminism. At that point, I will return to the problems of values and needs that lie at the heart of the dispute between poststructural and Frankfurt approaches to cultural studies, broadly understood. Although I argue against the relativism and nihilism of poststructural cultural studies, I am quick to admit that the Frankfurt cultural-studies agenda leaves a good deal to be desired, particularly in its original insensitivity to the realm of the popular. My own neo-Frankfurt version of cultural studies corrects and improves the Frankfurt approach with insights and theoretical practices from Birmingham, poststructuralism/postmodernism and feminist cultural theory without papering over some basic disagreements among these approaches.

This book has two purposes: it is intended for newcomers to the field of cultural studies; for these readers, Chapters 3–7 will provide an adequate descriptive background, coupled with this opening frame-setting chapter. As well, this book is an exercise in synthesis and a sharp argument for a particular version of cultural studies – perhaps one that is far from being realized in the variety of critical practices today. One might say that this book represents a cultural studies approach to cultural studies, risking the infinite regress that such a posture invites. In any case, cultural studies is one of the most fertile interdisciplinary regions of theoretical and interpretive intervention. There is no single 'cultural studies'; nor is anything and everything done in the humanities and the softer social sciences worthy of the name. Instead of simply defining the field of investigation termed *cultural studies* I want to exemplify a cultural studies approach in the way I unfold and interrogate alternative versions of it. Of course, this is a dialectical process: by the end of it, the reader will be better able to judge just what is, and is not, cultural studies, as well as decide which are the best variants of that generic approach. That dialectical unfolding is precisely the nature of the cultural practices of reading and writing, central topics of cultural studies today.

Chapter 2

Popular Culture as Serious Business

Before I continue with an exposition and analysis of the various approaches to cultural studies, on my way to a concluding argument for a politicized version of cultural studies in Chapter 10, let me pause here and consider just how culture has become a crucial site of political contestation in the late twentieth century (see Levine, 1988; Shiach, 1991). Although this may be apparent to those steeped in critical cultural theory, it is less obvious to four groups of people: consumers of popular culture, defenders of traditional high culture, orthodox Marxists and cultural dystopians. I will deal with the first and second groups at greatest length inasmuch as they are by far the largest; orthodox Marxism has a kind of subterranean existence in remote corners of the university and in certain political sects, but almost nowhere else. For their part, cultural dystopians are certainly not predominant, although their argument bears close examination. The first group of people comprises those who watch *Entertainment Tonight* and read *People* magazine *as entertainment* – the episodic chatter of pop-culture diverting us from the serious, sobering issues of geopolitics, the despoiled environment, homelessness and many others. The second group of people includes high-tone cultural doyens who believe that culture is a vehicle for rehabilitating the taste of the masses by imparting important moral and civic lessons. The third and fourth groups are composed of various marginal figures on both the left and right.

This chapter is divided into responses to four sorts of claims: one, that popular culture is basically fun but insubstantial, distracting people from the ordeal of workaday existence yet not bearing closer scrutiny except by quotidian television and movie critics; two, that popular culture betrays traditional cultural values and should be edified; three, that popular culture is simply a big business that can be understood in the strict terms of Marx's economic analysis of capitalism; and, four, that popular culture is imposed from the top down and has a certain totalizing, impermeable quality that cannot be dislodged. Although popular culture is diverting and profitable, it is much more than that, as cultural studies shows.

Popular Culture as Diversion

The dominant version of the pop-culture-as-fluff line goes something like this: the exploits of megastars, their star vehicles, their ample remuneration are merely the stuff of chatter; they do not matter. Today's stars will soon be yesterday's has-beens. Television shows and movies endure only as long as notoriously fickle public opinion has patience for them. Culture is amusing, perhaps necessary, even cause for the odd critical essay, but it is not the real stuff of intellectual analysis or criticism. It should not be glorified or elevated. It should merely be consumed, indulged or ignored, subject to those remote-control units that channel nightly entertainment for most people in 'developed' nations.

The culture-as-fluff line suggests that only mordant intellectuals with nothing better to do expend themselves in 'deconstructing' these episodic pieces of chatter. Indeed, this is an argument I make in a somewhat different context in Chapter 8, where I discuss the methodologization of cultural studies as merely a self-reproducing technique for endless, theoretically groundless close readings of various cultural artifacts. Yet I make the case not because I believe that culture is fluff but because culture matters so much that I want to give it the full critical attention it deserves.

The defense of popular culture is mounted not only by the captains of Madison Avenue who use the media to sell products, nor by the huge studios and networks that churn out entertainment 'product'. Popular culture is also defended by those within cultural studies who incline in a populist or poststructural direction and who reject the apparent mandarinism of the Frankfurt School. The cultural studies defense of popular culture seeks a certain intellectual and political redemption in the arts of the people, for example Walter Benjamin's (1969) defense of art in the age of mechanical reproduction, noted earlier. Theorists like Benjamin argue that the popular is not willy-nilly a realm of unfreedom or unconsciousness but can, indeed, be a launching-pad of all sorts of valuable oppositional projects. Cultural studies proponents who hold this view spend time poring over the mass media in order to detect the heartbeat of dissent, however irregular, as well as to subject popular culture to the sorts of ideology critiques characteristic of political versions of cultural studies.

This defense of popular culture somewhat contradicts the culture-as-diversion line in that it valorizes the intellectual analysis of popular culture. Those who defend popular culture as usefully diversionary but reject its methodical examination, let alone deconstruction, are not the same people who defend popular culture as politically relevant today. The publishers of *TV Guide* would find *Camera Obscura* a strangely obsessive periodical. For them, television shows are to be watched and celebrated, not scrutinized closely for ideological and other content. Nevertheless, these two periodicals have a good deal in common in that both take entertainment seriously, the one to purvey it and the other to challenge and perhaps enlighten it. Neither the editors of *TV Guide* nor those of *Camera Obscura* apologize for being riveted by television: they recognize that television matters, if in very different ways. But mainstream television criticism has little patience for the intellectualization and politicization of this cultural form. Television journalists and critics ridicule the academic obscurantism surrounding what they take to be good, clean fun.

Popular Culture as the Subversion of Values

This line suggests that a preoccupation with mass-market movies, books, television and journalism will lead to an erosion of civilizational values, substituting ephemeral entertainments for more substantial morality lessons. Of course, this has been the argument of conservatives since Edmund Burke. Allan Bloom (1987) in his *The Closing of the American Mind* articulates this neoconservatism well, blaming youth culture and leftist academics for the decay of traditional culture. Popular culture is not only blamed directly for the decline of public intelligence and a weakening of the collective moral fiber. Beyond that, critics of popular culture are seen to exacerbate the problem. The role of cultural criticism should be redemptive (and, for the left version of this position, avant-garde).

By now, the conservative and neoconservative assaults on popular culture are well known – and largely discredited on the left. Obviously, popular culture matters inasmuch as it affects billions of people. Obviously, popular culture has a crucial imprinting impact on young people. Obviously, popular culture is a central vehicle of ideology. Arguably, popular culture is a relevant venue of radical interrogation and contestation. But for me to say that conservative attacks on popular culture have been discredited is to fall prey to the typical leftist projection of its own wish fulfillment onto everyone else. For every cultural studies person in an English or Comparative Literature department, there are probably a dozen or more 'straight' scholars, the kind raised on Leavis-era literary criticism or on the New Criticism. It is extremely tempting for the cultural left to exaggerate both its own number and its own importance. The culture industry is flanked by a high-cultural rump comprised of intellectuals and critics who keep it honest, reminding people to watch educational television as well as CBS, promoting the latest show at the Museum of Modern Art and touting foreign films.

This cultural elite cannot be wished away, even if it is theoretically and critically superannuated. The Hilton Kramers (1985) call the critical tune where establishment art criticism is concerned (see Luke, 1991). *The New York Times* dispenses redemptive cultural criticism designed to provide crucial depth to the mass experience of culture, provided by television, trade fiction and blockbuster movies. A recent (March 11, 1990, pp. 30–3) *New York Times Magazine* article about the new head of the art program at MOMA is typical of this position: Kirk Varnedoe is praised for negotiating the delicate balance between an establishment version of modernism and a trendier postmodernism. He is praised for ignoring the fashion of 'French critical theory, Marxism and feminism', preferring to stay outside the walls of 'ideology'. The long article preceded his first major MOMA show in October 1990, 'High Culture and Popular Culture', which, as *The New York Times* correctly noted, was already controversial among more antediluvian critics for its acknowledgment of popular culture at all.

This is not to suggest that what goes on in the halls of academe or the pages of highbrow cultural criticism has much impact on the general public. But in this chapter I am addressing four dominant dismissals of cultural studies. To the extent to which an interdisciplinary, politicized cultural studies is blocked by establishment intellectuals and critics, not to mention producers and consumers, it is worth considering why a methodical approach to the hegemonizing and liberatory forces of popular culture has gathered so much momentum. Although I am unashamedly a partisan of a radical version of cultural studies, it is crucial to note that more traditional cultural criticism holds sway in much the same way that so-called postmodernism, both as style and as criticism, has been safely metabolized by the culture industry (as I argue in Chapter 9).

There is a growing sense among academic literary and cultural critics that poststructuralism and postmodernism have 'gone too far', rejecting so much of cultural criticism's redemptive and educative role that critical practice becomes merely a technical exercise padding curricula vitae and promoting careers. David Lodge's (1982, 1984) academic novels sharply expose the trendiness of deconstructive critical methodologies. In his novels, deconstruction has become a medium for scoring points at academic cocktail parties, not a cultural intervention as serious as the deconstructed work itself. The backlash against theory in literary and cultural interpretation parallels the growing neoconservative backlash against the salacious 1960s generally (see Mathews, *The New York Times Magazine*, February 10, 1991, pp. 43, 57, 59, 69). Every deconstructor published by a university press risks being assailed by the numerous anti-deconstructors who not only plow a different critical turf but who have declared war on deconstruction as yet another subversion of cultural values (e.g., Newman, 1985).

This aversion to theory is especially common in popular criticism – *The New Yorker*, *The New York Times*, highbrow television. I suspect that a good deal of it reflects status envy on the part of popular critics closed out of the academy; to them, deconstruction is a code too difficult to master. Thus, they ridicule it, while incorporating some of its buzzwords into the text of their own writing. Local culture critics drop 'Derrida' as well as 'deconstruction' to show the academic community that they are their equal. But they also clearly resist the academization of their criticism as a betrayal of the popular, which they trumpet proudly as an excuse for the pedestrian level of their own reviewing. Of course, in this, they reflect the know-nothingism of the culture at large: pragmatism has reigned supreme in American intellectual life ever since continental philosophy threatened to overwhelm us with its Teutonizing constructions and labyrinthine meanings.

Although there is a theory renaissance going on in the American academy, as I noted in Chapter 1, there is also a growing counterreaction that reflects the long-standing effort to depoliticize culture while enlisting culture secretly in the project of moral and spiritual elevation. One would have to trace this project to Romanticism, although it is also possible to locate oppositional currents in Romanticism that differently give rise to critical theory's perspective on the possibilities of cultural resistance and criticism. Defenders of high culture attack what they take to be obscurantist theorizing for its failure to redeem misguided cultural taste. Perhaps ironically, they lampoon high theory for its elitist aversion to plain language while chiding plain folks for their pedestrian taste. Instead, careful ('objective') readings of Dickens should illuminate his enduring truths, neither pandering too much to the pedestrian public nor ascending to the Apollonian heights of high theory.

A good deal of deconstruction has become a fad, indeed a technical obsession. I deal with this issue directly in Chapter 6. But deconstruction is not the whole of cultural criticism, nor should it be. Deconstructors draw so much fire precisely because they have installed themselves as the main opponents to Leavis-era criticism as well as the New Criticism. And deconstructive versions of cultural studies tend to be found in humanities and literature departments, whereas the Frankfurt-inspired approach to cultural studies is somewhat more prevalent in social science and philosophy. Nor is this to assert that the Frankfurt School's argot, whether Adorno's or Habermas', is extraordinarily lucid (although, as I have argued elsewhere [Agger, 1989a], Adorno's short, punchy, densely packed sentences can be readily unwoven into an extraordinarily accessible and compelling argument).

The main issue here is not the prose style in which cultural studies is phrased. Cultural neoconservatives reject mass culture as a legitimate topic of theoretical and critical intervention because they favor bourgeois high culture, and their own places within it. It is arguable whether the New Criticism is any the less mumbo-jumbo than Yale deconstruction, Ransom (1941) more transparent than de Man (1979, 1984) or Fish (1980). The issue of incomprehensibility is either a smokescreen or worse: it often reflects the native resistance of academics to Continental discourses with which they are unfamiliar and by which they are threatened. It is clear that deconstruction falls on hostile ears in the American academy simply because it is a different, initially difficult language game. The graduate students who have mastered Foucault and Barthes are hard to impress by faculty trained at a time when Europe meant Flaubert and Faust (see de Man, 1986).

There is a final issue involved in the neoconservative aversion to cultural studies, related to prose style but extending beyond and beneath it. Establishment mandarins reject the flashy language of Europeanized cultural criticism and theory out of a certain puritanism; the complex, convoluted prose of Derrida and Adorno offends the moral sensibility of the plain-language people just as much as do native speakers who say 'ain't'. Their aversion to Europeanized cultural studies is an aversion to bad grammar and bad manners, reflecting the putative eclipse of civility in these bawdy, degenerate times. This is not only class bias: the Frankfurt critics were equally contemptuous of mass culture. It is deeper than that, representing a puritanical aversion to erotized expression of all sorts, whether Barthesian playfulness of the text or Marcusean rationality of gratification. This returns to the Nietzsche question raised earlier. Nietzsche, who was contemptuous of bourgeois morality, is perhaps the single most important common denominator in all forms of cultural studies (save perhaps the feminist). And no one intellectual figure is more despised by Anglo-American puritan-pragmatist philosophers than the redoubtable Nietzsche, with his wild flights of fancy and his foreboding.

Mass Culture as Profit and Pretense

Although I address the Marxist approaches to culture more extensively in Chapter 3, it is worth noting here that some Marxists do not even countenance such discussions, relying on a particularly economistic interpretation of Marx (e.g., see Slater, 1977). This version of Marxism rejects cultural studies because, it claims, Marxism already adequately explains culture as a direct product of economic dynamics underpinning it. Orthodox Marxists disdainful of cultural studies argue that culture is the realm of the superstructure that functions to conceal capitalism ideologically. They also argue that cultural commodities are worth analyzing as commodities pure and simple, whether in the realm of mass-market fiction, movies, television or journalism. Of course, they are correct in both these observations, although I differ with the base/superstructure hierarchy that allows orthodox Marxists to derive cultural phenomena mechanically from the functional needs of the so-called logic of capital. The theory of ideology needs to be more complex than that, especially inasmuch as culture is (and, I submit, for Marx always was) more autonomous than that model suggests (see Horkheimer, 1972).

Indeed, it is the theory of ideology that a leftist version of cultural studies proposes, especially in the Frankfurt formulation. After all, Horkheimer and Adorno (1972) understood that culture has become an industry; they differ from orthodox Marxism in that they more autonomously theorize the practices and products of cultural ideology both in terms of its institutional features and in terms of its subjective meanings. It is not enough, according to them, simply to derive ideological representations from the functional requirements of capitalism, especially where capitalism is not a single monolith but a complexly structured system full of fragmentation and discontinuity. Although, as Marxists, they agree that culture is big business today, they analyze cultural products and practices in their own terms, insisting on their differentiation. To offer only one example, they insist that there is no single 'culture' but all sorts of cultures – high, low, regional, gendered, racialized, national, neighborhood. It is empirically incorrect to homogenize all of these as alleged reflexes of a singular logic of capital; instead, they must be addressed in terms of their relative autonomy as well as their differential manifestations and meanings for these different groups.

Thus, neo-Marxist cultural studies attempts to use cultural studies as an occasion for retheorizing ideology in late capitalism. It also extends the original Marxist focus on the economic circuitries of cultural production, distribution and consumption, updating Marxism in this way. It does these things by taking culture seriously, refusing to slough it off as an epiphenomenon. Whether neo-Marxists theorize culture in terms of relative autonomy (Althusser, 1970, 1971), hegemony (Gramsci, 1971) or its contribution to total administration (Adorno, 1973b, 1974a), Marxist approaches to cultural studies refuse to accept that culture and cultural politics are somehow irrelevant intellectually and politically. Simply to view cultural commodities as commodities is insufficient. As Marx understood, the commodity form also contains reifying, ideologizing components, notably commodity fetishism – the ways social relationships appear to be relations between things. It is insufficient simply to view the culture industry in terms of dollars and cents; mass culture also makes a significant contribution to the deepening of false consciousness.

Orthodox Marxists disdain the study of culture for much the same reason as cultural neoconservatives: they are puritans who resist the 'softness' of culture and cultural studies and instead prefer the 'hardness' of Marxian economics (where cultural neoconservatives prefer the solidity and nobility of so-called traditional values). To call them puritans is not to engage in psychological reductionism; I do not know or care whether these orthodox Marxists had problematizing childhoods that predisposed them to view cultural expression and abandon with distaste. Rather, cultural neoconservatives and orthodox Marxists alike view the popular as a region of trivial pursuits. The action is elsewhere for orthodox Marxists, notably in the economic sphere. But this assumes that economics and culture can be cleanly separated, a notorious mistake among orthodox Marxists from the beginning, as Horkheimer (1972) has argued.

The either/ors of bourgeois society are repeated by Marxists who choose between economic and cultural theorizing. The latent productivism of orthodox

Marxism only imitates the productivism of capitalist economic theory. Work is good and leisure is bad: Calvinism straddles both sides of the fence, left as well as right. Cultural analysis is seen as a diversion from political work, the sort of critique leveled at the Frankfurt School (e.g., Slater, 1977). But the Frankfurt theorists argue that culture is both business and politics. Hence, they theorize cultural politics as well as suggest a cultural or literary political economy (see Agger, 1990). To ignore culture is to ignore the source of capitalist reification and false consciousness in the commodity form itself, the linchpin of all Marxist analysis. But left-wing puritanism allows orthodox Marxists to overlook culture except as another component in the capitalist accumulation process. Unfortunately, it is not that simple.

Automatic Culture

The fourth and final objection to cultural studies is that popular culture is a barren wasteland created from the top down – or from the center outward – and thus cannot be changed from below. Although this objection is sometimes associated with the Frankfurt School itself, I argue in Chapter 4 that this is not really the Frankfurt position, which was phrased pessimistically for strategic reasons. The automatic-culture argument is found on both left and right. But it is typically an argument of technological dystopians who do not fall along the left-right continuum at all. It can be derived from extremist versions of cultural neoconservatism, which hold that there is a syncopated conspiracy of cultural levelers who get together to depress the collective sensibility; it can also be derived from neo- and post-Marxist arguments about how in late capitalism the system must freeze everyone into place lest they stray too far from the straight and narrow (e.g., see Debord, 1970).

The automatic-culture argument combines some of the three aforementioned objections to cultural studies. Where popular culture is meaningful at all, it is too readily coopted and commodified to be a serious venue of political contestation. It is clear that the original Frankfurt thinkers like Adorno tended in this direction (although Marcuse [e.g., 1969], in his Americanized post-World War Two phase, markedly differs). They were Marxists, to be sure, but Marxists who shared the *fin-de-siècle* cultural pessimism of Freud, Weber and Wittgenstein. The difference between Frankfurt pessimism and the pessimism of these other figures is that the Frankfurt theorists refused to ontologize it, instead referring their political pessimism to empirical circumstances in the evolution of capitalism that diminished and defused opposition. Yet it is sometimes difficult to disentangle their empirical reading of capitalism (e.g., see Agger, 1991a, Ch. 2) from a seeming ontology that denies the possibility of political intervention altogether, even on the apparently apolitical terrain of culture.

But I think it is clear, as I demonstrate in Chapter 4, that the Frankfurt School encoded their political theory in their aesthetic theory (see Marcuse, 1978; Adorno, 1984). They were not resigned to the closure of the universe of discourse but suggested that politics was displaced into seemingly apolitical realms. Thus they argued that political struggles had to be fought on those fronts, repoliticizing the seemingly apolitical. The decline of public discourse (see Agger,

1990) makes this repoliticization imperative, even – no, especially – if politicization happens in realms like popular culture heretofore ignored by classical Marxists, who faithfully cling to Marx's outmoded political sociology that locates opposition unproblematically in the region of political economy. This is not to deny that the culture industry has its own literary political economy, as I just said. But it is also to understand that literary political economy discloses not only commodification and accumulation processes but also hegemony and reification.

The automatic-culture line does not necessarily endorse high culture as a solution; indeed, the automatic-culture concept suggests that there are no solutions: things are too far gone for that. But it does not shy away from high culture, especially modernist forms of theoretical expression and cultural criticism. Adorno's music-thought could almost be viewed as an aesthetic gesture in its own right. He struggles to defy the simplifications and linearities of positivist thought through a practice of allusion and indirection designed not simply to please himself and his narrow coterie of readers but rigorously to free thought from its positivist encumbrances.

One might usefully distinguish, thus, between two versions of the automatic-culture thesis. The first is an outright rejection of popular culture as a critical and liberatory medium. People of this persuasion view mass culture as a vehicle for mass stupefaction; they tend to be elitist in the sense that they posit the necessity of elite culture for purposes of moral education and civic elevation. The second version of the automatic-culture thesis is more nuanced; it is typified by the Frankfurt pessimism about the culture industry. Sometimes it is hard to separate Adorno's (1974a) pessimism from an ontological negativity; I would like to think that critical theory is empirical theory that sometimes unfortunately tends to blur with a more ontological skepticism about the possibility of social change.

Revaluing the Popular

These four objections to cultural studies provoke a sustained response requiring me to retheorize and revalue the popular as a significant region of politics and hence critical activity. Only on that foundation can actual cultural studies work proceed. But this whole book is devoted to revaluing the popular as a relevant arena of cultural politics and hence political theory. The ways in which I valorize the popular inform and are informed by my own version of cultural studies. That is, a poststructural cultural studies differs from a more Frankfurt-oriented cultural studies in its approach to defending the relevance of the popular. In some sense, then, the rest of this chapter anticipates my concluding chapter, where I spell out my program of cultural studies, drawing on the various strategies of Marxism, Birmingham cultural studies, poststructuralism, postmodernism and feminism as these complement and extend the Frankfurt program. Yet that last chapter presupposes this anticipatory framing, to be carried out mainly in the form of theses that summarize my responses to these four objections to cultural studies. In short, I need to defend claims about the political and hence intellectual relevance of the systematic study of popular culture in order to quiet doubts raised by these four critiques.

1. Poststructuralism provokes serious questions about the very boundary between popular and high culture. The high/low culture distinction is increasingly problematic in an age of the mechanical reproduction of culture (e.g., Benjamin, 1969; Levine, 1988). For this reason, cultural studies refuses to restrict its interpretive and evaluative purview to 'crass' or 'mass' cultural forms, excluding elite culture. It can employ exactly the same theoretical approaches with regard to so-called high culture that it uses in its analysis of television and mass-market movies. Once the high/low culture distinction fades under interrogation, all sorts of analytical and political opportunities open up. In particular, by placing all cultural forms along the same continuum, cultural studies refuses the claims of high culture to be high and of mass culture to be trivial. Both are important in the late twentieth century. And both can be studied similarly, with the same theoretical and technical apparatuses. In itself, this poststructuralist broadening of the range of cultural studies is extremely liberating in the way it resists the claims of elite culture to be inherently privileged with respect to popular culture.

This issue cuts both ways. Critics who reject the supposed Archimedeanism and elitism of the Frankfurt School, equating popular culture with populism, hence idealizing it, are challenged by the very poststructuralism that gives them license. Although poststructural cultural studies deconstructs the high/low culture distinction, it also tends contradictorily to favor popular culture as a privileged realm, simply reversing the hierarchy favored by cultural neoconservatives. But this deconstructive reversal must be reversed in turn so that the realm of the popular is not privileged a priori simply because it *is* more popular (as well as more theoretically neglected) than elite culture. That television matters culturally, politically and economically does not mean that television somehow deserves to matter more than opera. The strict deconstructive logic of postructuralism suggests that hierarchies of all kinds are wrong-headed – the hierarchy of the popular over the elite as much as the more traditional hierarchy of elite culture over mass culture. As I explore in Chapter 6, deconstructively-oriented cultural studies people too frequently ignore this deconstructive irony, inadequately theorizing their well-taken anger about the hegemony of elite culture over popular culture and thus failing to learn from it.

One of the most important contributions of poststructuralism to a wide-ranging cultural studies is this suspicion about cultural hierarchies and evaluations of all kinds. But cultural studies splits into two wings here: one wing, doctrinally and methodologically rooted in American deconstruction (e.g., see de Man, 1979, 1986), rejects all cultural judgment as logocentric and elitist. The other wing, embracing Marxist approaches to cultural studies like that of the Frankfurt School, allows cultural judgments but resists the logocentrism of cultural neoconservatism; (whether it does this through a direct reading of Derrida or via Adorno is immaterial). One might note a contradiction here: poststructuralism helps all versions of cultural studies deconstruct the high/low culture distinction without necessarily precluding cultural and political judgment. But poststructuralism also authorizes resistance to what Lyotard (1984) called 'metanarratives' that decide questions of truth, beauty, freedom and justice.

This seeming contradiction represents the difference between strong and weak programs of cultural studies. Both programs derive from essentially Derridean insights into the epistemological and evaluative illegitimacy of high/low culture distinctions in the first place. But the weaker version, developed by

American literary deconstructors (see Culler, 1982), is only one among a number of possible extrapolations of Derrida's strictures on logocentrism, undecidability and difference/differance. This weak version takes the deconstruction of the high/low culture distinction to be equivalent to a rejection of all cultural evaluation. The deconstructive cultural studies program thus transvalues all cultural values, reflecting a debt to Nietzsche that I noted above.

The stronger cultural studies program accepts the Derridean deconstruction of the high/low culture distinction without ruling out the possibility of cultural evaluation, which is permitted with reference to some sort of philosophy of history, philosophical anthropology or universal pragmatics of communicative discourse (see Denzin, 1991). In other words, it is possible for cultural studies to accept that there is no clear demarcation between elite and popular cultures while at the same time endorsing certain 'true' needs and values that make differential cultural comparisons and evaluations possible. In Chapter 8 I phrase the difference between these two programs of cultural studies in terms of their differing positions on human needs.

This stronger position borrows notions about the undecidability of cultural judgments from poststructuralism while going beyond it – toward Marxism, notably – for resources with which to render the concept of undecidability itself undecidable. The relativity of relativism makes more definitive judgments possible, if only situational ones. A Nietzscheanized postmodern cynicism – 'anything goes' – is rejected by a version of cultural studies that is above all political. Here is where the intellectual rubber meets the political road: *a left cultural studies wants to change the world via interpretive and analytical interventions*. This requires cultural studies proponents to develop a full-blown aesthetic politics that situates cultural expression and judgment in the larger political scheme of things. Obviously, Picasso's *Guernica* has a certain political intent and impact. Less obvious is that both television and trade fiction matter in a political sense, with television perhaps mattering more in light of the televisionization of reality today (see Luke, 1989). Even less obvious is that political resistance can be represented and hence reproduced aesthetically; although the examples of this are few, they are frequent enough to offer some support for the non-relative theory of needs implied or stated in left-wing versions of cultural studies.

2. The argument that popular culture is ephemeral and thus unworthy of sustained critical attention misses the fact that pop-culture is at once ideologically encoded and encoding. A large and rapidly growing literature (e.g., see Gitlin, 1980; Rachlin, 1988; Hallin, 1985) suggests that mass media are crucial circuitries of what Jameson (1981) called ideologemes – pieces of political and social recommendation concealed in cultural expressions. The mosaic of these fragments constitutes the whole of popular culture as we know it. Together, they comprise worldviews that have become largely hegemonic. For example, advertising (Williamson, 1978; Wernick, 1983; Leiss, Kline and Jhally, 1986; Goldman and Papson, 1991) instructs us not only which differentiated commodities to consume but to want them at all, thus stoking the engine of capitalism; the portrayal of women in fiction and magazines suggests appropriate gender relations and representations of women; academic writing in the social sciences (which is surely part of popular culture in an era of mass education) suggests an immutable, law-like social world depicted on the model of the 'hard' natural sciences.

All of these cultural forms are sent, received and enacted through the language games (Wittgenstein, 1953) comprising the dense fabric of everyday life. Whether they have subliminal impact is somewhat beside the point: these cultural forms structure experience politically if only in the sense that they construct a relatively narrow range of social and political possibilities in the ways people develop and satisfy their needs (see Kellner, 1989). It is not so much that Paul McCartney promotes VISA credit cards but rather that viewers lose sight of just what is being sold – McCartney's concert tour, his version of reality, rock music, VISA cards, credit cards and/or the ontology of credit buying? The answer is probably all of them, although one might distinguish among the advertising's various levels of text and subtext. In losing sight of the specific claims made by advertisements, viewers assimilate and thus enact ads as total horizons of their possibilities. The particular validity claims made by ads are covered over in the sense and sentience of their total representation of reality and hence they cannot be falsified, for example by showing that McCartney's music is socially regressive or that credit buying is a dangerous trap for consumers.

One of the specific formulations of cultural studies is media studies. These media studies focus on ways in which the media both constitute and are constituted by hegemonic interests, at once creating audiences and consumers and responding to administrative imperatives flowing out of corporate and state power centers. What Luke (1989) calls 'screens of power' comprise a wide range of media practices that are in turn the topics of critical cultural analysis. These media studies refuse to ignore the text of media, nor do they accept that this text is depthless, transparent. Rather, critical media studies refuse to take the text of media on its own terms. Instead, they argue that *the text dissembles* in that it hides from view its own authorship – its having-been-written from the vantage of authorial interest. Critical media studies focuses less on outright falsehood (although that kind of analysis has a place, too) than on the subtle falsehoods that the positivist media purvey by appearing to present news and entertainment in unmediated, deauthored ways.

One of the central tasks of this version of cultural studies is to *restore the author*, showing the corrigibility and undecidability of these cultural texts that are in principle no different from science or fiction. Science is a kind of fiction in that it attempts to convince the reader of its own credibility; fiction differs from science only in that it does not need to authorize its attempt at verisimilitude from the outside, with the aid of methodology and credentialed discourse. Cultural studies approaches all texts as ideologically encoded and encoding, participating in the discourses of power transacted in the circuitries of production, distribution and reception/consumption characterizing media-ted life in late capitalism. Cultural studies refuses to grant popular culture an exemption from the general drift of ideology-critical analysis, ignoring sitcoms and weekly news magazines simply because they traffic in the quotidian.

Indeed, it is precisely the everydayness of popular culture that makes it so forceful in the transactions of power. Stuart Hall (1980a, 1980b) and his group at Birmingham pioneered a non-positivist media studies that does not rely on quantitative audience-research techniques for eliciting the political force of mass media. Instead, they theorize media in a way that implants media in the institutionalized practices of late-capitalist everyday life, inseparable from the other sites and sources of power. For his part, Foucault (e.g., 1977; also see O'Neill, 1986) offers his own distinctive perspective on how the everydayness of power can be viewed deconstructively, notably in his important studies of criminology and sexuality. The issue is not simply *message units* in which ideological claims are encoded but the *social ensemble of media-ted practices* that have enormous impact on the ways we live our lives.

Perhaps the most notable fact here is not the many hours people spend in front of television, videos and cinema. Although it is important to plot these shifts in 'leisure' time through survey research, critical media studies emphasizes that culture is a kind of work, too. It blurs the line between production and reproduction in much the same way that left feminists have shown that domestic activity is a kind of productive labor whose distinctive feature is its unwaged character (see Shelton and Agger, 1991). Culture is production as well as repro- duction; indeed, a deconstructive account of their relationship would show that reproduction *is* a production: the line between them blurs to the point of virtual indistinguishability. Cultural studies in this way deconstructs its own apparent limitation to the realm of the cultural, suggesting that culture encompasses a region of otherness thought to be excluded by it, notably work. By the same token the realm of work is also a region of the cultural in the sense that media-ted imperatives help organize it along the lines of total administration. Michael Moore's film *Roger and Me* makes this dialectical interpenetration between the spheres of production and reproduction extremely clear, interweaving, as he does, themes about General Motors' civic celebration in Flint, Michigan, and more directly economic themes regarding its plant closings and the effects these have on laid-off workers.

One might say that popular culture is political discourse, even where the interlocutors are not equally powerful. One of the main empirical facets of modern mass communication is that sender-receiver relations are both one-way and highly skewed. Nevertheless, people construct the discourses they receive just as they are constructed by it. A critical media studies is not utterly resigna- tory, although 'solutions' are few and far between; it is somewhat disingenuous simply to call for more and better public television, as if the media-tedness of late capitalism could be resolved in that singular way. Nevertheless, this is not (yet) a regime of total administration; I suspect that the original Frankfurt School imagery of 'the closing of the universe of discourse' (Marcuse, 1964) was only intended to be a tendential analysis in the first place. They realized quite clearly that the occasion of critical theory is the inherent possibility that one- dimensionality can be cracked open, deconstructed.

3. It is arguable that remediating (or demedia-ting) popular culture is politically hopeless. The impermeability of culture to oppositional challenges is an empirical question. Short of total planetary annihilation, there is always the possibility that one-dimensionality can be undone, especially in an advanced industrial society. This is not wishful thinking but a sober reckoning with emancipatory possibili- ties. Although I do not go as far as Ryan and Kellner (1988) toward a view of culture (in their case, popular film) that highlights audience resistances to hege- mony, 'the audience' is not a monolith and must be addressed differentially.

By the same token, the artifacts of popular culture are not all deadening, especially where poststructuralism has already blurred the boundary between higher and lower cultures. The fact that writers write is reason enough to suppose that the cultural universe is not closed to critical interventions. Some artists and writers are political, even if there is hot debate about what constitutes the region of the political today. Such debates are themselves cultural activities, as much of the discussion of postmodernism suggests. The 'safe' establishment postmodernism of MOMA and downtown architecture diverges significantly from the renegade postmodernism of critical social theory (see Best and Kellner, 1991). Essentially, one can read postmodernism as a debate about the relationship of culture to politics. Wherever one stands, the issue is not closed. Indeed, to imagine that the universe of cultural discourse is closed quickly becomes a self-fulfilling prophecy; the post-modern description of the end of politics is confused with its celebration (e.g., Kroker and Cook, 1986).

4. Cultural neoconservatism's argument against popular culture on grounds of alleged universalism (encoded in the Great Books and Works) is dishonest. Cultural neoconservatism merely substitutes one perspective for another; as post-structuralism tells us, perspectivity is inescapable in the realm of cultural and political evaluation. Although neo-Frankfurters like me agree with cultural neoconservatives that it is important to stipulate and then debate certain found-ational values (e.g., socialism over capitalism), we differ from neoconservatives who claim to have transcended perspective altogether in an act of Promethean interpretive will. Perspective endures long past the announcement of its demise by absolutists (see Rorty, 1979, 1989). The totality always threatens to dissolve into the fields of heterogeneity and difference characterizing human existence and language. That does not mean that we should abandon the project of totalization – social change – in the fashion of some postmodernists (e.g., Lyotard, 1984). Rather, we should insist on certain important values without losing sight of our own contextualization by history and interest. The absolutist rejection of relativism must recognize its own corrigibility lest absolutism lose a sense of irony, thus making way for yet another species of authoritarianism.

Cultural neoconservatism is a false universalism. Allan Bloom's (1987) hatred of the Nietzscheanized academic ex-New Left (e.g., Marcuse and his followers) is cast in the usual Straussian fashion: the Greeks are installed as eternal truth tellers. But this raises all sorts of foundationalist problematics. Why did the Greeks get it right? How do we know? What sort of epistemological privilege do Straussians like Bloom claim for themselves that is implicitly denied to others of different political ilks? Cultural neoconservatives who rail against popular culture for its idiotic ephemera and relativism are, of course, correct. Marcuse's own analyses of repressive desublimation (1955) and false needs (1964) converge with much of Bloom's own analysis of the closing of the American mind – the same Marcuse attacked by Bloom as an enemy of free speech and moral rectitude. Yet cultural neoconservatives do not go beyond assertion where they argue for certain 'right' values, books, cultural forms and political structures. They lack a ground for their substantive political theory.

As a result, there is a certain arbitrary quality to the iteration of Great Books and Works offered as resources for civic rehabilitation by the cultural right. The politics of curriculum building are resolved with reference to tradition, not by debate about the relationship between culture and politics of the sort entered into by cultural studies proponents. Of course, this has been a tendency of all conser-vatism since Edmund Burke. It is far from arbitrary: it protects the status quo.

The great-white-male classics are offered as cultural sustenance at a time when the power elite is threatened from all sides. The return to liberal arts education, urged by the right, is a thinly veiled attempt to return to the intellectual and cultural priorities of the past, when gentlemen were gentlemen and women knew their places. The conclusion is inescapable that cultural neoconservatism embraces a certain cultural politics that is far less universalistic than meets the eye; the Great Books which say 'man' when they mean all of humanity are encoded to convince readers that men should be in control. And the right empowers the cultural custodians of the academy to protect these putative universals through their cultivation of certain allegedly timeless works.

Whether works are timeless or not is entirely an empirical question, to be resolved only from the vantage of distant retrospection. The endurance of cultural expressions has everything to do with the sociology of cultural knowledge and nothing to do with intrinsic merit, whatever that might be. Greek essentialism is ad hoc; it reflects the endurance of Greek cultural hegemony over the years, now returning with a vengeance in the polemics of the cultural right. We misidentify Greek cultural standards as timeless simply because antiquity is so old, thus inflating the past into eternity. In the depthless, shifting, impermanent world of fast capitalism (Agger, 1989a) there is a tremendous urge to secure a toehold in the solidity of enduring values and standards. The alternative seems to be the quicksand of postmodernity (see Harvey, 1989). But it is unnecessary for us to seek this solid foundation in the past, especially where it is possible to deconstruct Greek culture as highly perspectival in its own way (e.g., its exclusion of women and slaves from the *polis*).

Thus, I want to develop a concept of cultural politics that does not risk being read as nihilist simply because it opposes the false universalism of cultural neoconservatism. To refuse to go backward in search of cultural standards is not to endorse standardlessness. As left utopians like Brecht and Sartre have always insisted, if in very different ways, those standards lie ahead in the future. And they must be prefigured in the standards we enact in the here and now. To imagine that the Judgment Day lies in the future is as misguided as to suppose that it resides in Greek antiquity, having only to be cultivated by culture doyens in order to release its educative force.

5. The analysis of the culture industry need not foresake ideology critique simply because it focuses on cultural commodification. Dualist Marxism falls into the same trap as dualist non-Marxism, endorsing the either/or of bourgeois civilization. Cultural commodification is bound up with cultural commodity fetishism, thus chilling cultural representations into a tableau of inescapable necessity – a world littered with McDonald's restaurants, horror movies vacuous television sitcoms and the values they all encode. Lukács' (1971) reification culminates in the administered society (Horkheimer, 1973) of the present; in Baudrillard's (1983) terms, it is difficult even to distinguish between reality and the simulations that portray reality. The crisis of representation is caused by the cultural and psychic crises of late capitalism, forcing popular culture to fill the gap by offering us simulations utterly replacing substance with style (see Ewen, 1988).

In this context, the whole meaning of ideology changes, making it harder than ever to separate profit and power from false consciousness. The culture industry blurs these lines, at once bleeding off potentially revolutionary dissent through simulations while contributing to the accumulation of capital. Bourdieu's (1984) notion of cultural capital is an overly mechanical expression of all this: he implies that cultural capital (e.g., factual knowledge about the world, credentials, manners) is simply banked in the way that real capital is accumulated. Although strictly true, this implies that culture is an object instead of a process of production, circulation and consumption, what Althusser (1970) calls a lived practice. I prefer Althusser's terminology to Baudrillard's because it is not enough to say that ideology consists of simulations (of reality). Rather, ideology is built into the interstices of everyday life itself, having been dispersed from the erstwhile tomes and texts of ideology like religion and capitalist economic theory originally targeted by Marx.

These dispersed texts become con-texts, everyday practices that are infused with the cultural imageries consumed daily from television as well as textbooks. Our adaptation to the 'given' is routine, automatic. It is not mediated by the kind of devotional study necessary for people to become religious acolytes or champions of bourgeois economics. Thus, the ideal and material dimensions of culture merge to the point of near identity. Cultural commodification and cultural reification are inextricably linked in the various cultural lifeworlds comprising the international-capitalist global village or what Horkheimer and Adorno call the culture industry. Con-text is another name for what Wittgenstein (1953) called language games, the local scenes of communication and consumption through which people reproduce the material and ideal conditions of their existence. False consciousness is not something 'done' to people as much as an alternation between encoded and encoding that marks the subtle, slippery nature of fast capitalism. In McLuhan's (1967) terms, the medium is the message.

In this light, it makes little sense to separate the economic aspects of popular culture from their ideologizing con-texts. Baudrillard (1975) attempts a political economy of the sign, although his later work on simulations (1983) largely regresses behind his earlier, more unified approach to the relationship between material and ideal aspects of culture. Baudrillard is currently such a fad (e.g., see Kroker and Cook, 1986; for a critique see Kellner, 1989b) because his theory of simulations somehow moves us into a post-capitalist, post-Marxist analytical framework according to which the mode of production ceases to matter. In Poster's (1989) terms, we have entered an era of the mode of information. But this is precisely the same idealism found in Bell's (1960) end-of-ideology argument, as well as in other analyses of 'technological society' (e.g., Ellul, 1964; Touraine, 1971). We have not transcended capitalism, although our capitalism is perhaps qualitatively different from that of Marx in the sense that the lines are even more blurred today between the realms of economy and culture. As a result, the site or con-text of ideology has shifted: ideology is dispersed from the realm of pure textuality into the world itself, encoded in the various language games preoccupying everyday life for most people. Ideology has become ontology, a veritable theory of being enacted in the various modes of being human.

From the vantage of Marxism, the post-capitalist framework of simulation theory seems to demand a sharp rebuke. But such rebukes ought not to regress behind Marx's own dialectical understanding of the relationship between ideas and material practice. Mechanism is the other face of idealism; both short-circuit the non-identities that make social change possible at all. If the world is not a gigantic advertisement (Baudrillard), neither is it merely a factory. A poststructural Marxism helps interrogate the thin boundaries between these two realms, deconstructing (without effacing) their difference. Only through such differentiated analyses – cultural studies! – can we avoid both idealism and mechanism, the pitfalls of undialectical attempts at totalization. Cultural studies offers a non-identical theory of culture that shows the interdependence of ideology and material practice, thus making way for a cultural politics that aims at total transformation.

6. The poststructural emphasis on difference and non-identity should not become such an absolute commitment that relativism is enshrined ontologically. I insist that cultural evaluation is possible, but according to different criteria than moral elevation. Cultural evaluation is possible only within the frame of a total social theory. I frankly align myself with the Frankfurt version of cultural studies, preferring their non-identical totalizations over the anti-totality stance of post-structuralist cultural studies. I reject Lyotard's suspicion of metanarratives because only through such metanarratives – philosophies of history – can we pull together heterogeneous resistances into the whole cloth of social change. In this sense, I believe that cultural evaluation is not only possible but necessary. Cultural studies need not eschew evaluation out of the fear of absolutism. Absolutism can be tempered with a historicizing self-consciousness that turns texts into contexts, as I have indicated.

These are essentially slogans – con-text, historicization, totalization. They have particular meanings in critical theory and yet they cry out for exemplification, notably in what they exclude from themselves. Much of the work of cultural studies has been overly descriptive, if not downright methodologically fetishistic. Cultural readings are rarely theorized in a way that suggests their contribution to totalizing understandings of the world and then attempts to create new totalities through cultural and political practice. Like deconstruction, cultural studies has tended to become a cottage industry without any theoretical or political center. Theory and politics, yes, but a peculiarly decentered kind that is too wary of laying claim to totality. We can easily see this on the part of men who write critical theory in light of feminist thought (see Connell, 1987): they are so gun-shy about their own territorial tendencies that they essentially abandon the region of gender to feminist theorists, thus localizing their own general theories in an inadvertently sexist way. Of course, this is precisely the postmodern agenda: the aversion to the Enlightenment is so strong that we fall back into the disconnected 'subject positions' (Lacan, 1977) that make no claims to articulate with those of other subjects, whether women or people of color. Thus, postmodern social theory ironically reproduces the factionalism bred by capitalism, taught to fear totality by a totalizing system that desperately wants to blunt the effort to form alliances out of decentered resistances.

Cultural studies is too often a fall-back position for frustrated critical theorists who write in the shadow of the masters like Adorno and Habermas. Failing to achieve their own encyclopedic scope and lacking their synthesizing versatility, people who pursue cultural studies retreat to regional readings of cultural texts that reproduce themselves in a flurry of deconstructive activity. Media studies, film theory and women's studies all become sites of this specialized, regionalized activity. Courses are established, journals founded, conferences organized around one or another culture-critical theme, together giving the impression of substantial consensus about both theory and method on the left. But there is little consensus; postmodernism serves as the unifying theme, where to be postmodern means that one eschews the unifying grand narratives that attempt to make sense of everything. Humility and irony replace the self-confidence of the European theorists. Cultural studies reflects the domestication of French social theory and German critical theory in the academized rituals of the British and American universities and cultural communities. Everyone 'does' deconstruction, even if few have read Derrida (let alone Marx).

But doing deconstruction virtually assures that one will be done in by it, without recourse to a larger social theory that employs cultural theory within a more articulated political theory and strategy. Too much of cultural studies is an exercise in avoiding theory – the conceptual work that ties together film theory, media studies, literary analysis and the sociology of science. If these pursuits remain fragmentary, they refuse to reach the level of the political; they are hobbies, occupying members of the academic leisure class who get double mileage out of their avocations. Where a burst of developments in European theory made cultural studies possible, cultural studies risks losing touch with those theoretical developments, drifting off into the hyperspace of the academy. I oppose that tendency precisely because I believe that cultural studies can do important theoretical and political work, notably in opening mass culture to dehegemonizing and thus reconstructive accounts. Through it, we can understand and hence reverse the hold culture has on us. In itself, cultural studies contributes to the rebuilding of culture, particularly through its democratization and despecialization. Ultimately, as I explore in my concluding chapter, cultural studies can become a mode of everyday life, transvaluing the typically passive role of the cultural consumer into a much stronger version of reconstructive reading and writing. But this is a case that I have to make. It is not enough to assert the possibility of cultural studies as political practice. In the meantime, I will devote the next five chapters to surveys and critiques of different approaches to cultural studies, after which I will consider the ways in which cultural evaluation can only take place within a theory of human needs that helps us decide for and against various cultural forms.

Chapter 3

Marxist Theories of Culture

The Absence of a Coherent Cultural Politics in Lukács' Realism

Although cultural studies explicitly emerged with Richard Hoggart's establishment of the Birmingham Centre for Contemporary Cultural Studies at the University of Birmingham in 1964, the social study of culture predates 1964. I would trace the beginnings of cultural studies to the Marxist sociology of culture, while immediately noting that there are a host of different versions of this approach to culture (see Hauser, 1982). In this chapter I lay out the central assumptions and methodological approaches of the Marxist theory of culture. This discussion will lead into my consideration of the Frankfurt School in the following chapter; this is especially appropriate inasmuch as the Frankfurt theory of aesthetic politics is formulated in response to some of the more mechanical Marxist and neo-Marxist orientations to culture and cultural politics.

Let me begin with a bold assertion: by and large, Marxist students of culture do not have a cultural politics! Or, better, their cultural politics are formulated in counterpoint to the dominant Marxist economism and thus exist in somewhat contradictory relation to it. For a Marxist even to have a notion and practice of cultural politics is strange: culture for economistic Marxism is supposed to be epiphenomenal, a region of experience and expression basically derived from economic imperatives. Admittedly, there are few truly economistic Marxists who have significant theoretical voices today. Indeed, as I indicated in my preceding chapter, Marxism is altogether passé among many students of cultural studies, creating a strange lack of articulation between two traditions that ought to speak to each other.

Nevertheless, the fact that Marxists since Lukács and Goldmann have developed highly self-conscious approaches to culture indicates that, at some level, culture matters to them. Lukács' (1962, 1963, 1964, 1971, 1974, 1980) realism may not be a very effective cultural intervention at a time when the crisis of representation is upon us (i.e., the positivist notion that words and images unproblematically depict reality without also distorting it). Yet there is no denying that Lukács was among the first Marxists to have given serious attention to issues of culture in a way that suggested the relative autonomy of literature and art as important realms of social and political investigation. Although he did not effectively theorize this relative autonomy in a way that was genuinely dialectical, showing the interpenetration of political economy and culture, Lukács gave sufficient attention to the study of culture that subsequent debates among the left about cultural politics are scarcely imaginable without reference to him, and later to Lucien Goldmann (1964, 1972, 1975, 1976, 1981).

The fact that Lukács struggled to elaborate a coherent cultural politics shows his allegiance to what one might call an orthodox Marxist perspective on art, represented in Bolshevik-era Zhdanovism (socialist realism). Although it is arguable that Marx would have endorsed socialist realism as an adequate theorization of culture's relative autonomy, the existence of socialist realism suggests that Marxists since Marx felt the necessity of elaborating a theory of culture that was not simply implied in Marxist economic theory (see Fischer, 1963, 1969). After all, Lukács in 1923 (1971) helped put the study of ideology on the emerging Marxist agenda, giving rise to all sorts of western-Marxist forays in the next half century. In *History and Class Consciousness* Lukács (1971) responded to the political as well as intellectual failures of Marxism in a way that could recoup them. It is no accident that the Lukács of *History and Class Consciousness* was also concerned with art and culture, both on political and theoretical levels. Although Lukács' influence on cultural studies today is negligible, it would be a serious mistake to underestimate the transformative impact his work on class consciousness and cultural expression had on the original project of western Marxism (see Agger, 1979; Arato and Breines, 1979). He helped liberate Marxism from stagnation by reintroducing themes of voluntarism, consciousness and praxis that have become central commitments of western Marxism (e.g., Gramsci, the Frankfurt School, Paris left-existentialism, etc.). Although some of these themes were largely contradicted by his realist theory of culture, the influence of his Hegelianization of Marxism has been enduring.

The efforts of the likes of Lukács and Goldmann to free Marxism from an economistic straitjacket constituted a major upheaval within orthodox Marxism (e.g., see Jacoby, 1981). Studies of the dominant scientific Marxism of the Second and Third Internationals (Lichtheim, 1961) indicate the extent to which Marxism since Engels had become incredibly scientistic and mechanistic by comparison to Marx's original works. Of course, the issue of fidelity to Marx is ambiguous: for every reader of Marx there is a different Marxism. There are passages galore in Marx where he seems to endorse a positivist conception of social theorizing, including an objectivist theory of representation that reduces the constitutional roles of both theory and practice. These passages can be balanced against the places, especially in the *Economic and Philosophical Manuscripts* (1961), where Marx endorses a more dialectical model of the interaction between social and economic structures, on the one hand, and subjective and intersubjective agency, on the other.

Intellectual uses of Marx derive from the political interests readers have in reading him (e.g., Althusser and Balibar, 1970). Poststructuralism makes the case convincingly that there is no royal road to a definitive 'Marx', only different, often quite heterogeneous versions. This does not mean that we can hallucinate readings of Marx that bear no relationship to the sense of his text; the extent to which we can be playful with Marx, or any text, is certainly governed by obdurate material limits placed upon such interpretive extravagances. It is much more important to situate readings of Marx in interpretive interest than to worry about how one can approximate a transparent Marx, exposing him representationally as if he can be reflected presuppositionlessly, by every reader. Indeed, the notion that there is a singular transcendental reader is challenged by postmodernism in a way that has significant impact on the development of a non–positivist cultural studies.

The positivist Marx is a construction of positivists who pretend not to write when they read. But writing cannot silence its author or authorial interest altogether. Eventually, the subtext obtrudes up through the surface of the page, deconstructing the smooth linearity of the argument for all to see (Derrida, 1976). The contradictoriness and differential character of Marx's oeuvre only attest to the difficulties faced by positivizing interpreters of him. Althusser's (1970) attempt to find an epistemological break in Marx serves his interest in periodizing Marx's alleged maturation from adolescent philosopher to adult scientist. But no *coupure epistemologique* can be forced on writing from the outside. Oeuvres, even self-styled scientific ones, defy linear comprehension; instead, they leak out all over the place, making it difficult to publish those notorious doctoral dissertations submitted to university presses by graduate students hoodwinked into believing that 'scholarship' can capture a life and mind inertly on the page.

The sheer undecidability of writing makes cultural studies possible, particularly a Marxist version. If we could show that Marx's economism is all of a piece, then cultural analysis would be merely the extension of the analytic logic of capital to the realm of cultural commodification. Although that is important work, it is insufficient because, as I suggested in the last chapter, it fails to comprehend both the interpenetration and non-identity of commodification and commodity fetishism (or ideology). Cultural Marxism turns Marxist economism upside down not in order to reverse the putative structural priority of base over superstructure (with culture now becoming predominant 'in the last instance') but to win for culture a realm of theoretical and political autonomy denied it by economizing readings of Marx (see Ross, 1989).

Ultimately, what must settle these questions of revisionism made possible by the poststructural insistence on interpretive plurality are empirical argument and evidence. Even if Marx was certain that culture derives epiphenomenally from the mode of production, he could well be wrong today. I happen to think that Marx always recognized the dialectical non-identity of the economy and culture, dialectician that he was. But the issue for us today is whether culture is simply 'Culture, Inc.' (Schiller, 1989) or whether, in fact, culture is a crucial factor in the perpetuation of domination in the sense of facilitating Gramsci's hegemony as well as serving as a wellspring of surplus value. That it can be *both* is the main claim of non-orthodox cultural Marxists. They make this claim stick by demonstrating the empirical applications of a critical cultural theory that adds crucial nuance and depth to Marxist political economy, a vital necessity at a time when conventional class politics have taken a rightward turn (e.g., see Kellner, 1990, on television).

The very acknowledgment that there should be a Marxist theory of culture suggests deficiencies in orthodox Marxism. But the shadow of Marxist economism is sufficiently extensive as to obscure the effort to develop a systematic left theory of culture that, in effect, serves as an extrapolation of the theory of ideology found in Marx. The reprivileging of culture as a relevant political arena began with, but was not completed by, Lukács. Lukács could not break through the hegemony of Marxist dualism sufficiently to grant culture an independent status as both a region of domination and a crucial political battleground in the struggle to create socialism. Marxist cultural theory was doomed in the early years by the extremely powerful momentum of Marxist economism which, almost inexorably, turned matters of culture into issues of political economy per se. Even Lukács' Hegelianization of the Marxist theory of ideology in *History and Class Consciousness* (1971) was insufficient to break Marxism out of the mold of scientism and economism. Not until the Frankfurt School did left theory develop a sufficiently independent theory of culture that, in its own right, reconnected with political economy to forge a powerful new analytical apparatus for analyzing emerging monopoly-capitalist contradictions (see Lowenthal, 1961, 1975, 1984, 1986).

Lukács' realism recognized that bourgeois hegemony took all sorts of important cultural forms. Against orthodox Marxism, he recognized that the socialist revolution could be effectively forestalled by the development of ideological forms and practices that defused dissent either by portraying the social world falsely or by suggesting the possibility of non-materialist transcendence that obviated the need for radical social change. But he still harnessed art to the representational role of political education and critique laid out by Marx and Marxists immediately after him. Culture was to be a tool of political struggle, arousing working-class desire to overthrow capitalism. Although culture was relatively autonomous in the sense that culture was not merely the sum total of ideological validity claims about social reality but also an expressive realm in which unfulfilled desires could be expressed, Lukács did not theorize the ways modernism and postmodernism heighten awareness by breaking through representation pure and simple.

As such, Lukács read bourgeois literature (e.g., *Essays on Realism* (1980)) for its class truths; his ideological deconstruction of these truths rested in his own counterfactual claims. He aimed to show that the aesthetic depiction of the bourgeois world expressed a certain class standpoint that was particular, not general. He argued that bourgeois culture *gets the world wrong*, as if one can formulate the world culturally without distorting it. By contextualizing culture in this way, Lukács could expose its false universality in a way that breaks through the habitual acceptance of the quotidian and denies the narcotic function of this high art. Cultural criticism was to show the class perspectives encoded in allegedly universalist art, historicizing it. In this sense, cultural criticism was to function as ideology critique, reading cultural expressions as class texts written in order to deceive.

Although this mode of cultural criticism is extremely compelling, it accepts the positivist possibility of cleanly representational readings and writings. Post-structuralism casts doubt on the possibility of cultural readings that debunk class particularism from the vantage of the supposedly universal – Lukács' (1971) collective subject of world history. The only way to debunk particularism is through particularism itself, albeit one that unashamedly reveals its own grounding in one interest or another. Lukács had the same problem in *History and Class Consciousness* (1971) where, following Marx, he anointed the proletariat as the identical subject-object of history. His anointing lacked a reflexive foundation in arguments about why his reading was any more universal than the particular readings that installed capital as historically universal. As I just indicated, Marx also had this problem: Lukács inherited it from him. As a result, Lukács suggested a proletariat standard of cultural judgment – so-called realism – that could serve not only to debunk capitalist particularism but to orient cultural creation and judgment in a socialist future.

Realism is often attacked for deromanticizing cultural creation, reducing culture to politics. But this need not be so. Lukács' realism differed from Zhdanovite socialist realism, which glorified Soviet labor as the subject of cultural creation. Yet Lukács' realism was inadequate politically because he failed to respect the non-identity of culture and politics; he could read bourgeois art for its false universals but he could not develop an adequate oppositional aesthetic program that performed more positively. Lukács could read but not write culture. In this respect, his version of the Marxist theory of culture anticipated most other Marxist and neo-Marxist versions. All of these perspectives on cultural politics failed to capitalize on the non-identity of culture and politics (culture's relative autonomy in Althusserian terms), reading culture for its encoded politics but not politicizing cultural creation in a forward-looking, liberating way. In other words, Lukács' early version of cultural studies remained above history and thus politics, even though he historicized bourgeois cultural work through his own criticism. Like most Marxist theorists of culture, Lukács fails to recognize that criticism itself is a culturally constitutive and reconstitutive moment.

It was not until Frankfurt critical theory and poststructuralism that criticism was itself understood to be an act of cultural and political creation, albeit frequently a negative one (e.g., Adorno, 1973b). Lukács' original critical program debunked bourgeois culture but he did not understand that in doing so he was already prefiguring a non-bourgeois cultural milieu through the example of his own criticism. Lukács' critic – the realist – was a specialist intellectual; criticism was an esoteric, academic practice and not a part of cultural everyday life itself. In this sense, the relationship of criticism to culture could only be external. It was not understood that criticism had to deconstruct the whole metaphysic of representation that allowed Marxist criticism to set itself up as a transparent reading of bourgeois cultural contradictions from the vantage of objective interest. Lukács never understood the irony of his own positivist practice of cultural studies that allowed culture to remain an essentially determinate moment of political economy; he brilliantly showed the contradictions of capitalist existence concealed in European realism (as did Sartre (1981) in his studies of Flaubert). And yet he failed to understand that the realist criticism of realism succumbs to the same representationality that subordinates culture to politics and economics in the first place, hence only perpetuating its own heteronomy and unwittingly preserving the causality of economics over culture that is part and parcel of capitalism.

Culture as Truth and/or Transcendence?

The Marxist sociology of culture founders not only because it fails to understand the constitutional role of the critic but, indeed, of the artists themselves. This is because an essentially positivist Marxist sociology of culture has viewed culture as a repository of veiled truth claims (e.g., about the superiority of the bourgeois worldview or, indeed, about the alleged absence of authorial perspective in art). This is not wrong, only insufficient, from the point of view of cultural studies. As the Frankfurt theorists indicate, culture is both a realm of truth claims and a transcendental and constitutional project in its own right, making a purely epistemological investigation of culture narrowly one-sided from the outset. This is a central point of departure for the Frankfurt version of cultural studies. They both suggest and exemplify a mode of cultural criticism that takes into account not only expressive but also critical constitutionality, refusing to be straitjacketed by the narrowly epistemological traditional Marxist mode of critique, after the fashions of Lukács and Goldmann.

This epistemological or representational model of cultural criticism focuses on the truth content of works of culture. Thus, Lukács can show that bourgeois realism represents the world falsely from the perspective of the universal interests of the proletariat as spelled out by Marx. Admittedly, Marx established this representational model of criticism where he forged the terms of the critique of ideology in books like *The German Ideology* (Marx and Engels, 1947). Culture in general, like philosophy and economic theory in particular, can be read as a text proposing truth claims that can be falsified. The texts of bourgeois ideology err where they pretend that particular class truths are in fact general or universal truths, hence concealing the class standpoint of objective interest from which they are deceptively developed. Ideology is the proverbial *camera obscura* that inverts reality in the interest of the ruling capitalist class. Hence, both cultural criticism and cultural production are to be developed with an eye toward establishing counterfactual claims that give the lie to the bourgeois truths encoded in a variety of critical and cultural expressions. Culture can be falsified and 'true' culture created anew – one that represents the true interests of humanity, i.e., of the world-historical collective subject of the proletariat.

As a Marxist of sorts, I have no trouble at all with the notion that there are certain objective universal interests in freedom, justice, beauty, etc. To be a Marxist requires one to have some investment in such transhistorical rationalist notions. Indeed, what separates poststructuralism and postmodernism from Marxism is precisely this notion of the universality of objective reason. But the assertion that there are certain true societal and personal interests does not imply that culture is to be seen and practised simply as a repository of these incontrovertible truths. That is the problem with what I am calling the representational model of culture uncritically adopted by most Marxist theorists of culture (and one reversed by a poststructuralist version of cultural studies). A representational concept of culture fails to acknowledge and then harness the emancipatory potential of culture in projecting and hence enacting a qualitative otherness that, I would contend, is vital to the project of collective liberation.

This raises an irony of sorts, to be more fully addressed when I discuss poststructuralism and postmodernism in Chapter 6. On the one hand, Marxism corrects the poststructuralist and postmodernist relativisms with an objective perspective on universal reason. In other words, Marxism helps raise poststructuralism and postmodernism to the level of political critique. But, for its part, poststructuralism corrects Marxism by showing that culture is not only artifact but also practice, not only text but also con-text. These mutual correctives threaten to cancel each other out where Marxists and poststructuralists continue to talk past each other; there have been few serious attempts to show their possible convergence and to develop that convergence as a theoretical as well as political practice (see, e.g., Ryan, 1982; Agger, 1989a).

Poststructuralism exploits the crisis of representation to its advantage: the critical practice that emerges from the crisis of representation transcends the purely validity-oriented concerns of traditional Marxism. It is not enough to notice that cultural truths are class truths, nor to exhort the creation of a universalistic culture without specifying the grounds for such a recommendation. This is not to say that poststructural cultural studies has been particularly political; it has not been, and that is one of the ironies of its corrective of Marxism, which often seems more like a dismissal. Be that as it may, it is impossible to conceive of a Marxist cultural theory and politics outside of Derridean antifoundationalism. That is, Marxism can no longer rest assured that representational questions about validity can be easily resolved, especially in the realm of culture. Simply to taxonomize the great works of culture with respect to their political truth content ignores the whole modernist and postmodernist deconstruction of truth claims that are made unironically, without reference to the con-texts of texts (and the textuality of con-texts). Although (see Huyssen, 1986) I am more modernist than postmodern in my political sensibilities (in the same sense that Marx and Adorno were modernist: modernity as the revolutionary end of pre-history), traditional Marxism regresses too far behind sophisticated theoretical discussions of the cultural politics of representation to be of much use today, at least in its unrevised form. One of the projects of a politicized cultural studies is precisely to redevelop a Marxist cultural theory that avoids the fatal mistakes of representationality while holding fast to one or another absolutist version of left-wing critical practice and politics.

This discussion repeats the growing conviction on the left that what it means to be a Marxist is increasingly up for grabs. Theoretical iconoclasm and revisionism reign as never before. I am worried that much of this left-wing reflexivity, carried out under the signs of postmodernism, poststructuralism and feminist theory, goes too far toward abandoning Marxism in total. A postmodern Marxism may be too post-Marxist as well as post-modern, an issue I have considered elsewhere (Agger, 1990). The reaction against Marxist representationality threatens to lose the political vigor of the original Marxian project. To date, no emancipatory theory or movement remains as effectively totalizing and energizing as Marxism, no matter how often the western press revels in the 'demise' of Communism, as if that said anything about Marx or Marxism. At issue here, then, is the extent to which the Marxist theory of culture retains its political acuity while reconsidering some of its basic positivist tenets regarding the objectivism of critique and the representationality of cultural expression generally.

If culture can simply be read in terms of its encoded validity claims, as Lukács implies, then culture is a political factor only in the sense in which culture can be conceived as a series of transmissions. Cultural politics would want to change the content of these transmissions, moving away from the veiled particularism of bourgeois culture toward the universalism of proletarian culture. But I would argue that culture can also be read and written in terms of its transcendental properties, notably the way in which it focuses attention on the insufficiencies of history. In this sense, where culture represents a bad reality, that very representation constitutes a resistance of sorts, as well as hope. This is the character of art that Marcuse (1978) calls *Schein*, its illusory quality in itself preserving, even fostering, rebellion and, over the long term, transformation. Marcuse's aesthetic politics (see Agger, 1991a, Ch. 9) in this way corrects the tendency of orthodox Marxists to read culture simply as a set of propositions but not also as a rebellious or prefigurative practice that in itself effects some degree of social change.

Art's transcendental properties are more important than its class truths, according to this view. What Marcuse (1968) calls affirmative culture reduces art to mere reflection of the quotidian, thus ignoring its emancipatory properties. This is especially crucial where cultural criticism itself becomes mere representation-of-representation, not an intervention in its own way fully as constitutional as the cultural artifact itself. But this gets back to the perennial problem of Marxian scientism: the same people who view Marxism as incontrovertible economic law also tend to reduce culture to sheer representation. Ideological and cultural critique are seen as a kind of unmasking, a making present. They service political enlightenment by removing the barriers to clear perception and hence class action.

This essentially positivist model of cultural criticism is favored by many Marxists since Lukács. It is insufficient in light of the poststructural critique of the subject-centeredness of our traditional models of knowledge. In particular, it assumes that culture can be reflected presuppositionlessly and that the act of reflection itself need not be treated as a constitutional moment in its own right. Derrida's critique of the philosophy of presence – a world supposedly present to the presuppositionless, stable subject – shows that the whole positivist metaphysic of pre-ontological reflection is self-deceiving. The Frankfurt critique of science (e.g., Horkheimer and Adorno, 1972; Habermas, 1970, 1971; Marcuse, 1969; see Agger, 1991a, Ch. 11) adds a political twist to this Derridean critique of positivism by showing the ways in which the positivist metaphysic reinforces power in late capitalism, even on the left. A positivist cultural studies (see Denzin, 1991) that emerges from positivist Marxism is no less a feature of the general unconsciousness than the positivism of bourgeois social science. Worse, it loses its own precious opportunity to crack the codes of bourgeois mystification and representation.

Marxism and the Crisis of Representation

Let me amplify these remarks about the veiled positivism of Marxist cultural theory since Lukács and Goldmann. I am saying that this closet commitment to a representational model of cultural reading is the other side of a deep-seated economism that has plagued Marxism since Engels and then the Second and Third Internationals (and now reflected in Althusserianism as well as the rational-choice Marxism of Elster and Roemer). Left critics of left scientism have tended to ignore this positivist cultural theory largely because they were so preoccupied with economism, which seems like the more important enemy. But this represents a tendency for the critique of economism to be economistic itself, missing other dimensions of Marxist positivism that are equally debilitating in the long run. Where the Lukács of the 1920s is clearly an opponent of economism (e.g., Lukács, 1971), he did not extend his critique of economism into the realm of cultural theory. Indeed, the critique of economism should reasonably have produced a non-heteronomous theory of culture as a counterposition, as it did for Gramsci (1971; see Morrow, 1991), redeeming both cultural expression and cultural analysis as relatively autonomous media of critical political constitution. But Lukács and Goldmann did not adequately think through the crisis of representation in a way that would have allowed them to understand the depths to which positivism had sunk in early twentieth-century capitalism. Instead, they simply duplicated cultural representation in their own representational cultural criticism, falling back on more traditional models of political edification that failed to challenge bourgeois hegemony at its deepest source – Enlightenment subject/object dualism (see, e.g., Horkheimer and Adorno, 1972, who theorized the depth of this bourgeois hegemony in a much more compelling way).

The crisis of Marxism in the early twentieth century was not resolved in a way that anticipated the later crisis of representation addressed by poststructuralism. Lukács assumed that discourse was a more or less straightforward vehicle for uncovering mystification, whether in economistic or cultural forms. For him not to have anticipated the poststructuralist critique of the positivist philosophy of language is reasonable enough; philosophical trends and fads change overnight in some instances. But it is strange that a Hegelianizing theorist like Lukács, who took ideology and consciousness so seriously in developing his critique of Marxian economism, would neglect the implications of his revaluation of the realm of culture for his own analysis of culture. Surely at some level culture is a world apart – precisely the wellspring of emancipatory critique and practice needed to deconstruct the automatic Marxism of Engels, Kautsky and the Bolsheviks. As Marcuse (1964) argued, there needs to be a 'second dimension' along which critique and resistance can be conceived, the realm of imagination and desire.

Culture can convey utopia. Similarly, cultural criticism can exhume the utopian potential of culture where it is not explicit. This is precisely the modernist agenda – at least the critical modernism of Adorno and his Frankfurt colleagues, if not the mainstream modernism of architecture and urban planning that has transformed our cities into selfsame monoliths reflecting the homogenizing gigantism of capitalism (see Huyssen, 1986; Harvey, 1989; Soja, 1989). Mechanical Marxists do not so much purge culture of utopia as fail to see it there already; cultural expressions are read for class truths and untruths, neglecting their marginal existence as worlds apart from the capitalist quotidian. Of course, much mainstream culture embraces its own integration: that is what Horkheimer and Adorno (1972) meant by the culture industry. It not only allows itself to be sold; it sells out, unashamedly. The 'American century' is glorified (by *Time* magazine) for all of its glorious contributions to popular culture that signify fundamental social and intellectual progress. The Frankfurt dismissal of mass culture is occasioned by this romanticism of popular culture in the hands of the end-of-ideology crowd (e.g., Bell, 1960, 1976) who dismiss modernist mandarinism for its supposedly anti-populist overtones. Instead, they bizarrely laud the achievements of popular culture delivered from on high by advertising agencies, networks and publishing conglomerates.

I would argue that the crisis of representation today is an outgrowth of the crisis of capitalist accumulation and reproduction generally, a point that should be obvious to Marxists of all stripes. Positivist representation is an ideologizing response to the advanced needs of legitimation and consumerism (see Habermas, 1975) at this stage of capitalism: it repeats and hence relives the world 'as it is', that is, as it is given to us through the various texts of culture and science. Representation is no longer simply an epistemological or aesthetic stance but a veritable political theory. In reflecting the historically momentary, it wants to freeze the present into eternity, inducing people to rehearse the allegedly ontological routines of subordination depicted for them as nature-like by the authors of culture and science. This is the general drift of the Frankfurt analysis of the culture industry, albeit one that is also indebted to the poststructural critique of the metaphysic of representation.

It may be unfair to criticize Lukács for not anticipating the crisis of representation in terms of its implications for social and cultural theory. Indeed, it was Lukács who gave the original impetus to later Frankfurt and Derridean critiques of the metaphysics and politics of representation through his pioneering book *History and Class Consciousness* (1971). But although Lukács ought not to be criticized through the convenient lenses of 20/20 hindsight, reductive Marxist sociologists of culture continue to ignore the constitutional roles of culture and cultural criticism, addressing cultural validity claims counterfactually. Although some of this work is interesting and important (e.g., Marxist critiques of media and mass entertainment for their egregious misrepresentations of the world), it fails to theorize *itself* as a constitutive moment of representationality. Thus, it loses a ground in constitutionality that can help it push beyond the mere appearances hoodwinking consciousness into identification with the quotidian as a plenitude of human existence.

Representation is in crisis because it has been politicized, notably through critical theory and poststructuralism. There is no going back: we can no longer read images, words and codes as presuppositionless, pre-ontological screens on which Being is imprinted. Reading writes, just as writing is a reading. Habermas (1971) puts this differently. He says that Marxism has always lacked a ground in self-reflection that could help it avoid the instrumental rationality of the hard and technical sciences, propelling it into the fray of history and hence historical becoming. That is one way to put the problem. I do not favor it because I reject his Kantian dualism separating the rationalities of instrumental and self-reflective/communicative action. It seems to me that poststructuralism would radicalize the Habermasian program to the extent to which it was no longer feasible at all to make such sharp categorical distinctions between qualitatively different types of action, instead blurring them to the point of virtual identity.

Of course, that raises all sorts of other problems, notably the so-called dialectic of nature. Are technology and science simply discourses? The adjudication of that issue will have to await a different treatment, a poststructural reading/writing of science more extensive than my own reading of science texts (Agger, 1989b). For my purposes here, I want to point out the parallel between Habermas' knowledge-and-interest argument and the poststructural critique of left economism. They both conclude that representation is constitution (and constitution a kind of representation). To raise these issues in a sober discussion of the Marxist theory of culture will cause more traditional Marxists to raise their eyebrows. Impatient with metaphysics, they choose physics – the supposed laws of economic crisis sketched out by Marx (1977) in Volume One of *Capital*. And where Auguste Comte developed bourgeois sociology as 'social physics', Marxist cultural criticism is a kind of cultural physics, debunking the false representations of bourgeois cultural expression from the vantage of unsullied objectivity.

The poststructural crisis of representation is above all a crisis of criticism, as Fish (1980) and Jameson (1984b) have indicated in different ways. Where artistic representation is no longer unproblematic, so critical representation-of-representation must be argued from the ground of antifoundational interest, not the impregnable Reason endorsed by Hegelian Marxists. Fraser (1989) has nicely developed the ironies of the antifoundationalist assault on objective reason from the point of view of feminist theory and critical theory. Her critique of Rorty (1979, 1989) is particularly telling. But Marxist sociologists of culture do not learn from these developments: they persist in presupposing the possibility of vantageless criticism from which they evaluate cultural artifacts along the continuum of Marxist epistemological verisimilitude. But the attack on representationality typically, as in the case of Rorty, takes a politically anti-Marxist bent, conflating the lack of left critical reflexivity with the alleged failures of the Marxist political program itself. This is characteristic of a creeping academic neoconservatism that rehearses Bell's (1960) end-of-ideology strictures through the mouthpiece of Lyotard's (1984) critique of Marxist grand narratives. Postmodernism becomes yet another version of liberal pluralism, as ideologically driven as ever.

Where postmodernism denies the possibility of evaluation per se, indulging the whirling play of multiple signifiers as its form of what Barthes (1975) calls *jouissance*, Marxist cultural theory attempts evaluation from the ethereal heights of Apollonian dispassion – the impossible vantage of the transcendental collective subject of a teleological world history. Where postmodern cultural studies denies that subjectivity is any factor in cultural analysis and evaluation, the deterministic cultural physics of Marxism installs a transcendental collective subject as the Archimedean arbiter of cultural forms and forces. But in this age of the crisis of representation, such objectivist postures appear hopelessly out of date. To read culture for class truths (or untruths) from the privileged vantage of epistemological vanguardism is thoroughly anachronistic, leading either to Zhdanovism pure and simple or to the arbitrary objectivisms of Lukács, Goldmann and perhaps even the Frankfurt School (e.g., Adorno's infamous dismissal of jazz). It is one thing to resolve the crisis of representation with an utter retreat from validity claims, as poststructuralism does. That simply capitulates to the purported end of politics, hence ensuring it. It is another thing to pretend or presume that validity is unproblematic from the vantage of class standpoint. That rehearses all the old problems of vanguardism, from which the left cannot escape except through the heroic politics of the cult of personality.

Criteria of Aesthetic-Political Correctness

There are three possible left positions on the truth content of art – orthodox Marxism, poststructuralism (Chapter 6) and the Frankfurt School's critical theory (Chapter 4). (Since feminist theory [Chapter 7] falls along a somewhat different continuum, I will discuss it separately, below.) Poststructural cultural theory suggests that there are no stable grounds for evaluating the truth content of cultural artifacts or expressions. Indeed, the talk of truth, characteristic of the Enlightenment and its scientism, is silenced by Derrideans, who instead appraise cultural forms in terms of their own internal aporias, undecidability and relations of difference. Poststructuralism challenges Marxism to demonstrate the unproblematic grounds of its own validity from which it can confidently evaluate cultural works according to criteria of political correctness. In this respect, as I develop further in Chapter 6, poststructural cultural theory essentially eschews critical evaluation of a directly political kind.

Orthodox Marxism for its part suggests that aesthetic-political correctness must be assessed from the point of view of class, notably the class supposedly at the leading edge of historical unfolding. This is the general thrust of Lukácsian aesthetics and continues to ground Marxist aesthetic theory. It is to this line of argument that poststructuralism is an address, as one can ascertain if one examines the emergence of French poststructural thought after May 1968 as a counterpoint to the dogma and scientism of French Communist Party epistemology. Derrida suggests that the confidence Marxists have about foundation is false; the aporetic nature of language enmeshes both the cultural producer and cultural critic in the infinite regress of difference/differance. Theory becomes an activity of playful agitation from within texts, showing the weak spots in discourses that posture themselves as seamlessly self-sufficient and impervious to deconstructive challenges.

The poststructural critique of orthodox Marxism has been extremely persuasive, at least judging by the cast of characters doing cultural criticism in the university. A good deal of the critical field has been taken over by poststructural and postmodern cultural theorists, with occasional challenges from neo-Frankfurters and feminists. For their part, even Frankfurters and feminists often drink deeply of the poststructural challenge, incorporating aspects of Derridean critique within their own critical and political practices (see Fraser, 1989). But for the most part a kind of antifoundationalism reigns in cultural theory; Marxism is seen as hopelessly out of date, arrogant, authoritarian. One of my interests here is in developing new criteria of aesthetic-political judgment that help me chart a safe course between the Scylla of orthodox Marxism and the Charybdis of poststructuralism.

In this sense, it is important to recognize that the poststructural challenge to Marxist cultural theory is at once correct and misleading. It is surely correct in its deconstructive analysis of the imbeddedness of criticism itself in the aporias and forms of life of language; there is no Archimedean stance from which we can wash away the constitutional nature of language. But poststructuralism is misleading where it utterly abandons the project of aesthetic and political evaluation. Marxist cultural theory is above all intended as a political intervention, not simply an exercise in *jouissance* designed to please the critic, let alone build academic careers. Lukács and Goldmann were committed intellectuals, in Sartre's (1965) terms, even though they failed to understand the deconstructive spiral within which their own cultural evaluation was inevitably ensconced.

Although Lukács can be read as arbitrarily prescribing cultural and political values from the outside, notably in the ways that the world-historical mission of the proletariat is either foregrounded or obscured by cultural expressions, all Marxists (to be Marxists) recognize that culture is a powerful factor in both domination and liberation. That minimal criterion of a political aesthetic need not entail the non-deconstructive cultural physics of Lukács-style cultural theory. It is possible to elaborate an aesthetic that neither eschews commitment nor pretends stancelessness. In fact, as I will argue later, that is precisely the balance struck by the Frankfurt School in their appreciation and further development of a modernist political aesthetic (challenged unsuccessfully by Lyotard's postmodernism).

The poststructural critique of Marxist foundationalism typically leads to antifoundationalism. There are other possibilities: the critique of foundationalism might argue for different, more inclusive, reflexive and dialogical foundations approached with the humility and irony of people who recognize that the truth is inherently ambiguous (e.g., Merleau-Ponty, 1964; Habermas, 1984, 1987b). The critique of Lukács does not disqualify Marxist aesthetics altogether but could conceivably provoke new formulations of cultural politics, informed variously by poststructuralism, Frankfurt critical theory and feminist theory. That is precisely the project of cultural studies as I understand it.

Proletkult

Lukács falsely universalized the proletariat as the identical subject-object of world history, thus ignoring other agents of liberation. But that is different from saying that there are no universal subject-objects – agents – of totalizing social change. The poststructural critique of foundationalism confuses the particular foundations claimed by orthodox Marxism with foundations in general. I would argue that one can be a Marxist – a critical theorist in the largest sense – without reifying the Euro-American, largely male proletariat. One can hold onto foundations, albeit different foundations from those claimed by orthodox Marxists. The empirical revision of Marxist theory suggests a reconfiguration of the collective and singular subjects of a progressive world history, addressing a host of levels and victims of domination heretofore ignored by orthodox Marxism, notably including women and people of color. *Proletkult* has little, if any, relevance in the 1990s.

For Marxist cultural theory not to be hopelessly anachronistic today, it must rethink Marx's mid-nineteenth-century assumptions about the likely patterns and agents of social change in international capitalism. This is not to dismiss the proletariat, as post-Marxists and postmodernists do. It is rather to encourage a thoroughgoing rethinking of Marxism in the light of global as well as psychic developments in capitalism since Marx's death in 1883. This is precisely the project of the Frankfurt School, mediately reflected in their modernist version of aesthetic politics (e.g., Adorno, 1984; Marcuse, 1978). They do not throw out the working class as a central focus of Marxist theory, analysis and cultural resistance; like Gramsci, they retain a concept and practice of class. However, they refuse to retain the relatively undifferentiated class theory of Marx, risking the charge of apostasy. Instead, they grapple with empirical changes in capitalism and the world system that occasion fresh thinking about social change. Theirs is a shamelessly revisionist project.

The issue here is fundamental: is Marxism only or mainly a theory about the exploitation of workers' labor power or is it a more general theory of all domination, oppression and exploitation? The Frankfurt theorists argued that Marxism is a version of critical theory, not the other way around. They do not privilege class domination but trace the origins and depth of domination to the epochal subject philosophy that realizes itself in the conquest of the objective Other, whether nature or other people. This is the argument laid out in *Dialectic of Enlightenment* (Horkheimer and Adorno, 1972), perhaps the most important statement of Frankfurt critical theory. If Marxism is only or mainly a theory of (white male) class exploitation, then the *Proletkult* stance makes sense – the idea that art and culture must somehow express class truths. But if Marxism is larger than (white male) class theory, then cultural politics must be substantially broader than that. What, exactly, it should be is an issue that will have to await my concluding chapter. Suffice it to say here that the Lukács position on cultural politics is far from exhaustive of possible Marxist stances; indeed, his relatively mechanical theory of cultural resistance tends to provoke the post-Marxist counterposition in response, thus confusing his particular Marxism with all possible Marxisms.

Marx gave little guidance here; his authority legitimates all sorts of twentieth-century extrapolations, particularly in the realm of cultural politics. It is simply impossible to read Marx as a guide in a world where cultural transmission and hegemony are reproduced through television (see Fiske and Hartley, 1978; Fiske, 1987; Miller, 1988; Luke, 1989; Kellner, 1990; Harms and Kellner, 1991). Things have changed too much for that. This is not to deny that theoretical insights can be found in the pre-culture industry theories of various leftists, including Lukács. But one cannot derive a 'correct' cultural politics from theorists who lived so far in advance of electronic mass culture that they could scarcely imagine the sorts of political and psychic implications that these cultural innovations would have for both theory and practice. Indeed, a good deal of cultural revisionism on the left has concerned the appropriate theorization of mass culture.

The *Proletkult* position – that art must somehow serve the interests of the proletariat in its world-historical struggle – was probably wrong even in the nineteenth and early twentieth centuries. Marxists never faced the crisis of representation; they never understood that cultural readings were themselves strong writings, involving criticism not only in representation-of-representation but in what Althusser (1970) called theoretical practice. Lukács was never correct to claim a secure foundation in a proletarian philosophy of history that enabled him to stand outside of history in pronouncing judgments on the various cultural artifacts of the time. There is no *standing outside* for a deconstructive cultural studies: cultural criticism is strongly constitutional, not merely representational. The critic by criticizing is already changing the world, already creating and recreating culture. Ideology critique is political practice, if insufficient practice. The proletariat cannot simply be spoken for by cultural artisans or critics in their attempt to provide cultural enlightenment from without. There is always a dialectical relationship between cultural criticism and cultural production that forces the critic not simply to assume an impregnable foundation outside of history but to argue for one's claimed foundation in a way that acknowledges one's own historicity, hence fallibility.

In this sense, it is not the particular evaluations and cultural practices associated with Soviet socialist realism that characterize what I am calling *Proletkult* here. Lukács was at times hostile to this version of Marxist cultural politics, and for good reason. *Proletkult* is the broader strategy of distancing criticism from history in a way that sunders the two, recommending cultural practices that somehow stand outside of and speak for the local practices of the oppressed. *Proletkult* is not only a fetish of working people, concealing the intellectual's voyeuristic disdain; it is a form of cultural evaluation and prescription that fails to appreciate the dialectical nature of cultural expression, allusion and artifice: it judges art shabby if it fails to represent class truths. Although there are overt and covert class dimensions to art and culture, art and culture are also transcendental activities that in their very distance and difference interrogate the present.

Today, the position that I am characterizing as *Proletkult* is found everywhere in the left academy. But today the issues are not only class but now also race and gender. There is a growing movement to evaluate cultural works with respect to their authenticity as correct political statements on the part of victims whose suffering they represent; frequently, the artists themselves are from these embattled groups and their work is read as if it were constitutive of the 'voice' of the disempowered. This has resulted in the politicization, professionalization, and ghettoization of cultural studies done from the particular vantages of the subjects that cultural works depict: there is women's art and the art of people of color (in addition to class art, as in the original Zhdanovist version of *Proletkult*). Essentially, these positions all argue that culture can be judged externally from the point of view of certain mechanical requirements of political authenticity or correctness. Although feminist cultural studies and cultural studies done from a non-white perspective differentiate themselves from Marxism, they use orthodox Marxist criteria of representational evaluation in their own critical practices. In particular, they attempt to stand outside of cultural history and evaluate the works in question from the perspective of their political truthfulness, precisely the project of original Marxist cultural theory.

It is obvious that this sort of critical activity has politicized the study of culture as well as academic life generally. I am not denying that academic and critical work are already heavily saturated with values and assumptions; value-freedom is, as ever, a positivist ruse. But I would argue that cultural works are already political in the stance of detachment and evocation they take with respect to their subject matter. Every work of fiction is protest against the ritualized quotidian conducted from the point of view of a mute conformity. Although some novels are more or less effectively political, writing fiction is inherently a political statement, regardless of its content. To politicize culture from the outside denies that it is political in the first place. This ad hoc politicization serves a certain vanguard interest in the accumulation of cultural capital (see Bourdieu, 1984), authenticating those who are licensed as Marxist, feminist or African-American critics. In a sense, the critic's life is defined by his or her political commitments, which are seen to inform his or her critical practice from the outside, in terms of the overt judgments on political correctness made in the course of one's critical practice.

I will argue in my concluding chapter that cultural studies is inherently a radical activity in that it offers a method of reading and thus deconstructing cultural hegemony, thus enlarging the realms of freedom and imagination. To politicize cultural studies in terms of its particular ideological affiliations, whether Marxist or feminist, assumes that one can do cultural studies apolitically: the politics enter through the back door, as in socialist realism. But this assumes that critical practice is somehow other than cultural politics, a position that is essentially positivist. I will argue that any cultural reading is already an act of cultural creation and that to ignore this is to turn cultural studies into yet another professionalized activity with its own hierarchy over the topics and practices it addresses.

As a result, cultural studies ends up isolated in departments and programs defined by their particular agitational commitments (e.g., women's studies programs). There has been an explosion of feminist film criticism of this kind. I am not disputing the political and intellectual relevance of this work; in Chapter 7, I interrogate and appreciate these developments. But for cultural studies proponents to regionalize their critical interests in terms of their affiliations to particular social movements or interest groups detotalizes cultural studies, turning it away from a general theoretical address to things cultural and instead isolating it in a highly circumscribed area of critical interest. This is precisely the complaint leveled by feminists at Marxist cultural theorists: they ignore women. But feminist cultural studies tends to replicate this blindness, except in the opposite direction.

The political affiliation of a representational version of cultural studies undoes its focus on totality. This is as true of orthodox Marxism as of any of the other more recent affiliations of cultural studies. In the case of Marxism, the focus on class truth and class vantage tends to obscure the fact that Marxism should be a totalizing theory – a theory of everything – and not just an interest group perspective that focuses exclusively on the proletariat. Interestingly, Birmingham cultural studies has moved from an early preoccupation with working-class culture in the UK (e.g., Willis, 1977; Hebdige, 1979) toward a more general approach to popular culture (e.g., Hebdige, 1988), perhaps recognizing the limitations of classism when it comes to cultural studies. This is something that both Soviet and Lukács-era cultural theory never learned. Instead, they focused on the class roots of culture in a way that prevented them from understanding the complexity and differential nature of cultural hegemony, including the roles of women and people of color. Critical theory must confront the central dilemma of totality theories: on the one hand, they attempt to explain and thus transform everything; on the other hand, in so doing, they tend to reduce totality to a single axial dimension, whether class, gender or race, thus reducing the differential field of the totality one-dimensionally. This is the sense of Althusser's (1970) notion of a decentered totality (although Althusser ambivalently reinstates the logic of 'determination in the last instance', holding onto orthodox Marxism while contradictorily denying its reductionism).

Orthodox Marxism is typically countered by orthodox non-Marxisms. This is as true of cultural studies approaches as of more general tendencies in social theory. For that reason, Marxists and non-Marxist leftists (e.g., feminists) engage in a fruitless pitched battle which really conceals a deep defensiveness and territoriality. Of course, capitalism has always divided the opposition in order to conquer it. By pitting one reductive version of totality against others, we are assured that none of them successfully develops a truly total perspective on culture and society. By now, unfortunately, postmodernist resistance to Lyotard's so-called grand narratives like Marxism has become so prevalent in the cultural studies community that it is virtually impossible to advocate totality without putting the postmodern crowd on the defensive. This has the general effect of depoliticizing cultural studies at a time when the idea of a cultural studies might be the best available means for combating all sorts of tired orthodoxies on the left.

Chapter 4

The Frankfurt School's Aesthetic Politics

Marxism 'or' the Frankfurt School?

An assessment of the Frankfurt School's approach to cultural studies turns on the issue of its relationship to Marxism. By now, there have been numerous discussions (e.g., Jay, 1973) of this issue, although less with reference to their aesthetic theory than to their overall critique of capitalist domination. I am especially concerned here to address the convergence and divergence between the Marxist theory of culture and the aesthetic theory of the Frankfurt School. At once, I want to defend their work as Marxist while outlining some crucial differences they had with the Lukács-era sociology of culture.

To assess this issue of convergence and divergence it needs to be made clear that the political aims of Marx and the Frankfurt theorists were remarkably similar. They wanted nothing less than a thorough transvaluation of capitalist social structures and everyday life. The argument (e.g., Slater, 1977; Cleaver, 1979) that the Frankfurt thinkers somehow betray the revolutionary political theory of Marx and original Marxists is far-fetched, especially in light of the early statements of critical theory by the founders of the Institute for Social Research (e.g., Horkheimer, 1972). Rereading these original statements by Marcuse, Adorno and Horkheimer (see Arato and Gebhardt, 1978) suggests the close parallel between Marx's political aspirations and those of these early twentieth-century theorists. Yet it is understandable that commentators could miss this political convergence: the tone and substance of Frankfurt critical theory were very different from the political economic critique of Marx; in a sense, one has to read between the lines to get the full flavor of their political utopianism and commitment to socialist revolution. Frankfurt discourse became even more remote from the ringing declarations of Marx as their political pessimism deepened with the unfolding of fascism, the post-World War Two consolidation of world capitalism and the massive extent of the culture industry.

The Frankfurt School's revision of Marxism involved not an abandonment of his dialectical method or political utopianism but rather a fresh empirical analysis of the structural contradictions and crisis tendencies of capitalism. Writing in the 1920s and 1930s, the Frankfurt critics confronted some massive changes in western capitalism from the time when Marx composed *Capital* (see Mandel, 1975). Of course, much Marxological effort is devoted to sifting out what is essential from original Marx and what is historically episodic. Indeed, to be genuinely an orthodox Marxist today means that one accepts literal Marx in total. Thus, unsurprisingly, there are few orthodox Marxists inasmuch as few can dispute the fact that capitalism has changed in a host of ways only dimly predictable by Marx. Yet given the spreading neoconservatism in intellectual as well as political life today, it is equally easy to read neo-Marxist revisionism, like the body of German critical theory up to and including Habermas, as a recanting of Marx's dialectical method as well as his political utopianism. Such work is read as post-Marxist and hence it is embraced as positive proof that Marxist prophecy has failed.

This whole discussion could be resolved more easily by attempting not to gauge the extent to which the Frankfurt theorists were bona fide Marxists (whatever that might mean) but rather by examining the extent to which Marx's Marxism was critical theory in the broader sense. Adorno, Horkheimer and Marcuse believed that Marx's critique of capitalism was insufficiently radical, insufficiently far-reaching, obscuring deeper structures of millennial domination that both preceded and might outlast capitalism. As I said in the last chapter, they attempted to produce a generic critical theory that addressed the epochal subject/object dichotomy as the axial problematic of western civilization, a problem that they articulated as the dialectic of enlightenment (Horkheimer and Adorno, 1972). If one accepts the merits of subsuming Marxism under critical theory rather than the other way around, one can then better develop a critical cultural studies in terms that go beyond Marx's rather mechanical theory of culture, discussed in the preceding chapter.

In particular, the Frankfurt theorists refused to believe that Marxist critique itself was somehow exempt from social and economic determination, above or outside of history. In depriviliging the Archimedean pretensions of theory that reads cultural artifacts and expressions for their class truths, the Frankfurt theorists recognized that theory itself is a cultural and political activity. As such, they interrogated what poststructuralists call the crisis of representation by refusing to phrase their own cultural criticism simply as a representation-of-representation, merely an assessment of cultural products' class-truth content. Instead, especially for Adorno (1945, 1954, 1974b), cultural criticism, indeed critical theory generally, was to be an active intervention into cultural politics, not a distanced appraisal rooted in a left-wing objectivism.

The Frankfurt theorists wanted to avoid the Lukács-era cultural theory that placed cultural criticism above the heads of cultural producers, distributors and consumers. Cultural analysis would not involve simply the assessment of the political truth content of cultural works but would take these works on their own terms without losing the perspective of critique from which it is possible to acknowledge the difference between being on the inside and being on the outside. For example, Adorno's voluminous work on musical theory and composition (e.g., Adorno, 1973c) did not simply dismiss a variety of developments in modern music because they were high-cultural or somehow bourgeois. Instead, he attempted to move back and forth between the social context of music and the tensions and continuities within musical oeuvres that articulated with, and thus shed light on, this context. In this way, he believed, the theorist could learn a great deal about both the society in which we live and about the transcendental possibilities exemplified and disclosed by cultural creations.

It is easy to ridicule the mandarin tone of Adorno's aesthetic theory as well as its apparent political disengagement (see Jay, 1984). But that would not acknowledge the failures of a supposedly more engaged cultural criticism that reads cultural works only from the objectivist position of transcendental class critique. Although Adorno was attacked for his stand-offishness at a time in the 1960s when political engagement was breaking out all over, Adorno in fact sought engagement with cultural works that he refused to evaluate only from the perspective of a mechanical theory of class culture or what I earlier called cultural physics. This was because Adorno had a total social theory that enabled him to situate all manner of cultural expressions, from atonal music to radio and television; it was also because Adorno (as a musician himself) had the ability to engage immanently with compositions – from the inside out, as it were. Thus, in spite of the popular image of his cultural condescension, Adorno was more populist than many of his allegedly more politicized critics.

The Frankfurt theorists often courted misunderstanding because they viscerally felt that one did not have to choose between Marxism and critical theory; they refused to be branded as apostate with reference to simplistic devotional criteria of allegiance. Of course, anyone can call a cultural analysis Marxist or feminist, as I (1989a) have pointed out. But these words become slogans repeated thoughtlessly. Over time, they lose any content they may have had originally. Adorno really listened to Schoenberg and Stravinsky, just as he really read Beckett and Kafka. He refused to be hemmed in by preformed categories of political taxonomy, instead choosing to develop a highly nuanced aesthetic theory that did double duty as both cultural and social theory.

This tendency on the part of the Frankfurt theorists to combine cultural and social theory has been profoundly troubling to orthodox Marxists who retain a more reductive base-superstructure model. The Marxist sociology of culture, discussed in the preceding chapter, refuses to grant culture relative autonomy and, at the same time, fails to integrate cultural and political-economic analysis in a dialectical way. Frankfurt aesthetic theory effectively combines cultural and economic analysis to the extent to which these separate categories blur and even merge. Orthodox Marxism separates cultural analysis from social analysis, reducing cultural analysis to the search for class truths that exist somehow outside the realm of commodity production per se. But this disregards the dialectical unity of Marx's original analysis of reification under the commodity form: like the later Frankfurt thinkers, Marx believed that reifying culture and human relationships were part and parcel of the commodity structures of capitalist society. In this sense, cultural analysis was at once economic and political analysis, aesthetic theory becoming simultaneously a form of social theory.

In any event, whether these theoretical tendencies in twentieth-century Marxism are 'really' Marxist is irrelevant given the continuing evolution of capitalism since Marx. Had Marx foreseen the remarkable extent of state intervention and reification, perhaps the issue of revisionism – i.e., apostasy – might be relevant. Surely it is telling that Habermas has sharply diverged from Adorno's, Horkheimer's and Marcuse's analysis of domination, recanting fundamental aspects of their utopian quest for qualitatively new social and technological relationships. But Marx did not foresee the extent of state intervention or the rise of the culture industry as crucial mediating agencies in late capitalism.

The issue of what it means to be Marxist largely turns on whether theorists (like Habermas) accept the full extent of Marx's political agenda, notably the creation of a socially and technologically dis-alienated society. But this may be more a matter of temperament than anything else, irreducible to fundamental theoretical positions (but perhaps nevertheless reflected in them).

The Thesis of the Culture Industry

Assuming either that the Frankfurt thinkers were Marxists in the sense that they sought a dis-alienated society or that the question of whether they were Marxists is historically irrelevant today, their major contribution to cultural studies remains the remarkably prescient theory and analysis of the culture industry, first developed in Horkheimer and Adorno's (1972) 1947 *Dialectic of Enlightenment*. This book originates a left-wing 'mass culture' theory that in many respects was the first serious and systematic articulation of what has later come to be called cultural studies (although, as I will suggest shortly, there are some crucial differences in emphasis). The culture-industry thesis largely responds to developments in late capitalism unforeseen by Marx that contribute to the surprising resiliency of capitalism.

In particular, the culture-industry argument helps explain how the commodification of culture, particularly in the realm of so-called leisure time, contributes to both profit and social control, lulling people into a somnolent stupor that preserves the system against internal challenges. This is most elaborately argued in Marcuse's (1964) *One-Dimensional Man*, a book in which he explores the new powers of ideology to hold people in its sway. This 1960s argument stems from the earlier Horkheimer-Adorno discussion of the culture industry, bringing it up to date and casting it in a more systematic form for an audience largely untrained in European social philosophy. The seeds for this kind of analysis were laid first in the 1930s when Horkheimer (1972) argued that it is impossible cleanly to separate the economic and ideological dimensions of capitalism, thus giving critical theory its own dialectical methodology capable of analyzing social life simultaneously on both levels.

All of this work buttresses the particular empirical and critical analyses of high and low culture offered by the Frankfurt theorists (e.g., Adorno's aesthetic theory [1973c, 1984] as well as his studies of mass media [1945, 1954, 1974b]). Their cultural critique of capitalism set the stage for the subsequent traditions of cultural studies elaborated by the Birmingham School as well as by poststructuralists, postmodernists and feminists. The culture-industry thesis makes the study of culture respectable on the left. On the other hand, it provides a counterpoint against which the subsequent poststructural and feminist traditions of cultural studies have developed their own distinctive perspectives on the possibility of politicized cultural analysis. It is important to capture this dialectical irony for it helps us read post-Frankfurt cultural studies in terms of its ambivalent relationship to the founding Frankfurt work on culture.

In this sense, the reception of Frankfurt cultural theory by later cultural analysts has been all-important in determining the various political and intellectual inflections of cultural studies. Some readers of the culture-industry thesis recognize the dialectical unity of Horkheimer and Adorno's analysis of cultural commodification in terms of its twin foci on both economic and ideological features of mass culture (e.g., Kellner, 1989a). They do not read the Frankfurt theory of culture as a recanting of Marx's political economy but rather as its extension in a newer stage of capitalism. These readers recognize that the Frankfurt analysis of culture opens up a whole new vista of conjoined economic-ideological analysis of late capitalism by way of cultural critique. It legitimizes the study of regions of experience and practice heretofore regarded as epiphenomenal by orthodox Marxists.

Others read the culture-industry thesis to offer a quite mechanical and potentially elitist account of popular culture. Most cultural studies proponents view the apparent Frankfurt cultural mandarinism with a good deal of skepticism, rejecting what they take to be the Frankfurt aversion to emancipatory themes in popular culture. It is no exaggeration to suggest that British and American cultural studies largely define themselves in terms of their differentiation from the Frankfurt culture-industry thesis in the single sense that they reject what they take to be the cultural elitism of the Frankfurt School's disdainful analysis of 'low' culture. The popular-culture analyses proliferating both across and within academic disciplines, all the way from Birmingham to Bowling Green, mark their difference from the Frankfurt School by emphasizing their receptivity to issues of popular culture supposedly ignored or condemned by Horkheimer and Adorno (see Nelson and Grossberg, 1988; Ross, 1989). They establish themselves in terms of their difference from what they take to be the Apollonian Frankfurt disdain for mass-cultural forms like television, mainstream music and blockbuster movies.

The Frankfurt culture-industry thesis is thus read both to legitimize the study of culture on the left and to constrain cultural evaluation in terms of elitist Eurocentric aesthetic values. Both may be true, although I am highly suspicious of the conventional post-Marxist reading of the Frankfurt analysis of culture (better, of the reading that homogenizes Frankfurt cultural theory into a neat package, collapsing Adorno on Schoenberg and Marcuse on youth music). Even in its own terms, the reading of Frankfurt cultural theory as oblivious to popular culture misses Adorno's own writings on radio, television and journalism. The Frankfurt theorists took popular culture seriously and studied it rigorously (e.g., see Lowenthal, 1961, 1975, 1984, 1986). If they disdained mass culture for its hidden political assumptions and narcotizing effects, at least they recognized that mass culture is an important venue of political analysis and critique. The fact that Adorno favored modernist high culture as a critical vehicle is somehow beside the point: he recognized that mass culture is extraordinarily effective in deepening late-capitalist hegemony.

Whatever the case, the culture-industry thesis helped politicize the study of mass culture at a time when orthodox Marxists failed to meet the challenge of explaining the global village in adequate terms. Cultural commodification involves both surplus value and the reification of social relations, as Marx outlined in his original analysis of commodity fetishism. For Marxists to focus only on culture as big business misses the ideologizing, hegemonizing and reifying forces at work in cultural commodification, notably the tendency of cultural commodification to destroy an authentic realm of public discourse within which people can mount challenges to the dominant values and institutions. Even Marx addressed the narcotic effects of religion in his famous phrase. For economistic

Marxists to ignore this aspect of cultural experience in the late twentieth century seriously weakens their perspective on political blockages and possibilities.

As for the culture-industry argument itself, one can identify at least five distinctive empirical theses.

1. The Frankfurt theorists argue that there is a general or *mass culture* in late twentieth-century America (and now western Europe and capitalist Asia). Marcuse in *One-Dimensional Man* (1964) suggests that this mass culture enables working-class and middle-class people to attain nearly the same level of creature comforts and entertainments as their bosses. Where nearly everyone can own a VCR and vacation at Disney World, explosive class differences are muted. This facilitates the development of a new class consensus, defusing the class polarization of early twentieth-century Europe and Britain. Mass culture is relatively undifferentiated: poor urban blacks are exposed to the same advertising and entertainment as the preppie children of suburban Yuppies. They develop similar consumer aspirations as well as a common material worldview, dominated by individualism and consumerism. This generic culture appears to level class differences, thus protecting them.

Horkheimer, Adorno and Marcuse contrast post-war mass culture to the more differentiated, regionalized and heterogeneous cultures of pre-industrial societies. Habermas later (1984, 1987b) argues that the 'system' has colonized the lifeworlds of people in late capitalism, subsuming them under the same logic of integration and accumulation. The nationalization and internationalization of culture are developments not expected by orthodox Marxists, who retain relatively rigid class distinctions in their approaches to culture. Although the Birmingham School focuses on the distinctiveness of English working-class culture, following the leads of Richard Hoggart (1957) and E. P. Thompson (1963), the general thrust of cultural studies is to reject pre-given boundaries delineating class cultures in favor of a more empirically agnostic approach to culture.

On the one hand, then, cultural studies people tend to reject the Frankfurt School's blanket assertion of a single, enveloping mass culture; on the other hand, they reject the Marxist divisions among class cultures. Instead, they are open to the *decenteredness* of popular cultures, accepting the possibility of their heterogeneity and irreducibility. Thus, cultural studies might focus on middle-class women's culture, Anglo-Asian culture, Mexican-American culture, etc. These decisions are not taken a priori but emerge in the empirical work devoted to the archaeology of cultural difference and sameness. Although the impression of the Frankfurt School's elitist reductionism – mass culture – is overdrawn by their post-Marxist critics, it is certainly true that the culture-industry thesis places more stress on popular culture's sameness than do various postmodern and feminist approaches to cultural studies, which are devoted to the postulate of radical cultural difference and otherness as well as to the practices of difference and otherness (particularly in the case of feminist cultural studies).

2. The culture-industry theory suggests that culture has been *commodified* in late capitalism: cultural artifacts are produced in order to be exchanged for money. This is thought to degrade culture and diminish its emancipatory possibilities. Even within the Frankfurt School there has been controversy over this point. As I suggested earlier, Walter Benjamin (1969) lauded the eye-opening possibilities

of what he called art in the age of mechanical reproduction, arguing that the technological reproduction of important works of art could democratize art's critical insights. Adorno (see Benjamin, 1969) for his part rejected Benjamin's optimism. He argued that for art to be mechanically reproduced robs art of its 'aura', the individual authorial signature that connotes a vital aesthetic authenticity and thus helps auratic art resist its absorption into the culture industry. For example, where Beethoven's music becomes Muzak, piped into offices and elevators in order to soothe people's alienation, the authorial signature of its live performance is removed – a signature that helps convey the passion and polemic encoded in art as an irreducible form of human protest and hopefulness.

Whatever the case here, the rate of cultural commodification rapidly accelerates in post-World War Two capitalism. The enterprises of books, movies, radio, television, journalism and advertising become gigantic industries, vertically integrated with other corporate endeavors in the impenetrable interlocks of corporate capitalism (see Coser, Kadushin and Powell, 1982; Schiller, 1989). In this context, the standard categories of aesthetic judgment and criticism no longer apply: as culture becomes a business, the role of the cultural creator changes. The 'author' is deindividuated where movies, television and even books are crafted by committee, mediated in ways that ensure both their fungibility and profitability. Where culture becomes an industry, cultural studies must now focus not only on cultural content but also on cultural production, distribution and reception. Indeed, these are inseparable where, as McLuhan said, the 'medium is the message' (a neo-Frankfurt sentiment if ever there was one).

The analysis of the culture industry recognizes that cultural commodification is the extension of the logic of commodity production within a commodity-fetishistic framework to a seemingly non-economic terrain. In this regard, Horkheimer and Adorno give the lie to a dualist-Marxist separation of base and superstructure or economics and culture. The business of culture is both business and ideology, just as ideology is encoded in the money exchanges that constitute the dominant semiotic force field of capitalism (see Baudrillard, 1975; Agger, 1989a). By refusing the either/or of bourgeois society – either economics 'or' culture – the Frankfurt theorists make a significant advance over the economistic and dualist Marxisms of the Second and Third Internationals. This unified stance helps them address a host of complexly interrelated phenomena simply not amenable to traditional economic analysis. For example, the Frankfurt cultural theory allows one to read popular-cultural forms like movies and television *at once* for economic and ideological content (as Miller [1988], Luke, [1989] and Kellner [1990] do). In deconstructive terms, this unites the analysis of texts and con-texts, cultural expressions and the institutional frameworks within which these expressions take place.

In the *Dialectic of Enlightenment* (Horkheimer and Adorno, 1972) this remains largely a programmatic posture. The epigrammatic and fragmentary formulations of the culture-industry thesis (e.g., Adorno, 1974a) are not exemplified in sustained cultural readings that help us make concrete sense of the commodifying and reifying tendencies of mass culture. Although it is perhaps unusual to read the Frankfurt theorists as programmatists, in a sense their culture-industry thesis only sets the stage for the particular textual and con-textual readings that follow from their influence. Although the whole cultural studies tradition is virtually unimaginable without Frankfurt cultural theory, in significant respects the

Frankfurt mandarinism is appropriately corrected by neo- or post-Frankfurt analysts who do not view mass culture simply as a *deus ex machina* but read it in a nuanced, differential way that allows them to detect counter-hegemonic impulses as well as the dominant hegemonic ones in cultural expression and reception (e.g., see Ryan and Kellner's [1988] *Camera Politica* for just this sort of nuanced reading of Hollywood cinematography from a neo-Frankfurt perspective).

Many of the family differences among cultural studies people involve personal and political temperament more than substance. The Frankfurt cultural theorists are read as gloomy as well as elitist. The hypermodernism of Adorno is hardly populist: Beckett, Kafka and Schoenberg do not play in Peoria. But this reflects Adorno's own cultural formation and his mood more than it does the internal dynamics of Adorno's own (1973b) negative dialectics, which methodically attempts to break through what he (1973b, p. 406) calls 'the objective context of delusion from within'. This reversal of Bolshevik vanguardism suggests a new vanguardism phrased in the mandarin terms of high modernism. It is difficult for garden-variety leftists to recognize the agitational value of this sort of work, although one can argue for the political relevance of Adorno's cultural theory in terms of the overall aims of his general social theory. In other words, it is beside the point that Adorno was circumstantially gloomy about the agitational possibilities of a committed literature, in Sartre's (1965) terms. His own dialectical stance belied his pessimism, which marks all sorts of *fin-de-siècle* cultural developments in western and central Europe all the way from Freud and Weber to Wittgenstein (see Schorske, 1981). After all, German Jewish intellectuals appraising the revolutionary possibilities in global capitalism after the Holocaust were bound to emerge with a good deal of civilizational pessimism. In this sense, the more pragmatic Anglo-American strains of cultural studies provide a counterpoint of sorts to the pessimism and foreboding of German critical theory. This makes it somewhat ironic that German critical theory gave birth to the very culture-industry thesis that provoked the more pragmatist cultural-studies tradition to turn its back on the supposed mandarinism of the Frankfurt School (while accepting some of the empirical theses on the culture industry that I am enumerating here; see Morrow, 1991, for fuller consideration of this point).

3. The culture-industry argument suggests that there are certain *false* (or manipulated) *needs* (Marcuse, 1964) propagated by mass culture in order to both reproduce capital and deflect people from recognizing their own objective interest in total social transformation. False needs are needs not arrived at through autonomous and rational deliberation; they are imposed and then self-imposed. I devote Chapter 8 to a fuller discussion of the aporias of judgment reflected in the thesis of false needs. It is undeniable that the Frankfurt postulate of false needs has drawn all sorts of fire (e.g., MacIntyre, 1970; but see Kellner, 1984), especially from liberals who argue against the arrogance of the adjective 'false'.

The Frankfurt argument goes this way: Late capitalism needs to ensure sufficient consumption to match production. It must also ensure social control, which is imperiled by the imminent prospect of a world in which basic needs can be met by deploying advanced technology rationally (see Marcuse, 1955, 1964). As a result, the culture industry bombards people with imageries (or what Baudrillard, 1983, calls simulations) that suggest the equation of the Good and goods. These imageries both stimulate consumption and deflect critical thought:

people identify themselves with their leisure and consumer lifestyles. Thus mass culture involves inseparable economic and ideological dimensions, addressed by a cultural criticism that understands cultural commodification to involve both material and ideational processes. The consumption of jumbo Hollywood movies produces corporate profit while it also depresses radical thought; people come to identify with the filmic characters through whom they live their lives vicariously.

The thesis of false needs is often attacked for its conspiratorial tone. But the Frankfurt theorists are not suggesting that a tightly organized cabal of Hollywood moguls or Manhattan studio heads gets together concertedly to plot the ideological defense of capitalism. Instead, they pursue their own corporate profits in the usual ways, attempting to get a jump on the competition without swerving unduly from the established direction of audience taste. The ideological outcomes of the culture industry are in a sense unintended: they emerge in the interplay of authorial, directorial and audience assumptions about the nature of the world. Taste is both reflected and reproduced in cultural artifacts. Thus it is facile to suggest that the taste-makers deliberately decide not only what we will consume but also what sorts of values we should hold. The culture-industry thesis gauges the falsehood of needs with respect to their heteronomy: needs are false when people do not arrive at them freely but rather have them imposed on them from the outside, through the subtle acculturation processes of capitalist everyday life. It is crucial to note that this process of need creation takes place within the capitalist marketplace in the sense that it responds to what authors and directors contend is the pre-given taste of cultural consumers. The standard defense of cultural banality is trivially, deceptively true: people are given what they want.

The culture-industry thesis stresses the ever-the-sameness of these wants. People 'demand' what they have been given before, which in turn reflects an even more distant past. This is not to suggest that a cultural *deus ex machina* created an originary set of needs that are endlessly reproduced through the circuitries of cultural demand and supply. The history of needs in capitalism is contingent and should be analyzed as such. There is no compelling reason why people 'want' video games and big-screen television rather than other sorts of numbing and profitable entertainments. Indeed, it is the arbitrariness of needs (see, e.g., Leiss, 1976) that indicates the arbitrariness of the cultural apparatus as a whole: we consume what we do because producers compete for markets within historically determinate parameters of taste (see Ewen, 1976, 1988). We elect to consume the movie *Batman* because we choose not to spend our entertainment budgets on other jumbo movies, symphony tickets, or a trip to Alaska. The historicity of human needs makes the culture industry possible without requiring an original conspiracy of taste-makers who once and for all established a set of tastes, and cultural products to satisfy them, that are optimally profitable and stupefying.

The culture-industry thesis departs from orthodox Marxism mainly in the sense in which it refuses to separate the analysis of cultural production for profit from the analysis of the false needs serviced by cultural production. Orthodox Marxism evaluates the falsehood of cultural creation – the encoding of certain class truths, with Lukács and Goldmann – rather than the falsehood of cultural needs. The falsehood of needs is manifested less in the choice of particular cultural contents – rock videos instead of ballet – than in the insatiability of cultural consumers who are hooked on cultural consumption and who are impossible to satisfy in a lasting sense. One rents a video for home use, returns it and rents another one. One uses the remote-control television channel changer to switch restlessly from program to program, reflecting a groundlessness to our fast capitalism as a whole (see Agger, 1989a). Not only are false needs imposed from the outside; they are impossible to satisfy with singular acts of cultural consumption.

This applies to all commodity consumption, not only that in the realm of culture. Capitalism is a system of planned obsolescence and insatiable consumer appetite. As Marx showed, consumption must match production for the reproduction of capital to continue apace. Although one might suggest that this argument demonstrates the determinativeness of economics 'in the last instance', in the domain of culture as well as in other productive venues, in fact Marx's own analysis of commodity fetishism shows convincingly that the commodity exchange relationship involves not only the production of surplus value but also the creation of false consciousness on the part of economic players who cannot recognize that the economic relations in which they are enmeshed are not nature-like but historical and thus can be changed. In the era of technological capitalism it is nearly impossible for cultural consumers to recognize that the electronic media are highly media-ted venues for political constitution. We switch culture on and off, rent and return our videos and otherwise treat the production and distribution of culture as unproblematic processes. In dehistoricizing cultural production, we fall under the sway of the very commodity fetishism targeted by Marx in Volume One of *Capital*. False consciousness is created at the very point of production, not simply in the subordinate and epiphenomenal sphere of the superstructure.

4. This is especially easy to recognize in the realm of culture. False needs are generated by the *one-sided relationship between cultural producers and consumers*, a relationship that is, of course, endemic to all capitalist exchange relationships. The lament that television makes people passive is in fact a structural feature of cultural commodification: people accept their subordinate relationship to the giant colossi of corporate cultural production as second nature. Indeed, cultural commodity fetishism ensures that we do not even consider these media-ted relationships because, instead, we treat culture as something that comes out of a black box, switched on and off by the cultural consumer. The extent of the cultural consumer's constitutional involvement in the cultural acquisition process is a trivially technological one: we as cultural consumers switch the electronic receivers on and off; we rent videos; we purchase tickets. In these senses, we fail to recognize the historicity of culture – the fact that culture comes from somewhere else and that we are in thrall to it, indeed, that *culture could be different* (including our relationships to it).

This is the nature of all commodity fetishism, according to Marx. When we drive the new car off the dealer's lot, we do not think twice about the vehicle we have purchased as a social construction. Its imbeddedness in an international economy (e.g., the resources needed to produce it), its inherence in a particular Fordist workplace organization, and its corporate nature are all invisible to the untheorizing consumer. But these facts are not concealed purposely by the automobile salespeople, who otherwise fear being found out for the capitalist functionaries they are. These acts of concealment are imbedded in the commodity itself, as well as in our relation to it. We take it for granted that the vehicle we purchase, like the movie whose video we rent, is an objectified piece of social nature, not a molten piece of history that could be accomplished differently, within different economic and institutional parameters.

The argument that television is peculiarly numbing is often overstated (see Williams, 1975; Hallin, 1985; Kellner, 1990). All commodity-fetishized exchange relationships in capitalism are structurally as numbing as television. Indeed the reception of television may be somewhat less numbing than the reception of cars in the single sense that television is a thick subculture comprising not only the programs themselves but the whole mosaic of information and gossip contained in newspapers, magazines and televised talk-shows. We feel that we have more access to the text and subtext of television and movies than, say, to the production of automobiles or microwave ovens. Television culture is peculiarly reflexive; as a collectivizing spectacle (see Debord, 1970) it perpetuates a certain common discourse about itself. And our 'tastes' are regularly and scientifically sampled through the various audience-measurement devices like the Nielsen ratings, thus determining what will be programmed in the future. This apparent control over product is deceiving; we have very little real input into what is screened, which, in any case, resembles what was screened last season and the season before that. I simply dispute the cultural-neoconservative notion that somehow television, as a central emblem of popular culture, is at the root of all evils, for which the antidote is a dose of the Great Books as well as a return to so-called traditional values reflected in 'better', more elevating programming.

Although popular culture is frequently narcotizing, narcosis is part and parcel of every commodity-fetishistic exchange relationship where consumers are dictated to, and disempowered, by producers. Marx was clear that the obfuscation of the real historical relations among the players in a capitalist economic system contributes to what he called commodity fetishism and what Lukács (1971) later called reification. Relations between people – here, cultural producers and consumers – appear to be relations between things, governed by supposedly nature-like laws. In this sense, the relationship between production and consumption is experienced as one-sided, with production driving consumption through the various media of advertising, family, education and religion. It is the one-sidedness of commodity relations that is the real problem with commodified cultural production, particularly the way in which consumption is subordinated to production.

Now Marx in fact did not theorize consumption adequately. His analysis of commodity fetishism was not extensive enough; it did not allow him to go beyond the economic implications of commodity fetishism toward a full understanding of the socio-cultural and psychological dimensions of commodity fetishism (although his original analysis of commodity fetishism in *Capital* blended these halves of the problem to the point of dialectical indistinguishability). For his part, Marx could reasonably say that he did not theorize consumption, consumerism or the consumer culture sufficiently because consumption had not become an obsession in his relatively early stage of capitalism. Better, needs were generally 'truer' than they are today in the sense that needs were primary and not secondary – about material necessities and not extravagances. Marcuse's later (1955) analysis of 'repressive desublimation' as a characteristic of a society that structurally requires consumption to be artificially stimulated (lest capitalism collapse) would have been far-fetched to Marx, writing in the mid-nineteenth century. In any case, Marx understood the one-sided relationship between production and consumption even if he did not fully realize the extent to which this would unfold in subsequent consumer capitalism.

Marx did not foresee the extent of the culture industry. He did not foresee that culture would become contested terrain, although he developed a theory of ideology that showed that consciousness matters in the ebb and flow of material history. The culture-industry thesis could only have arisen in a much later, more productive stage of capitalism, where the structural disproportion between production and consumption had to be addressed self-consciously by the state and corporations. Marx simply could not have foreseen the extent to which what Baudrillard (1983) calls 'simulations' (e.g., advertising) would come to play such a pivotal role in stimulating consumption and in rendering consumerism an attractive lifestyle. Marx would have been amazed that recent promotional literature from the city of Phoenix, Arizona, suggests that 'shopping is a way of life' in Phoenix. For Marx, shopping served the reproduction of life but was not a central source of people's identity or of the economy's rejuvenation. For Marx, shopping was a relatively unproblematic fitting of unmediated material needs to available goods at hand. Shopping did not have to be theorized because shopping (for basic necessities) just happens. Indeed, for Marx, the crucial trigger of capitalist crisis was absolute poverty – the outcome of the overaccumulation of capital in private hands, forcing many into poverty. Today, capitalism totters where people do not fill the shopping malls and automobile showrooms (although, of course, capitalism also breeds both internal and international uneven development of a kind that creates poverty for many).

5. Finally, the culture-industry argument suggests that culture has certain narcotic or diversionary properties that somehow transcend false needs per se. In effect, the culture industry *dehistoricizes* culture in a crucial system-serving way. This is really an extension of the commodity-fetishism analysis into the late twentieth century. Horkheimer and Adorno argue that the one-sided relationship of cultural consumers to cultural producers not only stimulates them to consume culture passively, hence against their own objective interests. It also transforms culture into a *deus ex machina*, a nature-like process that exists independent of human will. We orient to popular culture in an unproblematic way: we do not view popular culture as artifacts but rather we live and breathe it as an inescapable ether surrounding the planet of late capitalism. We lose the sense that culture has been authored (and hence that it could be reauthored), just as we lose the sense of our own constitutional efficacy as strong readers of culture who are capable of resisting its images of the world.

Marx explained all of this in his analysis of commodity fetishism. Human relations appear to be historically invariant. The culture industry appears not to be industry at all. Instead, we experience our common culture unreflexively: we are habituated to an endless flow of entertainments and information that we absorb unthinkingly, as constitutive of our common experiences of citizenship in late capitalism (see Keane, 1984). These common constitutional experiences range from television and movies to journalism and education, all the sites of cultural reproduction today. Although we can certainly authorize television by tracing its cultural outcomes back to certain authorial, editorial and transmission practices, this is a second-order practice; it is not built into the actual cultural reception process itself. We must struggle hard to elevate ourselves above, or beyond, the gripping hold of the television simulacra (the unreal world portrayed as real by it) in order to read them as the authored practices that they are. Although this is possible (after all, that is the very possibility of cultural studies), popular culture resists its own authorization and historicization in order to appear to be merely a piece of cultural nature pre-given to us.

Baudrillard argues that people consume not commodities per se but their 'simulations', their media-ted presentations. This is especially obvious in the realm of culture, where commodities are insubstantial to begin with. Thus, one consumes not the movie *Batman* but rather the various simulations of Batman-the-movie encoded in advertisements, reviews and the various Bat-paraphernalia surrounding the event itself. These encodings, or what Baudrillard (1983) calls simulations, desubstantiate culture even more than it is in the first place. Instead of reckoning with *Batman* seriously as a cultural text with certain imbedded claims, we lose our grip on what differentiates the movie itself from the various Bat-phenomena surrounding and encoding it. This is another way to understand the construction of commodities in advertising: advertisements represent the commodity in a way that helps us lose ourselves in it, failing to deal with it rigorously on its own terms. The longer we have it drummed into us that Hondas are snappy and maintenance-free cars, inherently superior to their American counterparts, the more likely we are to lose any critical distance from them that enables us to take these validity claims seriously (perhaps even noticing that many Hondas are now assembled in the US by American workers).

The dehistoricization of culture is a crucial part of the culture-industry argument, helping explain the enormous hold that cultural artifacts have on our imagination. Simulators work their magic without being seen as textwriters of commodity fetishism. After all, movie producers no less than car manufacturers purvey the image of the product as a way of selling the product. Where simulations blur with the realities they simulate (e.g., the Honda advertisement in a sense becoming the Honda itself or the Batman campaign becoming the movie itself), we not only forget who wrote the text but we overlook the difference between the text or simulation and the world to which it refers representationally (even if this representation is always constitutional in its own right). This makes it difficult to evaluate the specific issues at hand: how well the car drives, whether the movie was worth seeing, etc.

Where popular culture loses both its apparent authorship and its textual demarcation, it slips by us unchallenged. The cultural milieux of the moment are extraordinarily permeative in the sense that they engulf all discourse, experience, evaluation. Culture appears to come from nowhere and to be heading nowhere; it is objectified in the magazine racks at the airport, in the chain bookstores, in the endless television programs and movies at the mall. We expect culture in the same way that we expect the weather; although it varies, its existence is invariant. Thus, it is difficult to reauthorize and retextualize culture as a distinctive outcome of human artifice as well as critical evaluation. In this sense, the culture-industry thesis suggests that culture has become a haze, nearly impenetrable by traditional interpretive techniques or external political challenges. This is precisely what Gramsci meant by hegemony: a world of ideas and practices so routinized that we forget that we add value to these rituals at every step along the way. This is *our* world and it is difficult to imagine it differently, let alone write it and work toward it differently. Ideology has penetrated into every nook and cranny of everyday experience; we allow it to penetrate the interstices of existence because we allow ourselves to believe that culture lacks history, that it is only simulation and not also a piece and process of reality itself.

Frankfurt Cultural Readings

There is some distance between the Frankfurt School's culture-industry thesis, on the one hand, and their particular readings of culture, on the other. Their critical theory is not a method to be applied willy-nilly but rather an interplay between method and substance. For this reason, it is somewhat artificial to survey the particular Frankfurt readings of culture as if we can distance their cultural theory from their cultural analysis in the same way we might do in the case of deconstruction. We can at least summarize the areas of interpretive concern for the Frankfurt theorists, recognizing that there was no monolithic Frankfurt cultural theory but only particular inflections given it by the different people associated with the Institute for Social Research (see Jay, 1973; Agger, 1979; Held, 1980).

Frankfurt cultural studies focused on art, mass culture and the information industry. Only their work on art was highly theorized and voluminous. Adorno's (1984) *Aesthetic Theory* is probably the 'highest' work of Frankfurt aesthetic theory, although there are numerous other, and different, articulations of his basic perspective (e.g., Marcuse, 1978; Adorno, 1973c). One of the key Frankfurt insights is that aesthetic theory is a valid component of a more generic cultural studies in the sense that the same critical method can be applied to a wide range of cultural products and practices. This is a significant difference from other approaches to cultural studies, including that of the Birmingham School, postmodernism/poststructuralism and feminism. These latter approaches tend to ignore so-called high culture and instead concentrate more on pop-cultural artifacts addressed by media studies and film theory.

The Frankfurt approach to aesthetics suggests that art can be read both for empirical evidence of society's contradictions and for possible transcendence of these drab realities. In this sense, art, especially modernist art, is treated dynamically by the Frankfurt theorists. There is no single correct art, nor a single correct approach to reading it. Instead, critical method and evaluation must adapt themselves to the con-texts in which art arises. This aesthetic interpretation is immanent as well as contextualizing: it reads art in terms of itself – what it is trying to say to its readers, listeners and viewers – as well as in terms of the social environment within which it is located and to which it must be read as responding. Irrelevant, then, are the supposed truths (whether class or some other kind) represented or reflected passively in art. Art is not a cognitive act per se; although expression includes cognition, it goes beyond it, resonating both the stifled hopes of humanity and the outrages committed against it.

Frankfurt aesthetic theory refuses to render the reading of art mechanically political in the fashion of Zhdanovism and Lukács. Art not only encodes ideology; it is also a form of cultural practice and experience. This is not to deny the political relevance of art (and all culture) but rather to locate its politics elsewhere than in what a mechanical Marxist would take to be its overt text of ideological representation. Art may well be partisan in one direction or another but frequently its partisanship is less important than its ontological stance – its reading of and recommendation about social being itself. This notion of metaphysical partisanship is, of course, a modernist one; the Frankfurt critics not only take modernism seriously as an aesthetic trend but they practise modernist criticism in the sense that they refuse the representational aesthetic readings of orthodox Marxism in favor of these more veiled readings that recognize metaphysical partisanship for what it is.

Immanent and contextual readings of culture are politically valid, according to the Frankfurt theorists, because the whole notion of the political has changed since the dawn of modernity (see Habermas, 1981a). Politics is not frequently found in the established political arena per se. Instead, it transpires beyond conventional politics in the regions of experience and expression heretofore regarded as off-limits to political transformation. Although traditional Marxism might dismiss this view as existentialist, Sartre's (1965) existentialism interrogated the metaphysics of existence in a way that later helped him extend his more ontological insights into a coherent critical political theory. For Sartre, the perspective of the artist represents the commitment of passionate existence to its own inescapable contingency, if not to *Partinost*.

This is not to say that the Frankfurt perspective on modernism endorses the letter of French existentialism (see Poster, 1975). However, their discussions of aesthetic theory certainly trade on current modernist notions of the politics of the personal and of culture that definitely converge with some of early Sartre's own notions of aesthetic politics. Perhaps the best way to say this is to note that existentialism, like critical theory, is a moment of modernism (although the Frankfurt people, especially Adorno, were frequently and in my opinion correctly hostile to a variety of currents in existentialism – see, e.g., Adorno, 1973a). These modernisms unite around the notion that, as feminists say, the personal is political – that the creative gestures of the artist or cultural creator bespeak values which are critical and transformative in their own right.

Less important than ideological correctness assessed from the outside (with Zhdanovism and Lukács) is the immanent meaning of cultural artifacts and practices. Adorno can read Beckett as radical not because *Endgame* exhorts the proletariat or denounces rapacious capitalism but because Beckett understands the human condition of modernity, albeit without sufficiently historicizing it to suggest a utopian alternative. Beckett's angst is the angst of all critical intelligence under capitalism, just as his 'solution', if one can call it that, is inappropriately existential. *Waiting for Godot* is precisely hopeless: it evokes dystopia at every turn. Adorno's critical reading of Beckett raises Beckett's text to the level of social criticism by historicizing it, setting it in the context of its time and working through Beckett's own immanent intentions as a protest writer.

Sartre's (1965) term for political art is committed literature. Although Sartre and Adorno are both modernists, Adorno disdains Sartre's agitational intentions. Instead, he sees modernist cultural work as protest against a system that most modernisms only dimly understand from the point of view of world history. Schoenberg's dissonant music scarcely understands how it immanently reflects and sets itself apart from the dissonance of administered society; Adorno's reading of Schoenberg makes this interpretation possible. Yet Schoenberg is heard by Adorno as protesting. In other words, Adorno's version of cultural studies adds the political to protest work by historicizing it, setting it in a certain social context and unraveling its own immanent meanings that typically go untheorized. (The point of cultural production is to produce cultural meaning and not simply to reflect on its own constitutional practices; that is what critics are for!).

Although Adorno's disdain for mass culture is well known, I want to reverse the standard reading of Adorno by pointing out his instructive deconstruction of the high culture/low culture division. Where many post-Frankfurt cultural studies people thematize Adorno's mandarinism (and there is no denying this strain in his work) and thus read his aesthetic theory as a purposeful departure from the more catholic agenda of cultural studies, I prefer to read Adorno as an author of cultural studies who models all of his cultural readings on a totalizing social theory. Instead of splitting apart his high aesthetic theory from his 'lower' analyses of popular culture, I read Adorno as modeling his critical readings on the same immanentist/contextual model of interpretation that he brings to bear in his readings of Schoenberg, Beckett and Kafka.

In this sense, Adorno takes popular culture more seriously as a differential field of significances as well as a potential site of resistance than many on the left give him credit for. His studies of television, radio and journalism represent some of the best work in materialist cultural criticism, reflecting little of the disdain for the rabble for which he is famous. I would argue that the cliché 'elitism' has been overdone on the left. To be sure, Adorno did not reject bourgeois high culture, particularly Romanticism and modernism, out of hand. To be sure, he and his other Frankfurt colleagues wrote aesthetic and cultural interpretation densely and homogenized some of the broadest tendencies in popular culture, rejecting it as irremediably vulgar. But Adorno and his cohorts did not sharply differentiate their high-culture studies from their low-culture studies; they both drew upon the same immanentist/contextual model of criticism that Adorno developed as a veritable mode of social theory itself.

In fact, Adorno developed an extraordinarily strong program of cultural studies that claimed a status as critical social theory itself. He took the same approach to philosophical interpretation in his studies of German idealist thought as he did in his cultural readings. It is important to read his *Negative Dialectics* (1973b) side by side with his *Aesthetic Theory* (1984). They were written one after another and together they collect the variety of his approaches to social and cultural analysis that proceed from immanentist/contextual foundations. His deconstruction of Kant and Hegel in the former book could as well have been a critical reading of major literary works or films. Adorno was extremely adept at keeping one eye on totality while he developed the particularistic implications of various forms of cultural, philosophical and political expression, in this regard satisfying Stuart Hall's own (1980b) requirements of a cultural studies that joins what Hall calls *culturalist* and *structuralist* approaches. In an ingenious dialectical synthesis, Hall uses the terms culturalism and structuralism to refer to the moments of experience and determination present within any cultural practice. It is difficult to see how this is different from Adorno's approach, although certainly Hall's cultural criticism reads much more accessibly than do Adorno's two mature works, aforementioned.

For his part, Marcuse, alone among the Frankfurt thinkers, remained in the US after the end of World War Two. This both reflected and facilitated his openness to more popular developments in American culture and politics, notably his sympathy for the New Left that he theorized in his (1969) book *An Essay on Liberation*. This openness gave the impression that he was more positive about mass culture than were his other Frankfurt colleagues, although, as his (1978) *The Aesthetic Dimension* indicates, this impression is misleading: Marcuse was Adornoian in his aesthetic theory (although I would also argue that Adorno was Marcusean in terms of his own openness to popular culture). One of the reasons for the impression that Adorno was a cultural mandarin and Marcuse a veritable sympathizer with rock-and-roll was that people were generally unacquainted with the impressive array of popular-culture readings done by Adorno during his American exodus in the 1940s. By the time the counterculture's aesthetic politics bloomed in the 1960s, books like Marcuse's (1964) *One-Dimensional Man* and his later *An Essay on Liberation* were relatively accessible and spoke vividly to the circumstances of the new social movements bursting forth in the US, England and western Europe.

It is almost absurdist that Marcuse came to be tagged the 'guru' of the New Left and his *One-Dimensional Man* read as an inflammatory statement. Anyone familiar with Marcuse's American period knew that he was a patrician philosophy professor who took the high-European traditions of social philosophy and culture very seriously, although he also had the versatility to theorize and even participate in the New Left. Of course, nearly every other critical American intellectual was doing exactly the same thing at the time. Noam Chomsky, C. Wright Mills and Alvin Gouldner joined Marcuse in opposing the Vietnam war and supporting the civil rights movement. And to call Marcuse's 1964 book agitational reflects Anglo-American analytical philosophy's lack of engagement with the political. Only by comparison to that arid tradition could a book like *One-Dimensional Man* be read as a call to arms.

This account is not meant to harmonize the Frankfurt cultural theory so that all differences blur into a synchronous whole. In fact, Marcuse's engagements during the mid to late 1960s and early 1970s were somewhat different from those of Adorno and Horkheimer who, by then, had returned to West Germany. Where Adorno and Horkheimer were ridiculed for what seemed like accommodationist stances on the Vietnam war, Marcuse's opposition to that war as well as his concomitant openness to the cultural discourses of the youth movement was well known. Nevertheless, Marcuse's own aesthetic and cultural theory can be traced to some early essays that were originally published in the Institute for Social Research's house journal, *Zeitschrift für Sozialforschung* (and since translated into English in various places; see, e.g., Marcuse, 1968). His well-known (1968, pp. 88–133) essay on the 'affirmative character of culture' anticipates a host of later Frankfurt School forays in cultural theory. In no way did his 1960s exuberances get the better of his nuanced interpretive and theoretical eye, which he developed very much in concert with the perspectives of Adorno, Horkheimer and to a lesser extent Walter Benjamin.

Like Adorno, Marcuse sought to read cultural products and practices both immanently and contextually. He tried to historicize and politicize them in ways that brought out their rage against oppression and their utopian promise of a qualitatively different society. Even less than Adorno does Marcuse fit the caricature of Frankfurt cultural mandarinism, notably in his sympathetic appraisals of adversary youth culture during the 1960s. Marcuse's cultural politics was decentered and flexible, requiring no mechanical adherence to standards of critical evaluation grounded in rigid criteria of political correctness (however these may be defined). The illusoriness of culture (*Schein* – appearance) makes it inherently transcendental, a protest against *la vie quotidienne* and a call for a qualitatively new mode of existence. Marcuse, even more than Adorno, located this transcendental aesthetic activity directly in the ebb and flow of popular culture; he was less modernist than Adorno (or, better, more diversely modernist than Adorno, whose modernist standards were substantially more stringent than Marcuse's).

This ability to hear and read political resistance in ostensibly only cultural forms is a paramount feature of Frankfurt aesthetic theory. It breaks Marxist aesthetic theory out of the representational realism enforced on it by Lukács and the Bolsheviks. The explanatory theory of the culture industry is blended with the modernist interpretive framework of Frankfurt critical theory, both situating and immanently extending cultural expressions further toward the political light of day. The Frankfurt theorists believed that straightforward social criticism was all too easily absorbed by a system that claims to prize difference and diversity. Marcuse (Marcuse *et al.*, 1965) called this repressive tolerance. Only by working on a different, less discursive level could critique find its adequate voice and resist absorption into the maw of the culture industry that cheerfully transforms every half-empty glass into a glass half-full – the ontology of the Reagan years.

In this sense, Frankfurt cultural readings took difficult, allusive form. They defended abstraction as a vital indirection, thereby avoiding the trap of cultural and political banality. Although I (1990) have indicted all theories that contribute to the decline of discourse through their own obfuscations, Adorno and company composed their own critical readings and cultural analyses *as resistance itself*, wresting language free of the banalizing, one-dimensionalizing forces of what Marcuse (1968, pp. 88–133) originally called affirmative culture. Although some of the more empirically grounded Frankfurt analyses of mass culture are more accessible than the rarefied aesthetic theory of the later years, all of their work was thick with the dialectical echoes and innuendoes that preserved their own criticism from reduction into affirmative terms of common-sense discourse. They believed that this protected their own dialectical insights from absorption into the dominant consensus of late capitalism which reduces social criticism to ameliorable agenda items of statist social reform. When nothing less than the totality is at stake, a radical cultural studies must resist its own tendencies to be absorbed as harmless, even affirmative, cultural commentary (like the movie and book reviews that fill the newspapers and magazines as buyers' guides as well as cultural celebrations and heroizations).

Chapter 5

The Birmingham School of Cultural Studies

The Programmatization of Cultural Studies

In effect, the Marxist sociology of culture and the Frankfurt aesthetic theory that developed largely in counterpoint to it comprise the prehistory of cultural studies. Although I have argued that the culture-industry thesis of Horkheimer and Adorno (1972) grounds cultural studies' political-economic orientation (without sabotaging the dialectical-utopian modernism of Frankfurt criticism), one can properly date cultural studies as a more or less unified movement from the establishment of the Birmingham Centre for Contemporary Cultural Studies in 1964 by Richard Hoggart (1957) and later headed by Stuart Hall (1978, 1980a, 1980b, 1988), who, more than anyone else, has guided the programmatic and substantive development of British cultural studies. The Birmingham version of British cultural studies is owed to pioneering work by Hoggart as well as to historical work by E.P. Thompson (1963, 1978) and Raymond Williams (1950, 1961, 1966, 1975, 1977, 1980, 1981, 1983, 1989), the founder of the culture-and-society approach to cultural analysis. The term *cultural studies* itself is owed to the Birmingham group, although now it is claimed by a diversity of interpretive interests.

If there is a strong agenda of contemporary cultural studies, it is found in the work of the Birmingham School. Of course, one of the hallmarks of cultural studies is its antipathy to frozen definitions that replace creative thought and prevent flexible application. The Birmingham approach to cultural studies is found in the exemplary works of the people comprising the CCCS in Birmingham; programmatic statements have been few and far between (see Hall, 1980b; Johnson, 1986–1987; also see Leong, 1992). Nevertheless, we can reconstruct this agenda out of the bits and pieces of explicit programmatism offered by the Birmingham people as well as by a process of interpolation that helps us reconstruct the 'Birmingham approach' out of the various interpretive gestures comprising their broad critical canvas. In doing this, we must keep in mind that for Stuart Hall and his group cultural studies is neither a fixed method nor a discrete set of topics but rather an approach that is at once fluid and interdisciplinary.

Features of the Birmingham Approach

The Birmingham approach to cultural studies has the following features:

1. It is *interdisciplinary*. Although cultural studies and popular culture programs have been established at various centers, including the original program at the University of Birmingham, the cultural studies movement defines itself largely in terms of its resistance to disciplinary identification. It is argued that both the topics and methods of cultural studies defy easy categorization in terms of a single discipline. Although many traditional disciplines study culture (e.g., sociology, anthropology, English), they do so within the frames of reference of their own topics and methodologies. Birmingham proponents of cultural studies believe that this unnecessarily restricts the reach of cultural studies, failing to learn from a wide variety of disciplines as well as accepting pre-given disciplinary definitions of scope and method that unnecessarily curtail the search for new topics and new methods of study.

Virtually no one who writes in cultural studies would disagree with this characterization of cultural studies as genuinely interdisciplinary. This is the credo of cultural studies and will likely remain so. On the other hand, the establishment of cultural studies as a legitimate academic research area has tended to run counter to aspects of this more programmatic theoretical and methodological commitment to interdisciplinarity. Perhaps this is the tendency of any renegade intellectual movement to be institutionalized, against its original de-centering, disruptive purpose. In any case, the search for institutional legitimacy has tended to contradict the intellectual commitment to interdisciplinarity on the part of cultural studies scholars who are sorely tempted to establish their programs either within established departments or in specialized centers like the one at the University of Birmingham.

Research centers like CCCS can in fact be havens of interdisciplinary scholarship, as the Birmingham example shows. However, as I noted earlier in the book, there has been a nearly irresistible tendency for cultural studies either to seek niches in established disciplines, thus losing a cross-disciplinary focus, or to establish itself as a new discipline in its own right, thus fitting into the overall academic division of labor within universities. Thus, today, cultural studies exists almost as a separate academic sphere within the university, having enclaved itself within or beyond disciplines as a relatively homogeneous site of cultural analyses. Although certainly the theoretical and methodological orientations of people at these centers differ widely (e.g., the Bowling Green popular-culture program [see, e.g., Browne, 1980, 1989, as well as the *Journal of Popular Culture*, which he edits] differing from the Unit for Criticism and Interpretive Theory at the University of Illinois [see Nelson and Grossberg, 1988], both of which are quite different from the CCCS), there has been a marked tendency for people to cluster together in departments or proto-departments that complete with other academic departments for legitimacy, resources and students.

This is perhaps a necessary stage in the gestation process of any new intellectual movement. But in significant ways I think it betrays the original thrust of cultural studies, notably the self-conscious effort to break out of disciplinary confines, indeed to resist any and all disciplining. Of course, theory and practice are often divergent here: for intellectuals to defend and entrench new developments in their fields they often risk institutionalization, hoping that institutional legitimation does not backfire on them and lead to a suffocating conservatism. Although people who gravitate to cultural studies centers, like those at Birmingham, Bowling Green and Illinois, have diverse intellectual and disciplinary backgrounds, one wonders whether the cultural studies movement has not become simply another discipline or proto-discipline secure in its existence apart from other disciplines with which it shares space, resources and students in the contemporary university.

In any case, that is precisely the question I will take up in my last two chapters, where I argue against a disciplinary or proto-disciplinary cultural studies and for a more engaged version of it, even a non-academic one. One of the implications of the disciplining of cultural studies has been its loss of an interdisciplinary theoretical focus; I do not believe that this loss is outweighed by the benefits of institutional legitimation in the university. One of the most important implications of cultural studies' interdisciplinary program has been its serious attention to theoretical issues. Cultural studies borrows significantly from the explosion of interdisciplinary interest in interpretive theory, including postmodernism, poststructuralism, critical theory and feminist theory. These convergent influences on the project of cultural studies virtually guarantee that cultural studies will not become sheer method, encamped in disciplinary niches in the university. At least, this was the original promise of interdisciplinarity.

But, as I explore in Chapter 9, many cultural studies proponents have descended so far below the level of theory that their own cultural analyses have become shallowly formulaic, almost technical, in their canned approaches to issues of cultural interpretation. This has happened precisely because cultural studies has decamped into departments and programs that subvert the very interdisciplinarity originally promising to ensure that cultural studies would transcend sheer methodology and actively interrogate cultural artifacts and practices in structural, hence political, terms. Today, unfortunately, a great deal of Anglo-American cultural studies amounts to unfocused, ungrounded 'readings' that do not coalesce into a larger understanding of the social totality nor lead to coherent political interventions. In Chapter 9 I expand on the idea that the institutionalization of cultural studies may have been required in order to legitimate cultural studies in face of cultural traditionalists who reject media studies as the preserve of dilettantes and poseurs (see Miller's [1988] account of his own attempt to do cultural studies in an English department).

Interdisciplinarity has been most important for cultural studies where it has guaranteed the theoreticity of cultural studies. For example, some of the Frankfurt School's analyses of mass culture borrowed readily from economics as well as aesthetic theory, thus ensuring that their own particular cultural readings would in Hegel's terms illuminate the general through the particular – capitalism through its cultural gestures. Adorno built general social theory out of particular cultural readings illuminated by, and illuminating, total theory, which emerges dialectically as these particular interpretations cohere. But, as I will describe and lament later on, this symbiosis between general theory and particular cultural interpretations has largely given way to methodically-driven readings that are more technical than theoretical, focusing on *how* culture composes itself as a discourse rather than on *why* cultural discourse is a social and political factor in the first place.

Clearly, both the *how* and the *why* of cultural discourse are important; cultural theory remains too abstract unless it delves into the actual texts of culture that dominate our lives. These texts become lives, as I (1989a) have argued in a different context. What I call fast capitalism disperses these 'texts' into our everyday lifeworld; the claims of money, science, edifice and figure are encoded in ways that make it virtually impossible to recognize and then refute them as such. Books are obsolete, at least in the old-fashioned sense. Yet textuality is more powerful than ever – advertising, television, textbooks, trade fiction, journalism. Unfortunately, the line between world and text blurs so much that it is very difficult to recognize the secret, often subtextual claims made on behalf of the quotidian world (let alone to reformulate a different version of everyday life).

Yet this sort of structural analysis (e.g., my notion of fast capitalism) tends to be subordinated to the particular technical readings done in the name of cultural studies. Where in Chapter 9 I explore more fully the reasons for this shift in critical practice, let me here note the contribution that the disciplining of cultural studies makes to the loss of theoretical involvement on the part of cultural studies analysts. All things being equal, the institutionalization of cultural studies tends to deflect precisely the interdisciplinary focus of theory that could help to check the tendency for cultural studies to become a technical fetish in its own right. Of course, this assumes that interdisciplinarity's major contribution to intellectual life is in the realm of theory, blending the particular concerns of disciplines into an orchestrated whole. But others might view interdisciplinarity quite differently, valorizing it only as a sophisticated version of neoliberalism that attempts to reverse the putative laxness of American college curricula since the 1960s, as a result inculcating 'traditional' values through a renewed stress on the classical liberal arts. This emerges clearly in the Bloom-Hirsch-Cheney tradition of educational neoconservatism presently sweeping American college campuses.

2. Birmingham cultural studies stresses a *broad* (not a narrow) *definition of culture*. Culture is not simply a repository of high-cultural works and knowledges but the anthropological ensemble of learning and lived experience that makes us human. This perspective on culture is typical of an anthropological concept of culture (see, e.g., Linton, 1936) as against a moral or literary concept of culture more characteristic of Leavis' *Scrutiny* tradition in mainstream English literary criticism (see Eagleton, 1983). Culture is neither 'good' nor 'bad' for anthropologists. It is rather an enveloping context within which people learn identity, values and behavior. In this sense, cultural studies spills over into the disciplinary preserves of sociology, anthropology and English departments, taking up topics of cultural analysis addressed more narrowly by scholars in these traditions.

Of crucial concern for the Birmingham group is to establish what 'counts' as culture – the delimitation of the field of cultural studies analysis. Although there are a few programmatic statements (often found in the form of book introductions) by the Birmingham people (e.g., see Hall, 1980b), for the most part this question of the coverage attempted by cultural studies is not satisfactorily resolved, nor perhaps can it be, given the eclecticism and interdisciplinary focus of the Birmingham group. Perhaps the richest contribution of the CCCS and its affiliated scholars lies in the realm of the particular empirical studies of working-class and youth culture (Cohen, 1972; Hall and Jefferson, 1976; Murdock and

McCron, 1976; Willis, 1977, 1978; Hebdige, 1979, 1988; Brake, 1980; Clarke, 1990) and women's culture (McRobbie, 1981; Radway, 1984) published over the past two decades. This is not to say that the CCCS people are atheoretical in the sense in which I just suggested that a proto-disciplinary cultural studies tends to lack theoretical focus when it loses its genuine interdisciplinarity (assuming that interdisciplinarity is even possible).

The richness of this empirical tradition forged by the CCCS militates against theoretical reflexivity that could provide an adequate definition of both the terrain and methods of cultural studies, beginning with a decision about what counts as culture. One of the strengths of the CCCS group has been its thoroughgoing reflexivity, reflected in the series of stencilled papers, the numerous conferences and the regular published theoretical treatments. It is clear from reading through this mass of materials that the CCCS people recognize that a proper definition of cultural studies would have to emerge dialectically in the context of their own empirical and political work. Unlike the more empiricist tradition of popular-culture analysis in the US, the CCCS group has been continually concerned that their own empirical analyses were grounded in some larger theoretical interests, but that theorybuilding would not take place outside of the context of particular cultural readings.

There is a certain tension in most versions of cultural studies between empirical readings of culture and the larger theoretical auspices authorizing these readings in the first place. The Birmingham group more than American popular-culturalists managed to keep this tension firmly in mind, even if they never satisfactorily resolved it. Indeed, more than most cultural studies people, the Birmingham scholars have been continually energized by theoretical developments as well as by the effort to reconcile diverse theoretical traditions (e.g., Gramsci and Althusser). There is an extraordinary amount of theoretical reflexivity in the cultural readings done by the CCCS group, in spite of the fact that Anglo-American cultural studies in general has tended to be rather atheoretical. Although in certain respects the CCCS group has not adequately blended their empirical work with their overarching interests in Gramsci, Althusser, feminist theory, semiotics and poststructuralism, at least they recognize the need for doing so, which is more than one can say for American cultural empiricism (see Denzin, 1991).

For this reason, indeed, one notes a certain insensitivity to the CCCS work in the US except among converts. It is understandable that the heavily positivist American disciplines like sociology and communications have not bothered to acquaint themselves with the Birmingham School. British, Australian, New Zealand and Canadian sociologies are all more theoretically oriented than American sociology and concomitantly much more receptive to the ambitious Birmingham program.

3. The Birmingham School emphatically *rejects the high-culture/low-culture distinction*, instead treating all cultural expressions as if they lie along the same continuum of 'height' or 'depth'. For many, especially people familiar with the Lukács and Frankfurt approaches to cultural theory, this is the most notable and challenging feature of the CCCS group. Virtually everyone in the cultural studies movement rejects the cultural mandarinism of the Frankfurt School, which, as I noted in the preceding chapter, looked down on forms of mass culture like jazz

and rock-and-roll as degenerate, derivative expressions barely worthy of serious study (see Brake, 1980; Frith, 1983; Orman, 1984; Grossberg, 1986). Although I argued in the preceding chapter that the Frankfurt cultural theory can be readily applied to mass culture using the same categories and critical method employed by the likes of Adorno in his analysis of high art, it is clear that the Birmingham group emerged partly in counterpoint to both orthodox Marxist aesthetic theory and the Frankfurt School's mandarinism, stressing the political and aesthetic relevance of popular culture for people on the left.

The Birmingham School's flattening of the cultural continuum to make way for a unified methodological approach to cultural products and practices is sometimes taken to be an *endorsement* of popular culture per se. Perhaps it is for certain authors, especially more overtly political ones. Yet I do not read Hoggart or Williams to be partisans of popular culture per se but simply attentive to ways in which cultural hegemony works its way up as well as down the ladders of social and economic inequality. Nevertheless, Hall's engagement with Gramsci makes it clear that he shares Gramsci's stress on the possibility of populist/popular cultural resistance, indeed its necessity, as a vital form of 'counter-hegemony' in late capitalism. But Hall, like Gramsci, theorizes this point carefully. Others do not, and thus they give the impression that what they dislike about the Frankfurt position is simply their apparent mandarin *taste* in culture instead of the way they *theorize* culture – two quite different issues.

I return to this discussion, which is quite pivotal in deciding the future of cultural studies, in Chapter 8 where I address the problem of needs, values and cultural criticism. Suffice it to say here that what is important about the Frankfurt position on the politics of culture is not their own preferences for or against certain types of largely modernist cultural expression (e.g., Kafka, Schoenberg, Beckett, if not jazz or rock) but their insistence that cultural evaluation is possible, notably as political theory. Of course, orthodox Marxists have always accepted the possibility of external cultural evaluation – for them, in terms of art and culture's political correctness, their external validity as cognitive claims about the social world. Non-Frankfurt oriented cultural studies, especially its postmodern and popular-culturalist variants, rejects not only Marxist class reductionism for its arbitrary Eurocentrism but all political evaluations of culture, including those of the Frankfurt School.

The Frankfurt critics take popular culture seriously as a venue of political meaning and contestation. They dislike popular culture for its betrayal of the great modernist project of reason. But they insist on political evaluations of culture within the larger framework of political and social theories that make sense of the structural contributions of the culture industry to hegemony. Without such a cultural theory, both the Frankfurt and Birmingham groups are at a loss as to why late capitalism persists – why people in an age of possible technological surplus nevertheless adopt self-negating, self-contradictory material and cultural needs. The theory of false needs (e.g., Marcuse, 1964) is precisely equipped to provide a linkage between the level of personal choice in everyday life and the structural level on which larger dynamics of system reproduction take place.

Where the Frankfurt theorists rely on a Freudian version of human needs theory (e.g., Marcuse, 1955), the Birmingham group rely on a Gramscian version (later in their work to be blended with Althusser's theory of ideology, which in significant respects resembles that of the Frankfurt School). Both groups, the German and the British, insist that popular culture must be evaluated from a political posture in terms of its potential for knowledges, discourses and resistances that together constitute a crucial structural factor in the determination of social-structural dynamics at the most macro level of analysis. Although the Frankfurt people are more avowedly modernist than Stuart Hall and his cohorts (that is, they identify European 'high' culture as a repository of these critical knowledges, discourses and resistances), they share the Birmingham emphasis on cultural evaluation as a relevant mode of cultural politics in late capitalism. Both traditions deconstruct the high-culture/low-culture dichotomy as politically inappropriate in late capitalism, although the Frankfurt theorists leave themselves open to the conflation of their own modernist tastes, on the one hand, and their cultural-political theory, on the other.

By hinging their analytical work around Gramsci and not high-European modernism, the Birmingham group avoids the conflation of their temperamental cultural preferences and their rigorous cultural analyses. Gramsci's populism is an important part of the Birmingham texts' fabric, missing from the tenor of the Frankfurt work. This supports the impression that only the Birmingham group, and not also the Frankfurt School, held out the possibility of significant cultural resistance on the level of daily life. Although the logic of the Frankfurt position implies the possibility of the development of true human needs, including cultural ones (as Marcuse [1969] evidences in his engagement with the American New Left and youth culture of the 1960s), the Frankfurt theorists appear to deny this possibility in their cultural mandarinism, which emerges clearly in their choice of culture heroes like Kafka, Beckett and Schoenberg. Gramsci (1971) was never an important figure for the Frankfurt analysts, although he could have been, given the remarkable similarity between his hegemony theory and the Frankfurt critique of cultural domination (see Morrow, 1991). Had Gramsci been directly addressed in Frankfurt, perhaps the tenor of their cultural theory would have been different, thus avoiding the tendency to conflate their own situational modernism with their political logic.

In any case, the CCCS group energetically pursues the terrain of popular culture for all sorts of political encoding – the subtle and overt ways in which we reproduce our own victimhood, and sometimes resist it, through the language games and discursive practices of our everyday lives. Perhaps their most crucial contribution is a vigorous attack on the high-culture/low-culture distinction, thus broadening the neo-Marxist theory of ideology from the 'high' texts of bourgeois ideology (e.g., economic theory and official religion) to the 'lower' and more amorphous texts of everyday cultures which, as they and the Frankfurt group recognize, have enormous political impact in late capitalism, the era of false needs. Although a superficial reading of Birmingham work might suggest that they reject the implied elitism of the notion of false needs, in fact they agree with the Frankfurt critics that what is false about human needs in late capitalism is not so much their particular content but rather their heteronomy – the way in which they are imposed and self-imposed on people hegemonically, from both the 'top down' and 'bottom up'.

It is certainly not the case that the Birmingham implosion of the high-culture/low-culture duality also signals a relativist theory of needs, characteristic of postmodernism. Although the CCCS analysts have read widely in Foucault and others, they are not postmodern; they reject Lyotard's (1984) relativism as unpromising politically. That is, true needs are objectively and subjectively rational when they are freely self-determined. This opens the Frankfurt modernism to progressive cultural catholicity, where it is possible to valorize rock music as well as atonal composition, as Marcuse did. It is clear that CCCS' cultural studies approach is much more contemporary than Frankfurt cultural theory in terms of its openness to non-modernist forms of protest and resistance, and not only because Adorno and Horkheimer were highly threatened by the German New Left in the 1960s. The CCCS work shows that it is possible to be culturally pluralist while also endorsing a theory of needs that resists cultural hegemony on all levels of contemporary experience. Birmingham cultural studies has achieved this balance between pluralism and resistance in part through their theory of *subcultures* (Hebdige, 1979; Brake, 1980), which differentiates and regionalizes the portentous globalism of both high-culture and popular-culture arguments.

One of the central dilemmas of modern cultural studies is to hold onto a theory of needs and thus develop a theory of practice while flattening the high-culture/low-culture distinction into a continuum along which all sorts of politically relevant cultural analyses can take place. It is nearly irresistible for people who oppose cultural mandarinism to go so far in the other direction that they end up not only studying popular culture but also celebrating it. They lose the sharp edge of political critique that follows from a structural understanding of the role of popular culture in reproducing domination. The desire to avoid an Archimedean iteration of substantively true needs (Kafka but not Ken Kesey, for example) is well taken. But, as the CCCS group recognizes, this quickly becomes a positivist approach to the sociology of popular culture which has no relationship to political critique and practice. Although the Frankfurt cultural theorists certainly retained their sharp edge, based on a structural theory of the culture industry as well as an evaluative perspective on human needs, they too often appeared to itemize correct cultural choice in an inflexible way (even if the logic of their needs theory was actually more ecumenical than all that). And for the Frankfurt School the iteration of true needs took a largely modernist form, raising all sorts of questions about their inattention to non-white non-male forms of culture and politics.

Although, with Habermas (1984, 1987a, 1987b), the Enlightenment should not be recanted but fulfilled (against the Nietzschean strain in postmodernism), what it means to be modernist today is very much up for grabs, as Huyssen (1986), among others, argues. Frankfurt modernism is too limited as a standard of cultural evaluation. One might distinguish, albeit flexibly, between philosophical and aesthetic modernisms. The *philosophes'* dream of liberation from mythology, retained and rendered materialist by Marx, is the epicenter of philosophical modernism. Aesthetic modernism shares the goal of general enlightenment, to be achieved by critique and demystification, and yet it is historically specific to a variety of expressive gestures from within the heart of European capitalism. Cultural modernism typically resonates the bitter contradictions of capitalism. Adorno read these resonations both for what they tell us about the social world and for the imaginative, non-cooptable ways they express rage against the world. Cultural modernism is extended politically by the sort of immanent critique of culture that I described in the previous chapter on the Frankfurt School's aesthetic theory.

The problem here is that philosophical modernism can too easily be confused with the various gestures of cultural modernism that, by their very nature, are more allusive and episodic. Why should Kafka signify the insanity and unfulfilled promise of modernity where Ken Kesey does not? (I have no special knowledge of Adorno's view of Kesey, if he even had one. But I suspect that Adorno would have been impatient with his American counter-cultural fiction. Pynchon probably would have blown his mind!) Why should Berg be heard to evoke the harsh atonality of capitalism where the music of the Beatles or the Bangles is dismissed as generationally frivolous? Aesthetic modernism is a trap where it non-discursively substitutes for a philosophical modernism that necessarily spells itself out in unambiguous ways. For Adorno, of course, it is precisely the allusiveness of art and music that help them resist integration into the Muzak of commodified, hegemonized everyday life. One will never hear Berg piped into an elevator in downtown Manhattan or Kafka's words turned into advertising copy.

The CCCS group seems to have had less problem with the issue of cultural and political cooptation than did the Frankfurt theorists, who more rigidly differentiated high culture from low culture as an appropriate medium of critical transcendence. Although, as I said before, there is nothing about the culture-industry thesis that precludes its application to mass culture, it is virtually impossible to escape the impression that the Frankfurt School's cultural modernism was completely non-negotiable with respect to the possibility of non- or postmodernist forms of cultural expression. And because the first-generation Frankfurt critics never adequately delineated the boundary between philosophical and cultural modernism, they could not adapt their cultural politics to changing historical realities and resistances. They could have done so had they interpolated their cultural theory within the political framework of a strong philosophical modernism that keeps alive the Enlightenment's unfulfilled dream of real global enlightenment and hence liberation – precisely Habermas' (1984, 1987b) project.

One of the reasons why the CCCS people were able to avoid these pitfalls was because their own cultural analysis was carried out on a significantly lower level of philosophical abstraction than that of the Frankfurt School, even acknowledging their sometimes tortuous engagements with Gramsci, Althusser, Foucault and French feminism (e.g., see Hall, 1986). This is not a criticism of them but, if anything, praise! It is not that CCCS is theoretically impoverished but that, more than the Frankfurt School, they were driven by political concerns largely framed by the shifting dynamics of class cultures in Britain, both before and under Thatcher. This is not to say that Frankfurt critical theory was apolitical but only that their politics were highly mediated – necessarily so, they would contend. The Birmingham group wanted to understand how cultural class hegemony reproduces itself in everyday life and then to locate possible points of resistance to it. For the most part, the Frankfurt theorists gave up on the politics of everyday life because they thought that late-capitalist everyday life was nearly completely administered by what Marcuse (1968) called affirmative culture. The different perspectives of CCCS and Frankfurt toward the possibilities of political and cultural resistance in late capitalism do not reflect different theoretical assumptions decided a priori but acknowledge historical differences in the contexts within which they composed their cultural analyses.

The CCCS group argued that cultural analysis itself can be viewed as political practice. Although both Adorno and Althusser believe that 'theoretical practice' (Althusser's [1970] phrase) is inherently political, for CCCS this political emphasis is closer to the surface of structural social totalities than Adorno and Althusser supposed. Although I will comment on CCCS' own affiliation to Althusser below, suffice it to say here that the Birmingham group develops a version of his own attempt (Althusser, 1970) to ground a *politically concrete* cultural studies that, like Harry Cleaver (1979) in a different context, argues that Marxist and neo-Marxist categories both reflect and facilitate ongoing political struggle. CCCS takes 'low' or mass culture seriously because they view it as a contested terrain, not a monolithic entity.

4. For the CCCS group *culture is both practice and experience*, not a body of received wisdom, as in anthropology and sociology. Although, as I indicated earlier, culture in the cultural studies tradition is broader than high culture, it is not simply accumulated knowledge about the world but both experience of the world and practice within it. In this sense, the topic of cultural studies is not only cultural artifacts (texts, scripts, scores, films, etc.) but the practices and processes of production, distribution and reception comprising the cultural totality of a society. Cultural studies examines people at work making and experiencing culture; it is not simply a study of cultural works, libraries, studios or theaters – cultural objects and institutions, one might say.

This perspective on culture gives Birmingham cultural studies (see Thompson, 1963) a 'bottom up' perspective on the social world, much as the new historicism (Greenblatt, 1980, 1981, 1982, 1990) provides an innovative perspective on the role of real actors within history. Certainly, this broadening of the notion of culture stems from both the influences of Gramsci and Althusser (although Althusser, through Durkheim and French social anthropology, endorses the notion of 'history without a subject', contradicting the Gramscian emphasis on praxis, which is taken over by the Birmingham School). As Stuart Hall has noted, the CCCS perspective on what counts as culture may be so broad as to lack sufficient specificity in differentiating itself from the non-cultural. The Birmingham approach to culture as practice and experience responds to two influential perspectives on culture – orthodox Marxism and mainstream institutional anthropologies and sociologies of culture. Let me address the differences between the CCCS perspective on culture and these other two viewpoints as a way of framing the Birmingham concept of culture as practice and experience.

Against Orthodox Marxism

For deterministic readers of Marx (and, truth be told, for Marx himself in many places), culture was epiphenomenal, to be derived from the economic base of society. I have already discussed aspects of this perspective on culture in Chapter 3. The very idea of a cultural studies challenges Marxian determinism in the sense that it accords culture what Althusser (contradicting his history-without-a-subject position) calls relative autonomy – a structural and experiential force of its own. On this view, culture matters politically, and not only for a kind of class decoding in the fashion of Lukács and Goldmann. The Birmingham group has found the orthodox Marxist perspective on culture far too limiting, preventing them not only from studying empirical aspects of culture that bear heavily on class-cultural dynamics in Britain but also from theorizing culture in a way that invigorates Marxist social theory in the late twentieth century.

This is not to say that the CCCS group uncritically adopts Althusser's relative-autonomy thesis. Indeed, Althusser's argument for culture's relative autonomy also delimits this autonomy with the notion that economics is always determinate 'in the last instance' – admittedly a literal borrowing from original Marxism. A deconstructive perspective on the relative-autonomy thesis would suggest that the adjective 'relative' already decides in favor of determinism, not autonomy, albeit a closet determinism 'in the last instance'. Although it is certainly possible to defend the 'in the last instance' argument both empirically and theoretically, there are other versions of a non-deterministic Marxist theory of culture that do not endorse the deconstructively dangerous implications of the relative-autonomy thesis, interrogating its secret determinism in the context of the 'in the last instance' caveat. For example, the Frankfurt theorists (e.g., Horkheimer, 1972) reject the relative-autonomy model on the ground that, in fact, culture and economics are so dialectically intertwined and interpenetrating that even to suppose their difference – relative autonomy – is empirically invalid. For them, every cultural analysis is necessarily an economic one, and vice versa. Although the CCCS has engaged seriously with Althusser, I am not certain that they really endorse the veiled determinism of the relative-autonomy thesis, especially in light of their own Gramscian predilection (see Hall, 1985).

In any case, whatever Marxism 'really' says about the relationship between culture and economics, the CCCS group rejects a dualist, determinist Marxism in favor of a perspective on culture that stresses the dialectical nature of cultural practice and experience. There is no single structure of culture but rather continually overdetermined and overdetermining ensembles of cultural practice and experience that condition, and are in turn conditioned by, the logic of capital (notably through the nucleic relationships of commodity fetishism well understood by Marx). This perspective certainly helps the Birmingham School establish a flexible, dialectical method for analyzing cultural practices, notably one that does not choose between economic 'or' ideological factors. Although they never settled their score with Marx and Marxism in terms of developing a total social theory within which the theory of culture/ideology was only one component, they intended to move beyond the stale and counterproductive dualities that have characterized both Marxism and non-Marxism for too long.

There seems to be an inevitable trade-off between a flexible, useful interpretive method for analyzing cultural products and practices, on the one hand, and the sort of total social theory that the CCCS group lacks, on the other. In my last chapter I argue that one can, in fact, develop cultural studies within the framework of a critical social theory without sacrificing either the flexibility and applicability of method or a totalizing comprehensiveness. Indeed, I argue later that one cannot do cultural studies successfully without anchoring one's perspective on ideology in a larger social theory *and* that one cannot develop this larger social theory without the assistance of a cultural studies that functions as a theory and critique of ideology.

Why has the Birmingham School not developed the sort of comprehensive theory that is more typical of German critical theory (if not of French postmodernism and poststructuralism)? I have already touched on some of the temperamental as well as political factors influencing the intellectual differences among French, German, British and American scholars. This sort of sociology-of-knowledge-cum-culture can easily get out of hand and become a banal reductionism. On the other hand, it is notable that the British version of cultural studies, more than the French and German on the one side and the American on the other, has managed to wend its way between theoretical abstraction and atheoretical empiricism. While the CCCS' admixture of Gramsci and Althusser (or, in addition, Foucault and feminism) is not particularly convincing as an alternative to the totalization of German critical theory, the Birmingham group has managed to deploy itself both in concrete cultural readings and in an at least provisional theory-building that is far superior to the atheoretical work of the American popular-culture tradition and even some European versions of cultural studies that are heavily indebted to postmodernism and poststructuralism (including the Baudrillard [1983] of simulation theory).

Whether the Birmingham perspective can issue in a total social theory is as yet unresolved; the CCCS group continues to produce good critical work, if no resounding theoretical breakthroughs. The Thatcherite politics of the UK militate against the retreat from concreteness that would be necessary for the Birmingham people to attempt a new, more satisfactory theoretical synthesis than they have achieved to date (see Hall, 1978, 1988; Hall and Jacques, 1989). They are too politically desperate for that: Thatcherism must be opposed, and with it a regime of political, economic and cultural neoconservatism that has laid waste to whole sectors of British society, notably including intellectuals. Indeed, American cultural studies proponents may well envy the British the intensity of their political engagement. I suspect that that is one reason why people in the US (e.g., Grossberg, 1986; Fiske, 1987; Ryan and Kellner, 1988) are taking a closer look at British cultural studies for both political and methodological insights.

One might reasonably respond that the more atheoretical American popular-culture tradition has simply missed our own Thatcherite circumstance – the two Presidential terms of Reagan and now the Presidency of Bush. But Americans have always been more inured to class struggle than our British and European counterparts, even (perhaps especially!) in the academy. We have simply neglected the desperation of our political crisis in the US. The 1980s saw the utter decimation of the FDR-era safety nets protecting the underclasses against the ravages of capitalism, the further degradation of the environment and cultural life and attacks on personal and intellectual freedom at all levels. The most interesting question is why American culturalists, indeed social scientists generally, have not learned more from the burst of theoretical activity that has taken place in Europe and from which the CCCS group has learned so much. If the Birmingham scholars have not yet achieved a fully evolved social theory, diverted by the necessities of political resistance in a collapsing Britain, then American culturalists are even further behind in developing a structural understanding of the crises and contradictions of popular culture. Instead, we on the American side of the Atlantic remain peculiarly insulated from the kind of theoretical work that has remade the faces of social science and humanities scholarship in western Europe, Britain, Australia, New Zealand and Canada.

People in American humanities programs will object that they have already acknowledged and begun to assimilate the influences of Derrida, Foucault and Barthes. Yet the neoconservative paranoia about the leftist dominance of the American university (e.g., Bloom, 1987; Kimball, 1990) is simply not supported by evidence. Leading English departments typically sport a few deconstructors, leftists and feminists, notable for their flamboyance if nothing else. But for the most part American humanities remains dominated by the morally redemptive liberal agendas of Leavis and Arnold, who intended to civilize the business and leisure classes. Although it is easy to become obsessed with the extravagances of decon-speak that litter the program of the MLA annual meetings, the Europeanization of American humanities is often exaggerated – by both its partisans and its opponents. A careful check of recent university press publications in the humanities would be a more reliable way of assessing the extent to which American humanists have been as powerfully affected by the new semiological and interpretive developments from the Continent as have the British culturalists.

The American social sciences, for their part, have not been well fertilized by European theory. Anthropology (Marcus and Fischer, 1986) probably has been the discipline most affected by poststructural developments, notably in ethnography, with political science (Luke, 1989; Rosenau, 1992) and sociology (Brown, 1987, 1989; Denzin, 1986, 1990, 1991; Richardson, 1988, 1990a, 1990b, 1990c, 1991; Agger, 1989c) lagging somewhat behind. Of course, American social science disciplines have not yet assimilated Marxism fully; at best, Marxist social scientists are viewed as interlopers or half-baked. It would be surprising if American culturalists had already taken the full measure of Euro-theory, let alone been deeply affected by it in a way that would require them to retheorize their own interpretive practices. There have been a few exceptional Continental thinkers who have had significant impact on American cultural studies. Pierre Bourdieu's (1984) work on cultural capital has had some resonance in the American sociology of culture (Lamont and Larreau, 1988). Bourdieu has had more impact than other European cultural theorists because a good deal of his work utilizes techniques of empirical data analysis that are much more familiar to Americans than are the obscurities of Derrida.

In any case, the Birmingham people are far more theoretical than American popular-culturalists and, at the same time, far more flexible than orthodox Marxist students of culture. Although I would like to see cultural studies become not a distinct and isolated intellectual subfield but an arm of the totalizing project of critical social theory, functioning as a theory and critique of ideology that makes empirical sense in a stage of capitalism vastly different from the more rudimentary capitalism of the mid-nineteenth century, I am not persuaded that the Gramsci/Althusser (or .../Foucault) fusion fashioned by Stuart Hall and his cohorts is an adequate substitute for Frankfurt critical theory, in spite of Frankfurt's regrettable mandarinism. As I will suggest below, too much of Althusser is simply wrong, while for his part Gramsci is read as a delphic text in which one can find license for just about everything (given that Gramsci's writings were fragmentary). Of course, Gramsci has had enormous political relevance on the British left, suggesting, as I did earlier, that it is cavalier to ignore ways in which the particular national cultures within which left theory developed have produced quite different intellectual inflections in the hands of their practitioners. For his part, Althusser functions less dogmatically in the British context than he did in France, where he represented an unreconstructed French CP theoretical line that was uniformly rejected by revisionist political and cultural theorists there.

As the CCCS group has shown, it is possible to develop a non-orthodox Marxist and feminist perspective on culture that emphasizes the contested nature of cultural terrain. More than the Germans, French and Americans, the Birmingham group has managed not to lose touch with class struggle (although Hall would agree that the agenda for late twentieth-century leftists is precisely to broaden class struggle into a host of different theaters of struggle heretofore off-limits to the left). Although the Birmingham version of cultural studies is undertheorized, it is perhaps the best antidote to the stagnant Marxist theory of culture that either reduces cultural products to their class truth content or altogether dismisses the study of culture and ideology as pursuits of the privileged occupants of 'Grand Hotel Abyss', as Lukács once termed the Frankfurt theorists. The Birmingham analysts stress that culture is an ongoing practice that builds on the lived experience of the social world, requiring attention from the ground up as well as the top down. In this way alone, they reverse the mechanism and determinism of orthodox Marxism.

Against the Anthropological and Sociological Notions of Culture

It is clear that the CCCS people work with an extremely broad concept of culture. However, just as their concept of culture contrasts with that of orthodox Marxism, which makes culture epiphenomenal, so it contrasts with mainstream anthropological and sociological concepts of culture as an autonomous realm of knowledges and learned behaviors that can be separated out from other social institutions like the economy, family, polity, religion, education and even media. Although CCCS borrows from the anthropological broadening of culture beyond artifacts of high culture per se, they put distance between themselves and mainstream anthropologists and sociologists who render culture extremely diffuse by breaking or occluding its connections with other driving societal institutions, especially the economy and polity.

The CCCS group makes room for what I (1990) have called *literary political economy*, a way of approaching cultural practices and experience in an integrated institutional mannor. The anthropological and sociological definition of culture stresses mainly the experiential side of culture – the notion that culture is what we learn from a common stock of knowledge. Although Birmingham cultural studies does not dispense with this idea, it imposes the additional requirement that culture is a differential field of significances and activities that nest among a variety of overlapping, interlocking institutions including both the economic and political systems. By identifying culture everywhere, sociologists tend to lose the specificity of the concept of culture that stresses its interinstitutional nature as well as its active side – the possibilities of *making* new cultures from the ground up.

For sociologists and anthropologists, culture is everything we learn about, and from, our social world. The CCCS people extend this culture concept to include two additional themes. First, culture is not a monolithic or homogeneous entity but rather has differential manifestations across any given social formation and historical epoch. Second, culture is not simply received wisdom or passive experience but a host of active interventions, notably through discourse and representation, that may change history as much as transmit the past. By stressing the differential nature of culture, the Birmingham cultural studies perspective can relate cultural production, distribution and reception to economic practices that bear heavily on the constitution of cultural meaning. Culture is not a world apart from political economy, just as it was not for the Frankfurt School's version of Marx. By stressing that culture is practice as well as experience, the CCCS group follow Marx in theorizing the possibility of new cultural practices. Neither the sociological nor anthropological concept of culture allows culture to be differentiated in an institutional sense, nor do they make it possible to view culture as an ongoing set of everyday practices carried out by self-conscious agents.

Hall and his associates do not delineate the specificity of their culture concept sufficiently from the sociological and anthropological concepts of culture, especially with regard to culture's institutionally differential nature. Reading the CCCS often gives the impression that culture is the same sort of undifferentiated monolith – Culture – posited by sociologists and anthropologists. It is clearer that the Birmingham culture concept differs from those of sociology and anthropology with regard to the second issue – the active side of culture. This is especially apparent in the CCCS studies of working-class and women's cultures, where culture is treated not simply as imposed on mute victims but also as dialectically produced and reproduced from below. In other words, the CCCS culture concept possesses historicity in a way that the sociological concept of culture does not (which is not surprising, given sociology's original roots in Comte's positivism).

My (1990) notion of literary political economy could help explain the precise articulations between cultural practices and political economy, a crucial topic missed by the sociological/anthropological culture concept, which idealizes culture and removes it from its institutional housing. The sociological/anthropological culture concept in this regard hails from structural-functionalism (Malinowski and Radcliffe-Brown to Parsons, Merton and now Alexander), via Durkheim, in the sense that it stresses the normative component of societies. Although surely culture has a normative (and counternormative) component, to view culture ideally in this way occludes the relationship between norms and values, on the one side, and political–economic institutions, on the other. Marx opposes Durkheim where Durkheim splits issues of collective consciousness from those of what he called the division of labor in society (e.g., in his analyses of religion), a dichotomy that Marx overcomes in the development of his dialectical social theory.

For Marxists and neo-Marxists culture is at once a normative and material practice. Although culture transmits values, the encoding of these values is often subtle, even contradicting the express intent of particular cultural transmissions. For example, advertisements for alcoholic beverages that urge responsible use of alcohol (in the interests of personal health, road safety, etc.) clearly normalize a culture in which alcohol consumption is taken for granted, hence, in the long run, legitimating consumption of alcoholic beverages. The production of these cultural imageries of 'responsible' alcohol consumption is a thoroughly material practice, although it can also be read at its expressly normative level – e.g., what the advertisement 'says' explicitly about alcohol. The Birmingham perspective on culture suggests a distinction between cultural texts and subtexts (which become texts in their own right): culture conveys meanings and values explicitly while it also conveys them implicitly via what Baudrillard calls simulations that represent and reproduce reality through the frames of advertising and other forms of cultural expression.

Relevant to Birmingham cultural studies are not only cultural texts – what culture says on its surface. Also relevant are cultural subtexts, the hidden messages and values encoded in cultural gestures, from advertising to mass-market fiction. Also relevant are the actual material practices of cultural production, distribution and consumption that realize these cultural connections among authors, producers, distributors and consumers – readers, as they are called in deconstruction. Literary political economy addresses all three of these levels of meaning without reducing one to another, offering just the sort of culturally differentiated analysis that I spoke of before. Culture is viewed not merely as the transmission of values (let alone the values themselves) but as the decentered ensembles of cultural practice and expression constituting the everyday lifeworlds of people who, at least in this stage of capitalism, necessarily experience culture imposed from the top down.

The CCCS group's resolution of the theoretical interrelationships among cultural production, distribution, reception, text and subtext is not fully worked out. They have done better at spelling out the empirical ways in which these elements fit together in terms of their specific cultural readings. As such, they have made a vital contribution to the redevelopment of a materialist theory of culture and ideology. If they have not fully theorized their break with both orthodox Marxism and mainstream cultural anthropology and sociology, they have pointed in the right direction. Their version of literary political economy is a significant advance beyond both Marxist and non-Marxist theories of culture, especially in the sophisticated ways in which they read cultural practices as simultaneously material and ideal.

5. The Birmingham School *builds theoretically on both Gramsci and Althusser*. I have already alluded to their relationships to both of these figures, as well as to Foucault and various European feminist theorists. In many respects, the strangeness of their dual borrowing from Gramsci and Althusser signals the strength of the CCCS approach to cultural studies. On the surface, at least, Gramsci and Althusser are seriously at odds, one representing western Marxism and the other representing an antagonistic structuralist or causal Marxism. Of particular concern for the CCCS group are Gramsci's (1971) prison notebooks and Althusser's (1971) essay on ideological state apparatuses, from which they derived much of their impetus during the 1970s. Where Althusser stresses the 'relative autonomy' of culture and ideology, so the Birmingham people derive a relatively autonomous cultural studies that is not mechanically beholden to orthodox Marxism. Strangely, many Frankfurt-oriented thinkers have not been able to appreciate the relative-autonomy argument from Althusser, focusing instead on the structuralist emphases in Althusser (e.g., his notion of history without a subject). Clearly, the Birmingham theorists reject the history-without-a-subject theme while they accept a version of the relative-autonomy thesis.

Even this distinction oversimplifies a complex issue. The relative-autonomy thesis suggests that culture and ideology are determined by economic forces only 'in the last instance', relying on a more or less literal interpretation of Marx. But the rhetoric of 'relative autonomy' suggests that culture's autonomy is deconstructively belied by its subordination to the economic order of capitalism. For something to be only *relatively* autonomous means that it is not autonomous at all, a point I made earlier in another context. Nevertheless, even if Althusser's specific delineation of the relative-autonomy thesis leaves much to be desired, his heart was in the right place: he wanted cultural/ideological analysis to have a central role in Marxian theoretical practice, recouped from its totally derivative status for earlier species of orthodox Marxism.

Borrowing from Gramsci, the Birmingham thinkers derive a more fully-rounded perspective on cultural hegemony – the ways in which people participate in, and thus reproduce, the dominant cultural consensus and hence contradict their own objective class interests. Gramsci, like the Frankfurt thinkers, anticipated Althusser's later relative-autonomy thesis within a more nuanced non-reductive framework. In many ways, Gramsci remains the foremost Marxist theorist of culture, to which all sorts of left versions of cultural studies are indebted. Gramsci not only programmatizes cultural analysis but anchors his version of cultural analysis within a historical-materialist framework that explains and explores culture's utility in terms of its location in a wider nest of institutional arrangements, giving rise to the literary political economy I talked about above. One could say that there is no such thing as a Gramscist method, no definitive extrapolation of his own cultural and ideological analyses. Rather, Gramsci sets in motion the search for an appropriate cultural analytic within the general framework of his hegemony theory, which in crucial respects parallels Lukács' analysis of reification and the Frankfurt School's analysis of domination.

This is not to read Gramsci reductively or derivatively. After all, the literal Gramsci is full of exciting, innovative ideas about the complex interrelationships between ideal and material factors in the historical process. As much as anyone, Gramsci argues powerfully that there are no such things as ideal factors (e.g., sociology's concept of cultural norms and values) apart from the material practices within which they are encoded. Although he does not bequeath us a timeless method for exploring these aspects of imbeddedness – a materialist cultural studies – he gets the ball rolling in the sense that he shows the importance of cultural analysis for an overall understanding of hegemony or ideology.

That Gramsci's hegemony theory grounds the Birmingham approach more than does the work of the Frankfurt School is in large measure a function of the differential reception of Gramsci and the Frankfurt theorists in the UK. For both political and cultural reasons, Gramsci was the emblematic western Marxist for British neo-Marxists, where Adorno, Horkheimer and Marcuse were more central both on the Continent and in the United States (but see Smart, 1983; Dews, 1984, 1987). Part of this has to do with the simple contingencies of translations. It also has to do with the relative lucidity of Gramsci's writings, which are more easily received in the Anglo-Saxon tradition of analytic philosophy utterly scandalized by some of the Frankfurt School's more Hegelian utterances, especially in the case of Adorno. Whatever the ultimate reasons, it is clear that the CCCS group relied on Gramsci to give their approach to the venerable English culture-

and-society tradition (Hoggart, Williams, Thompson) a more theoretical and political twist, helping revivify the culture-and-society tradition at a time when it was running out of·steam. Gramsci opened the otherwise stagnant Marxist tradition to heterodox voices and enlivening perspectives, all of which, taken together, helped move Marxism into the late twentieth century as a program of cultural studies.

Chapter 6

Poststructuralism and Postmodernism on Culture

Deconstruction as Anti-Method

No intellectual developments have had more impact on cultural studies than poststructuralism and postmodernism; no cultural studies perspective is more ill-defined than the one(s) inspired by these two European traditions of thought. How can this be? In this chapter, I explore this paradox with reference to the various contributions that the two 'post's make to the emerging traditions of cultural studies. In the next chapter, I discuss the impact of poststructuralism, especially the work of Lacan, on feminist cultural studies. A good deal of the difficulty in sorting out these issues is definitional. Who fits where within these schema? I do not want to belabor definitions, and yet to dispense with taxonomy assumes that all readers will share my particular senses of poststructuralism and postmodernism, an assumption that is risky at best (for an alternative account, see Best and Kellner, 1991).

Poststructuralism refers to the theory of knowledge and language associated with the work of Jacques Derrida (1976, 1978, 1981, 1987). This perspective suggests that language users do not just pluck words out of thin air or a thesaurus when trying to convey meaning, fitting them to the objects or feelings being conveyed. Instead, the meanings of words are largely imbedded in language use itself such that *how* we talk, write and read largely determines *what* we end up saying. In effect, poststructuralism reconstructs the process of meaning in a way that gives fuller weight to the pre-given meanings imbedded not only in particular words but in the relations of words (Saussure's signs) to each other. As a result, Derrida argues that meaning is forever elusive and incomplete in the sense that language can never perfectly convey what is meant by the language user. In the next section of this chapter, I discuss Derrida's contributions to cultural analysis in greater depth.

Postmodernism for its part is a theory of cultural, intellectual and societal discontinuity that rejects the linearism of Enlightenment notions of progress. History is no longer conceived as going somewhere, from prehistory to the end of history. The present is no longer to be experienced as a way station en route to something higher or better. Nor is the past to be reconstructed as a dim period of myth and prejudice. Instead, postmodern culture draws on the best in a variety of historical epochs, indulging in a studied eclecticism. Postmodernism initially represented an architectural movement (Portoghesi, 1983; Jencks, 1987) designed to formulate alternatives to modernism from within a modernist frame of reference (see Huyssen, 1986). Whole cityscapes (e.g., New York City, Atlanta, Houston) have been postmodernized in this fashion as huge rectangular skyscrapers are adorned with a variety of gestures plundered from different, often incommensurable, historical periods. American shopping malls and strips boast identical postmodern fronts as the style has been standardized, ironically vitiating postmodernism's playful and pastiche-like irreducibility (see Harvey, 1989; Soja, 1989).

Having briefly described the two 'post's, let me suggest some of their contributions to cultural studies. Let me also suggest why such a summary is inherently difficult. Unlike all of the other perspectives on culture discussed in this book, the contributions of poststructuralism and postmodernism to cultural studies cannot be reduced to a singular method *because poststructuralism and postmodernism oppose their methodologization* – their reduction to formulae. They mistrust method because method postures as a value-free mechanism for resolving the aporias, ambiguities and ironies of language. Instead, the two 'post's insist that method itself is laden with significances that cannot be resolved outside of language. Method is not a royal road to meaning but a path every bit as rutted and circuitous as other forms of language.

The effort to apply poststructuralism and postmodernism to a methodical cultural analysis is resisted by the authors of these traditions like Derrida, Barthes, Foucault, Lyotard and Baudrillard (however/wherever we ultimately classify them). Deconstruction (see Culler, 1982) resists becoming a tool that one can use willy-nilly, without reference to its context or the intentions of its users. This is not to say that poststructuralism and postmodernism cannot be used to do cultural analysis, for there has been a great deal of work done under the aegis of Derrida, Barthes, Foucault and the French feminists. Indeed, the deconstructive approach to culture has produced a large number of cultural 'readings' that together comprise a rich and varied tableau of interpretations and interventions. In the US, at least, cultural studies people who reject positivist cultural empiricism are apt to be well versed in one or another version of deconstruction. Where left cultural studies in the UK has clustered around the CCCS group in Birmingham, theoretical versions of American cultural studies are more deconstructive than anything else, again reflecting cultural and intellectual differences between the UK and the US, particularly some of the different ways in which European theory has been assimilated in these two countries.

Deconstructive cultural studies has gathered the most momentum in departments of English, where poststructural literary theory has become well established. But it is important to distinguish between literary deconstruction per se and the more broadly cultural deconstruction of poststructural and postmodern cultural studies. The first focuses on the traditional literary text, where the second broadens cultural studies to include non-literary texts like film and television. Deconstructive approaches to media studies comprise a good deal of the current investment of American deconstructors, rejuvenating the highly quantitative and content-oriented approach of mainstream positivist media studies. This is not to overestimate the influence of this approach to cultural studies within the traditional literary departments like English and comparative literature but only to note interesting ways in which the deconstructive program has been broadened to address a host of meta-textual concerns, including those of social analysis and criticism (see Ross, 1988, 1989; Ryan, 1989).

The deconstructive approach to cultural studies is less method than perspective, a kind of interpretive self-consciousness. After all, Derrida never set down a singular way to read texts (against themselves, as it were). He did not theorize about reading but rather he read. Or better, he wrote readings, refusing to write 'about' readings as if reading and writing could be clearly separated. These distinctions blur to the point of indistinguishability when we view them deconstructively – precisely Derrida's point! Method can be found in anti-method, in the vigilant posture against method as a lifeless, stanceless reading that takes place outside or beyond the interstitial web of textuality. Thus, to read is inherently to write reading – to theorize it. Derrida's writing is singularly self-conscious in a way that flavors all deconstructive criticism, whether of traditional literary work or of media.

Deconstructive reading reads itself reading; it positions itself with respect to texts as con-texts, one might say. The deconstructive attitude suggests that every reading must be con-textual; it must be carried out in relation to the contingencies of literary language games and not done formulaically, in terms of general principles. For example, one cannot read 'film' deconstructively but only particular films or genres of films that cohere because they have in common a certain topic, author or reader (e.g., see de Lauretis, 1984; Mulvey, 1988). Frequently, deconstructive reading seems whimsically playful because it dexterously deploys itself with reference to texts that appear to possess little in common. The reading of texts gives them con-texts within which they take on a common intertextuality. This approach to finding sameness in difference is characteristic of the whole tradition of structuralism, against which poststructuralism is 'post' only in the sense of being more reflexive about its interpretive practices. In many respects, the difference between Saussure and Derrida fades where we consider that they both assumed that meaning is structured by the differential terms of arbitrary sign systems. As Lévi-Strauss (1963, 1966) demonstrates, mythology has structure because our readings of it give it structure, from which it derives its effectivity as a powerful social text. This power is conveyed in myth's iterability for those who participate in decoding it.

This language is difficult (for clarification, see Agger, 1991b, Ch. 2). Deconstruction often appears to endorse difficulty capriciously when, in fact, what it is really doing is forcing language to listen to itself do its work, thus shattering the myth of clarity that dominates the Anglo-American philosophy of language. Language does not stand or fall on its elucidation of opacity but rather on its ability to reflect on its own undecidability (Derrida's term) in a sustained and enlightening way. Deconstructive cultural criticism helps us to read, hear and view cultural texts in new ways, particularly illuminating the subtexts that drive them. By turning language upside down and inside out, deconstruction helps language interrogate itself, turning the act of reading into a strong act of writing or rewriting. A deconstructed text is reassembled in a way that shows some of its concealed meanings to be effective ones, thus helping us evaluate the cultural product critically and against common-sense receptions of it.

This sort of cultural reading shows the busy artifice that went into the cultural work but which is sublimated in the 'finished' version of it. Deconstruction shows that this sense of being finished is an illusion – that the final product, performance or draft is merely one among many possibilities. By reconstructing the cultural text in terms of its process of gestation, mediation and self-correction we better understand the authorial and editorial investments encoded in what we take to be the clean, final copy of the work – the last cut or the printed draft. In reauthorizing culture as an ensemble of authorial and editorial choices, we open it to different formulations and hence to different social relationships. By showing that these provisional choices could have been made differently, we demystify the aura of the final work, denying it permanence and unchallenged authority.

Some view this deconstructive intent as simply destructive – not 'positive' enough. But that is a misreading: deconstruction wants to democratize authorial possibilities, including the authorial possibilities available to readers. It wants readers to become writers and then to write for themselves. The deconstruction of canonical works that appear to be devoid of human artifice is tremendously empowering to readers who want to write as well as to readers who stand in awe of putative cultural genius. I am not saying that cultural genius is apocryphal but only that we must train ourselves to view culture's artifice as a process of deliberate human judgments carried out by people who are no different from you and me. The monopoly of cultural authorship and competent readership only reinforces the monopolies of wealth and power.

It is telling that poststructural literary critics generally eschew the label *deconstruction*. That already methodologizes an approach to reading that is con-text driven. The goal of poststructural cultural criticism is to produce *new* texts, new cultural artifacts, and not simply to leave old ones intact – venerated, canonized, explicated. Derrida recognized that criticism cannot fail to transform its object. At least, this is the strong version of poststructural cultural studies. Weaker versions have less grandiose aims. Predictably, deconstructive cultural analysis is affected by its own con-text, particularly its location in traditional literary departments in which objectivist criticism holds sway. Almost by osmosis the objectivist goal of traditional *Scrutiny* and New Critical criticism (see Fekete, 1978; Lentricchia, 1980) is internalized by cultural deconstructors, blunting their transformation of their critical objects.

This assumes that criticism *does* transform its object, opening it to new versions of itself by bringing to light its hidden assumptions and inconsistencies – deconstruction's aporias. One can easily see this with respect to descriptive, especially scientific, writing. It is harder to see this with respect to fiction – harder still with respect to television and film. In what sense can we say that Pauline Kael transforms the movies she reviews? Perhaps she does not because she is not a deconstructor. What can it mean for criticism to change a cultural text or artifact? Poststructuralism would suggest that criticism can rearrange our views of both the internal dynamics of the text (e.g., plot) and of the boundaries between text and world, showing that the text is in fact a combustible, contested terrain and that the text is not hermetically sealed off from its social site.

Deconstructive reading inserts itself into the flow and flux of the text's world, claiming it as its world, too. Reading familiarizes not only readers with text but text with world, showing all the places where the world seeps through. Thus, texts are turned into social texts – and social practices – by the strong reading practices of deconstruction. Reading is reconstructed as a social practice in its own terms, anchored in the variety of distribution and reception processes patterned for people in late capitalism. Reading is not simply a subjective act of textual appropriation but a socially situated and mediated practice that is inseparable from the social con-texts within which texts are produced as social objects. The drift of this discussion shows that textual interpretation becomes social analysis and critique when conducted through the lens of deconstruction, which sociologizes and economizes the practice of literary and cultural interpretation, turning texts into societies that can be read in much the same way that literary texts are read.

All of this sounds mystical both to literary traditionalists, for whom texts are texts and societies societies, and to mainstream positivist sociologists of culture, who do not problematize the act of cultural interpretation but rather view it as an objectivist process of reflection. Deconstructive cultural studies works beyond both of these traditional approaches to culture, implicating the reader himself/ herself – indeed, reading in general – in the cultural production and reception process. An obsessional (or simply misunderstood) deconstruction might go too far and conclude that reading produces the text independent of other productivist cultural practices. After all, movies are movies before we view them (even if, to become movies, they undergo many layers and levels of mediation, including actual viewings by test audiences). The reader does not become *the* writer but *a* writer, coexisting with the other writers who produced the cultural text in the first place.

Deconstructive cultural analysis rejects method in favor of politics (see Ryan, 1982, 1989). The politics of deconstructive cultural reading empowers reading, giving it equal status with the writing it criticizes, hence becoming new writing in its own right. Deconstructors must resist the temptation to view their reading as if it takes the place of writing. It is writing, but it is not the same writing as the writing it addresses: it is different writing – one might say writing with a difference. Cultural criticism in the deconstructive mode is different from other types of cultural critique in the sense that it is self-conscious of its literariness, its cultural production of meaning. The self-consciousness of the critic makes a significant difference to his or her criticism in the sense that it deprivileges the 'original' work, deauratizing it in Adorno's sense. This process of deauratization is democratizing in the sense that it opens the cultural field to new voices, one of the political goals of radical cultural studies as I envision it.

In this way, the political outcomes of deconstructive cultural criticism are somehow more important than the 'critical' outcomes, if one can separate these two things. One begins to change the world by transforming the relationship of reading to writing, and hence all power relationships in a technological stage of capitalism (see Poster, 1990). Cultural criticism of this kind intervenes in the cultural field not as a disclosure of truth but as a subversion of unchallenged authorial privilege, notably the privilege to determine one's own reception through the chicanery of authorial self-presentation in an age of simulation. Rare is the book, show or film that does not announce itself in its own terms, claiming a market niche (and, sometimes, a portentous intellectual significance) on its face – in its advertising, on its dust jacket, in its opening gestures, on the strength of the star status of its principals. Such writing preempts reading, hence closing off dialogue. Rare is the critic who can withstand the assault of these sorts of peremptory cultural self-presentations. Typically, the critic acquiesces to this cultural self-framing process by reviewing the work in its own terms, whatever those might be. He or she loses critical distance and hence analytical acuity.

What is Cultural Deconstruction?

So far I have described the textual and political contexts within which cultural deconstructors do their work. I have not yet examined the particular literary and interpretive assumptions made by deconstructors. Let me do that now.

1. Deconstructors assume that *culture is a text*. The boundaries of the literary text are expanded to include all manner of cultural performances and artifacts, from television and film to textbooks and science. Cultural deconstruction is possible only if we make the assumption that diverse cultural products can be 'read', in much the way that Derrideans read traditional literary texts. Derrida makes it clear that deconstruction applies to all manner of human expressions; we restrict it to traditional literary texts only out of canonical prejudices. This broadening of the possibilities of cultural reading is extremely powerful because it grants legitimacy to a host of cultural and media studies that are typically disdained in mainstream English departments. Once culture is expanded to include the media and entertainment industries, as the CCCS group in Birmingham has done, then the grip of traditional cultural mandarinism is commensurably weakened. Exemplifying the possibilities of postmodern cultural readings, Faurschou (1987) develops an intriguing postmodern-feminist reading of fashion.

   The notion that culture is a text is part of the basic theoretical and epistemological apparatus of deconstruction. Following Derrida, deconstructors claim that everything in the human world is textual – that is, everything can be read and rewritten critically from the point of view of a reader's intervention in a given text at hand. Although Derrida said that the text has no outside, I suspect that he did not mean by this that material reality evaporates into textuality, as with idealism, but rather that the boundary between the textual world and the social world fades once we subject culture to a deconstructive reading. Indeed, deconstructive reading intends to authorize cultural products in a way that one can read them and thus engage with them critically.

2. This process of textualization aims to *locate the author* of cultural products. Typically cultural authorship is concealed in a positivist culture, where texts of all kinds are purged of the dirty fingerprints of the people who have written them, through a variety of creative and editorial mediations. The cleansing of texts is fine for their superficial appearances, what people in media call their 'production values' or patinas of professionalism. But this cleansing robs writing of its grounding in authorial interest and con-text, suggesting a stancelessness to writing that deceptively discourages dialogues. Deconstructive work exhumes the author in order to engage that author in debate, conflict, sometimes friendship. In this sense, deconstructive work extends and rewrites extant texts by suggesting new versions of them that lie buried within the flesh and folds of their deauthored versions. Letting the author speak discloses surprising meanings, flying in the face of the sanitized versions of cultural texts.

This is especially relevant where we are dealing with cultural objects that have been heavily mediated, especially for the marketplace. Here, authorial vision may well have been subverted by the seemingly endless mediations imposed on the text by outside influences as well as by the author's own anticipation of what will happen if creative vision is not somehow hemmed in, domesticated. Locating the author helps readers see authorial purpose clearly as well as resist the overdetermined versions of the text that subvert this purpose in order to placate the audience. Cultural overdetermination is all over the place. Scarcely nothing is left untouched by editorial pens. This does not mean that various editorial mediations do not improve the final product; certainly, they often do. But just as often they mute authorial voice in a way that makes the finished cultural product more banal than it needs to be (and certainly more banal than the author originally intended it).

To view the author–editor relationship as inherently conflictual is not excessive at a time when there is growing pressure on editors to sign and produce profitable projects (see Curtis, 1989). Editors are not uniquely opposed to authorial vision; like faculty, they are bureaucratic workers in the culture industry. Often they fight indefatigably 'for' quality, protecting the original authorial vision against all challenges. But the process of cultural mediation is structurally adversarial in these times: authors struggle to make themselves heard over the din of banality and overdetermination deafening all of us. It is here that a deconstructive cultural studies can do its best work: it can reauthorize cultural products that seem to have lost any connection to the people who originally conceived and executed them.

This deconstructed text preserves the traces of mediation and conflict that issue in the clean culture available to us in the cultural marketplace. It is important to reconstruct the cultural production process as a process of administration and overdetermination because frequently it is: knowing this helps us read the finished cultural text in a stronger light. We try to recognize the regions of compromise and capitulation constituting the finished text – battlegrounds on which cultural vision bit the dust. By authorizing cultural texts, we reveal the possibilities of new cultural intervention and construction, wresting the power to mediate cultural expression away from editors and producers who respond slavishly to the demands of the marketplace. Deconstructive reading is empowering where it shows that the silenced author once stood his or her ground and resisted editorial imperatives, however unsuccessful these attempts may have been.

I am not demonizing individual editors here, or even the editing process in general. As often as not authors silence themselves; this is precisely what Gramsci meant by hegemony. They do so in anticipation of editorial mediation later on. Editors are not singularly opposed to cultural creativity or autonomy but merely occupants of role niches in the bureaucratic apparatus of the culture industry. Cultural hegemony occurs where cultural creators *self*-edit, succumbing to the literary norms requiring us to clean our texts of our own presences. Sometimes this capitulation is unconscious, having been routinized in the ways we present our work (e.g., in science writing). We deeply internalize the compromises we must make with 'reality' – the marketplace, editors, readers, producers – and do not think twice (or even once) about what we are doing. Authorial self-disciplining occurs almost naturally as we compose ourselves in our written work.

This sort of writing is valorized as writing done by 'professionals', people able to deliver clean copy on time. These literary professionals do not have to be chided or scolded; they rein in their own expressive extravagance: they are said to be good corporate players. Deconstructive criticism has to reckon with the realities of power here: cultural hegemony is so nearly total that successful writers do not have to be disciplined; they discipline themselves. Savvy writers deal with editors and producers on their own terms, fully recognizing the institutional pressures faced by them and capable of self-editing in a way that meets their requirements for a marketable literary 'product'. Professionalism is *realism*; only lunatics gleefully court rejection. Every cultural producer must reckon with 'reality' in this sense. They must compose themselves in ways that facilitate their editorial processing and production. To take literary risks is vainglorious at a time when the culture industry increasingly enforces the standardization of taste.

3. Deconstructors assume that *every cultural text is undecidable* and thus their critical practice takes this undecidability into account. What Derrida interrogates is the way in which the circuitries, ambiguities and conundrums of meaning cannot be resolved externally, from an Archimedean vantage of objective interpretation. Meaning is always elusive; in Derrida's terms, it embodies both difference and deferral: the more we attempt to triangulate meaning, the more it slips away, receding into the future. The principle of a text's undecidability is the zero point from which deconstruction as a critical practice proceeds. It forever transforms the nature of criticism from an objectivist practice of presupposition-less reading (e.g., the New Criticism) into a con-textual practice of the approximation and transvaluation of meaning.

Undecidability can provoke either nihilist ennui on the part of cultural readers (where we conclude that every reading is as valid as every other), or it can provoke a strong engagement of reading with writing such that criticism is in no way subordinate to the original text (rejoining my earlier discussion of the dehierarchizing textual politics of the Birmingham School's program of cultural studies). Deconstructive cultural studies is no different from literary deconstruction in that it faces this central dilemma, unresolved by Derrida originally. Does deconstruction lose its foundation (with Nietzsche) by claiming the undecidability of every text, including its own? Or can deconstruction be employed within a context of relatively stable values and politics as a mode of ideology criticism? The political Derrida would not conclude from the unavoidable nature of undecidability – the irresolvability of meaning outside of the con-texts within which meaning is produced – that a deconstructive politics is impossible. The apolitical Derrida (e.g., the Yale School – American deconstruction generally) would conclude from undecidability that any politics is impossible, the role of the critic being restricted to a kind of playfulness with texts (e.g., see Rorty, 1979, 1989) that makes no larger truth claims.

I am convinced that Derrida inclines in the latter direction; the effort to read or write politics into him indicates that the politics (e.g., literary and social dehierarchization) was not there in the first place. I politicize deconstruction in spite of itself because a deconstructive cultural studies avoids many of the blind spots of Frankfurt cultural theory and, as well, helps us conceive of cultural criticism itself as a mode of critical practice in the everyday life of the society of the spectacle (Debord, 1970). We can take these liberties with Derrida's program because, in effect, he has no program – his version of cultural and literary reading was itself so undecidable that it is possible to read and write any number of Derridas, depending on the pragmatic context within which we want to 'use' him (if not, also, be used by him).

After all, if undecidability blocks definitive versions of texts and cultural practices, then criticism itself is up for grabs. Deconstruction self-contradictorily becomes Archimedean when it sets itself up as a univocal interpretive method; the only really political deconstruction refuses its own methodologization in order to claim the status of political and critical theory, however labored this claim must necessarily be given Derrida's virtual silence on the politics of criticism (see Berman, 1988). When I talk about deconstructive cultural studies I am largely inventing a critical practice out of the many bits and pieces of literary and cultural criticism that proceeds using some, if not all, of Derrida's own interpretive practices as instructive examples. There is no school or method of 'deconstructive cultural studies' but only a number of regional versions (e.g., from within feminism) that could perhaps coalesce under the same name if we develop a reading of Derrida that makes this sort of common naming possible. I am not particularly interested in demonstrating a close reading of Derrida that makes this sort of interpretation or interpolation possible; suffice it to say that I am claiming Derrida for a project – radical cultural studies – that could well be so far from both the spirit and letter of his oeuvre that the naming 'deconstructive cultural studies' betrays his own opposition to method. So be it. Let others read Derrida in a different direction. And let them convict me of a pragmatic reading of Derrida that helps do useful analytical and political work.

The sort of radicalized deconstruction I am talking about uses the concept of undecidability to challenge objectivist readings of cultural texts and practices, disempowering traditional and canonical readings that sometimes disqualify counter-hegemonic cultural practices out of hand. Undecidability can be made to work for the radical critic even where it threatens to uproot all truth claims. Undecidability shifts the cultural–political balance of power, allowing the critic more room to move in the interpretation and interrogation of cultural products. Critics who defy conventional wisdom in their cultural readings can point to texts' ineluctable undecidability as grounds for their interpretations. No longer are critics hemmed in by canonical interpretations – deifications – of texts, nor bound to dismiss decanonizing, dehegemonizing works out of hand. If meaning is elusive and ephemeral, no critic can be sure that his or her reading is wrong. This is empowering where it helps critics on the outside gain confidence in the legitimacy of their own readings; it is disempowering where it unseats the time-worn interpretations offered by canonical critics who do not seriously challenge cultural hegemony as it frames both cultural criticism and cultural creation.

Methodologically, the undecidability of cultural texts and works prohibits a one-for-one translation of original creation into derivative interpretation. There is no singular code for translating cultural works, explaining their meaning trans-parently. There is no code for doing so simply because there is no pure language that can allow us to accomplish this translation process, no language devoid of its own lacunae, omissions, even contradictions. As Wittgenstein (1953) saw, one cannot stand outside language in attempting to clarify language. One can only do this through language, thus necessarily introducing the need for new translations. In cultural theory this has become ridiculous: primers designed to clarify original obscurities are every bit as technical and involuted as the works they purport to explicate, destining themselves as works that have to be translated in their own right. It is obvious to anyone with even a passing acquaintance with Euro-American cultural theory that the cult-theory business has become as obscurantist as the esoteric works cult-theory is designed to theorize. This is especially curious because a good deal of cultural theory proceeds under the sign of deconstruction, which should be especially alert to the undecidability – resistance to being translated – of every text, including the texts of criticism. The principle of undecidability is quickly learned and then forgotten when it comes to the opacity of one's own writing.

4. Cultural deconstruction *seeks the aporias* in every work or text. By aporia it means the ways in which works and texts at some level contradict themselves or leave a vacancy of meaning that needs to be filled. The aporetic nature of texts ensures their undecidability – their reduction to single, simple codes of meaning. Language is aporetic because, as Wittgenstein recognized, languages are composed of language games possessing their own rules of performance and interpretation that are incommensurable with those of other language games. The aporetic nature of language blocks attempts to reduce meaning into transparent codes that somehow lie beyond the vaguenesses, ambiguities and omissions of language. The language of criticism is necessarily as aporetic as the languages under criticism.

This is not a reason to eschew criticism as the project of explication and interrogation. The undecidability of aporetic language does not make language obsolete; indeed, it makes language all the more necessary, especially in an age of obscurantism and false clarity. Aporias are interpretively crucial because they can be exploited to allow writing's subtext to show through, helping explain and explore some of the internal pressures bursting forth from within texts but carefully suppressed in the interest of surface appearances. The undecidability of language destines every text to harbor these internal fissures and fault lines: every writer suppresses something or other in the way of what is intended to be said; not everything fits into one's argument and some things cannot be easily said with the rhetorical tools at hand. In some ways, deconstructors believe, these are the most telling pieces of (sub)text in the sense that to know what has been suppressed or conceded to the opacity of language helps one understand what lies on the surface of the page, pretending plenitude of meaning.

The best example of aporetic writing in this sense is science (see Knorr-Cetina, 1981; Agger, 1989b). The science writer buries the subjectivity of the writer underneath the heavy prose of methodology, allowing technical language and the figural gestures epitomizing science to take control of the text. The writer's deep assumptions about the nature of the world are suppressed underneath the technical surface of the text, hidden from the community of science and thus protected from external challenges. But the same thing happens in culture where, for example, we approach a film or novel as a 'finished' piece of work whose authorial imprint has been buried underneath the various editorial mediations that together conspire to give the work the aura of having been professionally polished. Literally, production values are the values added to the appearance of the text as deauthored, a piece of nature. The more production values are invested in a cultural work, the less one can tell that the work has been worked over busily by a scribe fatigued in the attempt to get it right – and always failing!

Aporias are not necessarily contradictions, where what is said directly opposes deeper concealments of meaning (e.g., the advertisement might say 'This cereal is health food' when, in fact, it is full of sugar and fat). Aporias can also include omissions, slips, ambiguity and glosses – all the ways rhetoric works to hide the fact that it is not solving fundamental problems of the world and science. I am not saying that rhetoricians are deceptive but only that rhetoric in its nature is fraught with the duplicities of meaning that haunt every human project. Nothing will clarify rhetoric, just as there are no meta-languages for getting us out of the hermeneutic circle, showing Being in Heidegger's sense for what it 'really' is. Nevertheless, the aporetic nature of language can empower as well as discourage critical thought and writing. It can help orient criticism to the weak links in texts and works that, if properly exploited, yield a treasure trove of meaning, even if it is meaning that reverses the text's surface direction of meaning.

Poststructuralists find aporias in all writing and cultural expression. However, this tends to flatten the concepts of ideology and ontology into the Wittgensteinian notion of language games: Marxists would concentrate on deconstructing texts in which ideology and ontology are encoded subtly, where non-Marxist deconstructors relativize aporia into a feature of all texts, thus muting the ideology- and ontology-critical project of Marxist reading. This is one of the main differences between Derridean and Marxist deconstruction, issuing in, and reflecting, a variety of crucial disagreements over matters of the philosophy of history. The problem with the Marxist critique of ideology is that it tends to compose itself in the presuppositionless tones and terms of positivism, paralleling problems of validity confronted by the orthodox Marxist sociology of culture that I discussed earlier. Marxist deconstruction too frequently conducts itself in a way that pretends to be non-aporetic (see Jameson, 1981, 1991). Where it locates the ideological and ontological suppressions of clean texts as a way of historicizing their stories, it too often implies that it is free of these deep claims and can be read at its surface. But Marxist stories (about positivist stories) must be conducted in undecidable language. A poststructuralist could deconstruct the aporetic nature of Marxist deconstructive language by pointing to omissions and tensions within Marxism's own text. This is a useful project where Marxists become so epistemologically and thus politically arrogant that they forget that their own assumptions about the nature of the world are never entirely lucid or transparent and have to be continually resurrected self-critically if they are to avoid the fatal combination of Archimedeanism and vanguardism.

A radical cultural studies, thus, must distinguish carefully between the inconsistencies, allusions, tensions and ambiguities that haunt every text, on the one hand, and the textual contradictions and suppressions characteristic of hegemonic, ideologizing, ontologizing texts, on the other hand. These are fundamentally different things. To confuse them, as Derridean deconstructors do, is to lose the political specificity of the neo-Marxist critique of ideology and ontology that is so vital today. One of the enormous contributions of poststructuralist literary theory to the Marxian critique of ideology is precisely the focus on ideology's literariness – the ways it takes a textual form and can be criticized as such. Ideology is rhetoric – subtext as well as text. For Marxist and feminist critics to be able to locate the fault lines in every hegemonizing text empowers readers to throw off the yoke of frozen history, concealed deceptively in the ceaseless chatter of popular culture. A left-poststructural cultural studies teaches people how to read culture for these dehistoricizing subtexts, instead raising pop-culture's advocacy to full view. This cultural studies treats pop-culture's imageries and promises as truth claims, as such subject to falsification. Is it true that Nikes will make us sexier as well as fleeter of foot? Will Hondas raise driving to an art form, thus aestheticizing our everyday lives? Will McDonald's food afford us family and community with all the other happy patrons there?

These are precisely the questions asked by a left-poststructural cultural studies that interrogates every text for its aporias – the places where it suppresses secret claims made about the world. When we treat popular culture as advocacy in this sense we are better able to resist its insidious seductions, even turning culture against itself by developing new cultural practices and experiences that make contrary claims: sneakers are an expensive rip-off; cars can kill as well as impoverish; franchised fast food makes us sick. Thus, we must produce new clothing, transportation and cuisine, transforming everyday life from the bottom up as well as the top down. The cultural forms of advertising, for instance, encode a variety of specious claims deceptively encoded in visual imagery and music that conflate the pleasure and promise afforded by this panorama of simulated experience with these truth claims, making it impossible to evaluate them for what they really are. By raising this to view, we can resist their subliminal energy and thus live (to fight) another day. Advertising is the highest form of simulation in that it makes the places where truth claims are encoded in texts virtually impossible to recognize, except to seasoned veterans of mass culture capable of reading back and forth between ads' words, music, images and the worlds they recommend.

It is more difficult to find these aporetic fault lines denoting the boundary between text and subtext in visual and aural culture than in textual culture. Learning to read film, music, theater and television deconstructively is more difficult than it is to read texts if only because the 'text' of visual and aural culture is more fleeting, harder to grasp, than the text of texts themselves; and, perhaps for that reason, visual and aural texts are the more compelling, the more captivating. It is possible to learn to read popular culture in all its formulations if one accepts the deconstructive program (see Fiske, 1989a). As I said earlier, this reading strategy is less method than a practised confrontation with the con-texts within which reading finds itself situated. One has to be agile and flexible, ready for any and all contingencies. One day one may find oneself staring at a jumbo Hollywood movie just packing in the captive audiences, trying to make sense of its philosophy of history: think of *Top Gun* or *Die Hard* as civilizational texts. Or one may find oneself at the supermarket checkout counter faced with the racks of tabloid newspapers, scanning the inflated headlines in order to find out how people in America and the UK are problematizing the big issues of the day – the Trump divorce, Charles and Diana's rumored marital indiscretions, the sexual preference of Cher's daughter Chastity. Cultural critics must be prepared to read culture where, and how, it is presented. Its tentacular force lies precisely in its difference from traditional textual culture, where ideas and values are propagated the 'old-fashioned' way.

5. Cultural deconstruction assumes that *reading writes* – that cultural criticism is itself a form of cultural creation in that it helps subvert the hierarchy of writing over reading as well as challenges the taken-for-granted assumptions purveyed in cultural texts and practices. Perhaps the most challenging contention of cultural deconstructors is that reading is fully as constitutional as writing, one of Derrida's main theses (see Agger, 1991a, Ch. 2). This is because writing requires reading, texts requiring con-texts, in order for them to be completed. There is no pure or given writing but only the perspectival writings that emerge in the con-texts of reading, reflecting the needs and interests of readers who bring to their reading values, attitudes and practical interests. This risks relativism where it might be heard to say that any text is anything we make it. Materialist Derrideans would step back from that extreme formulation; they would say that given texts constrain readings, but not decisively. Texts suggest limits to their interpretations, and yet these limits are themselves susceptible to being challenged. Deconstructive debate is centered precisely around this question of what constitutes the acceptable limits to interpretation – for example, Marxologists continue to debate what it means to read Marx, that is, under which rules shall the explication of Marx proceed (e.g., see Althusser and Balibar, 1970; Cleaver, 1979).

Deconstructors are as concerned with formulating the grounds for limiting criticism to certain acceptable interpretations as they are with 'what' certain texts say. These issues are fundamentally inseparable. What a jumbo Hollywood movie often 'says' cannot be answered apart from the issue of how criticism should gauge filmic meanings. As I will explore further in the next chapter, one of the most important contributions of cinefeminism as feminist social theory is to establish the grounds of what it means to create feminist culture, establishing rules for deciding what counts as feminist film and thus as feminist social practice. Inspired by Lacanian poststructuralism, cinefeminism refuses to assume that we can know a priori what it means to be a feminist, to write like a feminist, to write and read feminist texts, movies, television. Deconstruction makes available to readers a serious engagement with the opportunities and responsibilities of criticism in establishing its relationship to its critical object. It is not assumed that the point of criticism is presuppositionlessly to explain a text's or practice's pre-given meaning, as if that explanation could somehow take place outside of culture, textuality, language and meaning.

Reading writes because there is no way to develop readings outside of language and textuality. When one talks about cultural readings one is talking about writing (or speech) that aims to go public, to become writing itself. For poststructuralists, Pauline Kael's *New Yorker* movie reviews count as culture just as much as do the movies she reviews. She makes culture just as she interprets it. Indeed, it is difficult to draw the boundary between these two culture-making practices when one considers the effect Kael as a reviewer has on the way we view movies and thus live our lives – we who read *The New Yorker* before (or even after) we go to the movies. Cinefeminism for its part would argue that going to feminist movies involves one in a whole critical community beyond the movie audience per se – the community of women, of feminists, of feminist film critics, of feminist thinkers who theorize film in its relationship to the critical community. It is impossible to separate the meaning of a feminist film (whatever we might decide that is to mean) from the other discursive and lived practices involving us in a feminist community. One might even say that to be a feminist means that one takes seriously one's own investment and involvement in a community of other women and men in which these questions of interrelatedness take on significance.

The claim that reading writes is a regulative idea – it is what should be true. It is very important to separate two sorts of deconstructive claims here. On the one hand, Derrida argues that reading must exist in order to complement and complete writing – that there is no writing 'as such' apart from the con-textual ways in which people interpret and use writings (his blow against a positivist model of presuppositionless literary interpretation). Reading is never simply passive or reflective but is an active engagement with the undecidability of all texts – the ways in which they provoke our involvement in their aporetic senses as interpolators of meaning. On the other hand, a more political deconstruction would recognize that just because reading engages constitutionally with writing does not mean that reading is the same as writing. Reading is reading and writing writing. For reading to become writing it must go public as a text in its own right; it must be published or produced as an autonomous, if intertextual, cultural work. The vast majority of the world's readers are not writers and do not write their reading, except perhaps in marginal comments, unpublished letters and essays. They do not enter the realm of writing because they either do not see themselves as writers and thus do not submit their readings for publication (as writing) or because they have their work rejected. Obviously, most people do not live lives as writers; they do their reading in an everyday life in which they do not question the hierarchy of (published) writers over (unpublished) readers.

This distinction shows the difference between apolitical and political versions of deconstruction. The first is ahistorical in its assumption that all reading is writing; the second distinguishes between reading that remains private and reading that attains public visibility and thus enters into the power relations of capitalism. Although reading can be importantly political in that it energizes criticism and leads to public dissent, it is less transformationally political than reading that insists on its own writerliness – its own competence to enter public discourse as a counterforce to hegemonic versions of the world – and thus breaks into print. This is not to say that reading can simply will itself into being as a public text; all too often, publishing doors are closed to defiant and amateur versions. But surely there is a difference between private and public reading. The difference is this: public reading – new writing – changes the hierarchies of writing over reading and transforms the content of public discourse.

For Derrideans to equate reading and writing is ahistorical, ontological. But poststructuralists usefully challenge a positivist model of reading by insisting that reading is constitutional – that is, reading gives sense to writing by interpolating between its gaps of meaning and impasses, fleshing it out, contextualizing it, applying its sense pragmatically. There is no transcendental text, no writing 'as such'. There are only con-texts in which readers and writers come together and try to make sense of each other, writers anticipating what will make them understood to readers and readers reconstructing the writer's intentions and meaning from the given black-and-white or celluloid text. Poststructuralism helps change the way we think about cultural reception by showing that reading is a strong form of social practice. But, alas, it is not as strong a practice as writing – reading that goes public. Only through new texts can the world be changed. Reading changes only the reader, not the whole domain of public discourse and political action.

6. Deconstructive cultural criticism *turns the subtext into text*, reading the cultural object at its margins for its significances. Derrida's stress on texts' aporias (blind spots, omissions, tensions, circumlocutions, contradictions) suggests the methodological principle of deconstructive reading: search for sense in unlikely places, especially in rhetorical gestures that appear marginal to the main enterprise (prose, plot) of the text in question. In so doing, one can uncover the intended relationship between value and non-value – hierarchy – giving every text a certain direction of meaning. Thus, by reading footnotes or endnotes strongly, one can better understand why a writing relegates this material to secondary status by comparison to the primary status of what remains in the body of the text. Or one might read material placed in parentheses. Or, as I have done in my study of journal science (Agger, 1989b), one might read science deconstructively for the way in which the science text inscribes a powerful subtext of methodological gestures (number, figure, etc.) that become the main meaning of the science article, actually having more constitutional significance than the prose bits.

Derridean reading, then, not only restores the value of marginalia like endnotes, parenthetical material and figural gestures but also reverses the priority of main text over marginal text, text over subtext, in a dehierarchizing way. Derrida assumes that meaning is more clearly surfaced by examining these marginalia. For example, in the prefaces and acknowledgment sections in books one can find all sorts of telling first-person declarations about why the book was written, its topic, its progenitors and debts, its relevant speech communities (Hymes, 1974; Brodkey, 1987), the lifeworld of its author. One might read a whole book and not really understand its con-text, especially if it deeply suppresses the telling marginalia that give us clues about con-text along the way. Indeed, the citation style of the American Psychological Association (that I am using in this book) is gaining prominence as a preferred way of citing one's references, either abolishing footnotes and endnotes altogether or radically diminishing them. This citation style enhances literary felicity and economy; its downside is that it makes it harder to identify a text's subtext, unless, as in my writing, the writer self-consciously surfaces that subtext in a reflexive way: it should be clear by now that I am a political writer who wants to develop new and better ways of reading culture critically in order to change our whole public discourse. I am not a positivist; my political aims in this regard are not concealed underneath a densely objectivist style that moves linearly from one chapter to another. But, even here, the bad habits taught to us in graduate school and in the professional academic disciplines die hard! When I first wrote the section earlier in the paragraph beginning with the words 'Indeed, the citation style of . . .' and ending with '. . . one chapter to another' I encased the whole section inside parentheses, defeating my own claim to efface rigid boundaries between text and subtext. Luckily, in the age of wordprocessing, that was easy to fix!

Deciding just what is subtext as against text cannot be done a priori. Deconstructors do not assume that one can cleanly distinguish between two parts of a single text. Instead, they argue that there are many overlapping and cross-cutting texts – texts within, and beyond, texts, stories within, and beneath, stories. The use of the terms *subtext* and *text* violates deconstructive logic where they imply the possibility of clean distinctions. In fact, the issue of hierarchies of meaning within texts is a con-textual one, requiring methodical strategies for separating (and combining) these levels of meaning. A good deal of what passes for deconstructive literary criticism degenerates into formulaic analysis precisely because notions like aporia, difference, text and subtext are fetishized methodologically and cease to respond to the differential nature of writings that must be addressed in terms of their own local problematics of meaning. One could, for example, read a Steven Spielberg movie in the same way that one might read a Fellini film. Does that mean that one could then read a film produced by Alcoholics Anonymous (see Denzin, 1991) in the same way? Or a television mini-series? Unfortunately, American deconstructors have become so enchanted with the deconstructive program that they have subordinated their interest in reading to the development of deconstructive method, thus both losing sight of the cultural specificity of works in question and fetishizing method, which gains prominence over the work it is supposed to do.

Now I may seem to contradict myself here in that I am also involved at this very moment in iterating a set of what seem to be deconstructive principles of cultural reading. I am not against generalities or method but only the fetish of method across incommensurable con-texts of meaning. I am not entirely comfortable with the notion that one can 'read' film in the same way one can read a book, although I understand that it is important critically and politically to approach culture as the texts or meta-texts comprising it, hence opening its authorship as well as reception to public analysis and critique. Deconstruction has become enamored of its shiny new techniques, thus losing its own substantive contributions to both social theory and to local cultural analyses. In this respect, a Derridean cultural studies contrasts sharply with the Birmingham tradition in the sense that it has devoted much more attention to the development of critical method than to the building of substantive social and cultural theory that functions politically.

Strangely enough, deconstructive cultural analysis is nearly devoid of theory in this sense, contrasting with the impression that Europeanized cultural criticism is heavily theoretical, thus requiring a whole new convoluted conceptual apparatus to be used by people who 'do theory'. If by *theory* we mean abstract words and concepts, derived from the philosophical antecedents of contemporary social and cultural thought, then, certainly, Derrida, Barthes, Lacan and Foucault are theoretical in their work. But if by *theory* we refer to empirical generalizations about the social world, then Euro-thought is scarcely theoretical – dense, yes, but substantively theoretical, no. Deconstructors spend their time doing close cultural readings and improving their critical techniques, not developing theory in a way that could con-textualize these readings and interpretive strategies in a more holistic, hence political, way.

Two Postmodernisms

It is important to distinguish between poststructuralism and postmodernism in order to show their similarities as well as influences on a deconstructive cultural studies. Interestingly, this version of cultural studies owes more to certain Derridean notions about the reading and writing of texts than to the (scant) methodological insights of postmodernism, which remains more a socio-cultural theory than a set of epistemological and discursive principles. This is especially arresting because postmodernism is thought to be 'about' culture, whereas poststructuralism is about knowledge and language. At some level, they are so inextricably linked as to make simplistic differentiations impossible or undesirable (see Agger, 1990; but see also Best and Kellner, 1991). One would have to engage in a purposely simplifying taxonomy of names and their intellectual contributions in order to map the terrain of poststructural and postmodern cultural studies adequately – and even then the map would blur some crucial points of difference.

Suffice it to say that the deconstructive cultural studies I have been talking about owes something to people who are typically considered both poststructural and postmodern – e.g., to both Derrida and Foucault, respectively. At some level, the distinction between poststructuralism and postmodernism is too arcane or simply idiosyncratic to matter. I am not interested in producing a cognitive map of the cultural studies terrain because this terrain changes too quickly, responding to theoretical and critical developments that go into and out of fashion seasonally. Today's primer on Lyotard is printed on paper to be recycled in a few years to inscribe the words of a book on Baudrillard (or on some meteoric new theorist as yet undiscovered). Although cognitive maps (see Jameson, 1988) are crucial, especially for pedagogical purposes, one must not put too much stock in them. This book will be criticized for its own categorizations and namings; one could quibble with just about every distinction I have made between critical and theoretical schools, reflected in my structure of chapters, topics covered, chronology, examples and the like. After all, cultural studies flashes on and off before our eyes like the images on a television or movie screen. To harden it into taxonomic cement does not do justice to its dexterity and plurality. To do cultural studies means that one responds both to what is current in the way of mass culture and to unfolding intellectual developments that inform the way people study culture. This book is about the study of culture, although I am arguing that *these studies of culture become culture themselves*, informing the way intellectuals read and write cultural works. In other words, cultural studies is part of the overall culture, as a deconstructive reading would indicate.

Deconstructive cultural studies, drawing on both poststructural and postmodern insights, is especially capable of theorizing its shifting, evolving nature, resisting fixed definitions at every turn. It is not by accident that Derrida does not offer us a glossary of terms with which to translate his voluminous and circuitous writings into a common language replete with common-sense signifiers. Derrida is his own reader; he does not claim to read himself for others, on the outside. He would insist that they have to do their own readings, in their own interpretive and everyday con-texts of interest, desire, preparedness, national and regional culture, gender, race and class. To be Derridean is only to make sense of Derrida in one's own way; to be a Derridean reader means to read deconstructively, that is, in terms of reading's own constitutional strength, which must never be foresworn. Thus, a deconstructive cultural studies does not linger very long in the land of nomenclature, taxonomy, glossaries or conceptual refinements as if these events could somehow take place outside of the con-texts within which everything is subsumed under the rule of undecidability. Deconstructive cultural studies *studies* culture, including its own contribution to culture. It is not meta-theory.

As I said earlier, I prefer to understand postmodernism largely as a theory of cultural discontinuity, a philosophy of history short-circuiting the imagery of progress (see Raulet, 1984). It is another version of postindustrialism (see Bell, 1973), drawing on Bell's earlier (1960) end-of-ideology argument. Lyotard's (1984) postmodernist manifesto recycles Bell's attack on Marxism, albeit with a Gallic twist. Where poststructuralism suggests the ways in which language encodes and constitutes meaning, shattering the positivist model of a language user who plucks signifiers out of thin air and attaches them unproblematically to discrete things-in-the-world, postmodernism provides a larger philosophy of history within which it is no longer possible to project the possibility of substantive social change. What they have in common is a grounding in Nietzsche, drawing on Nietzsche's critique of the Enlightenment. This is not to say that they got Nietzsche right! After all, Nietzsche also inspired much of the work of the original Frankfurt School, particularly Adorno and Horkheimer (Horkheimer and Adorno, 1972).

I have discussed some of these issues in the first chapter of my *Decline of Discourse* (Agger, 1990). In particular, I argue that there are a number of contesting postmodernisms – an apologetic, Bell-like defense of late capitalism (that fails to distinguish between postmoder*nity* and postmoder*nism*, confusing description with endorsement), on the one hand, and a Frankfurt-like critical theory that provides a sense of dialectical continuity between capitalist modernity and a possible socialist and feminist postmodernity, on the other. I attempt to develop a postmodern critical social theory that can do useful analytical and political work; in significant respects, this version of a renegade postmodernism converges with Frankfurt critical theory in its critique of the Enlightenment phrased within a vocabulary that would preserve the basically progressive aims of the modern project (unrealized by the Enlightenment). Postmodernism adds to German critical theory a perspective on mass culture that is more ecumenical and less mandarin than some of the Frankfurt aesthetic theory, as such providing a valuable corrective to Adorno's cultural pessimism (see Huyssen, 1986; Aronowitz, 1990).

Again, as with poststructuralism's contribution to a deconstructive cultural studies, I am reading between the lines where I split postmodernism into affirmative or apologetic and critical programs. The question 'Who counts as a postmodernist?' is unanswerable without reference to certain assumptions about modernity. One can name anyone from Lyotard (1984) and Foucault (1977) to Hassan (1987) and Jameson (1991). It is worth keeping in mind that postmodernism, unlike poststructuralism, began as a distinctly cultural oeuvre, notably in architecture. It was not philosophically reflexive in the way that poststructuralism has been. Indeed, the notion of a postmoder*nism* only came to light in the past few years, mainly in the US (see Klinkowitz, 1988). Given these roots in architecture, it is even more difficult to recognize and make use of the incipient social criticism contained in postmodernism; the increasingly abundant 'postmod' office towers and shopping malls that dot the American landscape attest to the affirmative character of the postmodern architectural embellishment. Architectural postmodernism is an affirmative version of the dominant architectural modernism that lost any critical force it may have had with the Bauhaus. Huyssen (1986) explores the ambivalent relationship between modernism and postmodernism well in his *After the Great Divide*.

The argument for a critical postmodernism is really an argument for a radical cultural studies that is able to comprehend a variety of non-identical cultural expressions and practices in sympathetic and yet critical terms. What is genuinely liberatory about this version of postmodernism is precisely postmodernism's ambivalence about modernism. On the one hand, a critical postmodernism wants to get beyond modernity – the present built environment and socio-economic institutions of late capitalism. On the other hand, a critical postmodernism wants to fulfill the project of modernity, the Enlightenment's attempt to create a world founded on principles of universal reason. Where affirmative postmodernists like Lyotard (1984) argue that we must abandon the totalizing pretensions of the Enlightenment (viz. his critique of the grand 'meta-narratives' like Marxism that promise to change the whole world), critical postmodernists like Aronowitz (1990) and Kellner (1989a) argue that the Enlightenment must be completed in universal liberation of humanity and nature.

Critical postmodernism is able carefully to disentangle aspects of culture that serve the interest of liberation from the dominant cultural hegemony. These are not always easy judgments to make: as often as not, what appears liberatory is readily cooptable. And occasionally what appears to be cultural banality (or simply irrelevant) harbors emancipatory potential, even if this is initially unnoticed by either the producers or consumers of popular culture. A cultural studies founded on this renegade postmodernism rejects all aprioristic perspectives on culture, whether the mandarinism of the Frankfurt School or the affirmative stance of mainstream postmodernists who laud (and then discard) each and every simulation in Baudrillardian hyperreality. Such apriorism founders because it neglects the con-textual nature of cultural projects and reception. A critical-postmodern cultural studies relates its judgments about culture's emancipatory potential to the con-texts of production, distribution and reception within which cultural works and practices are located. In certain respects, this resembles the CCCS perspective on culture, although, unlike CCCS, it tends to phrase its cultural criticism in more self-consciously philosophy-of-history terms. Where Lyotard's postmodernism steps back from cultural and political evaluation, instead accepting the thoroughgoing indeterminacy of cultural products and practices as the distinctive signature of so-called postmodernity (utterly beyond ideology, values, judgment), a critical postmodernism theorizes cultural practice in a way that transcends both evaluative apriorism (e.g., aspects of the Frankfurt School's more mandarinist cultural theory) and the context-free eclecticism of mainstream postmodernism that accepts all versions and varieties of mass culture as more or less equivalent in their truth content.

There is no distinctive school or representative of this critical-postmodern cultural studies. The CCCS people have read and worked through Foucault and French feminism; perhaps one could locate some of their work in the category of critical-postmodern cultural studies. I am reluctant to do so simply because the agitational and local engagements of Birmingham cultural studies make it less theoretical (if more overtly political) than the sort of critical postmodernism endorsed and exemplified by Jameson, Aronowitz, Huyssen, Kellner and me. This is not to say that one can identify many common assumptions about theory and method in our work beyond a general commitment to redeeming the more radical promises of the Enlightenment within a post-Enlightenment (or what Jameson and Fish call a post-contemporary) philosophy of history that squarely confronts the problematics of postmodernism and postmodernity. In a way, the name *postmodernism* is misleading: most people use the term as a generic category of thought within which projects like so-called post-Marxism (e.g., Laclau and Mouffe, 1985; Block, 1990; Witheford and Gruneau, forthcoming) are located. I am decidedly not a post-Marxist; I believe that radical postmodernism is a version of critical theory, which is itself a category within which to locate the particular critical theory of Marx. At some level, this taxonomic activity gets out of hand. The really important issue is how different theorists relate to the cultural and political present in a way that helps them make distinctions among different versions of truth, freedom, justice and beauty. Critical postmodernism differs from its affirmative counterpart in the way that it preserves the possibility of cultural truth claims as well as the possibility of these truth claims' comparative evaluation. An affirmatively postmodern cultural studies refrains from these sorts of judgments out of the conviction that history has essentially ended, captured in the blitzed-out, bacchanalian cityscape of Manhattan.

As I argue further in Chapter 9, the postmodernism business is by now a growth industry. Everyone claims it, even if utterly ungrounded in the Continental social thought and criticism to which latter-day postmodernisms must inevitably be connected. Many writers of books and reviews claim the names Lyotard, Baudrillard, Foucault, Derrida, Deleuze, Guattari, Barthes, Lacan and Jameson without having read them. Their 'postmodernism' is claimed cheaply, having little substance beyond a certain superficial cultural currency. This is the fate of all theory in an age of instantaneity: it functions as embellishment, not as substantive social thought and rigorous criticism (see Newman, 1985; Jacoby, 1987; Agger, 1990). Postmodernism is the peculiar perspective that gives license to this thoughtless eclecticism, legitimating the use of theoretical icons within the pragmatic contexts of intellectual life as well as advertising and television. The local Buffalo newspaper says that David Lynch (director of *Blue Velvet*) has recently produced and directed a 'postmodern' television series. This claim is made good more on the basis of Lynch's own personal style than on grounds of rigorous examination of his directorial debts to postmodern aesthetic intentions (such as these may be). Postmodernism sells – itself and the products whose names it adorns.

I am reluctant to call for a postmodern cultural studies precisely for that reason: it sounds like an endorsement of so-called postmodern culture – the world of *Miami Vice* and Perry Ellis clothes as well as Lynch's imaginary filmic and television world. That is not my intention. By *postmodern cultural studies* I am describing *a critical stance toward current cultural practices that recognizes both the deficits and assets of the project of modernity* (see Conner, 1989), enunciated originally during the Enlightenment and then preserved in Hegel's and Marx's philosophies of history and later the work of the Frankfurt School. With Habermas (1984, 1987b), I want to fulfill the project of modernity. But this is only possible, critical postmodernism reminds us, if we recognize that the Enlightenment was peculiarly oblivious to its own Promethean self-confidence. Its hubris must be tempered by a con-textualizing theorization of science and technology that stresses their own corrigibility. This has been the program of western Marxism since Lukács (1971) wrote *History and Class Consciousness* in 1923. Western Marxists retain scientific enlightenment within a historical-materialist framework, grounding the truth claims of the human sciences in the extirpation of myth and ideology. Lyotard's postmodernism, like Derrida's poststructuralism (and both energized by a certain obvious reading of Nietzsche – if not Marcuse's [1969] version of Nietzsche's happy science), rejects science as yet another totalizing discourse corrupted by hubris. This resonates with the general pluralism of postmodernism and poststructuralism, the former a cultural and political pluralism and the latter an epistemological one. But that language is a prison-house (Nietzsche) does not prevent us from developing public discourses, including science, that are self-reflective and democratic.

A critical postmodernism aims to be a total social theory, explaining all manner of political-economic, cultural and psychological developments in late capitalism. Lyotard's postmodernism by contrast despairs of these totalizations, arguing instead that history has ended, or at least ceased to move forward, thus requiring us to give up the rhetoric and public practice of totality – social change movements designed to remake the world. Cultural studies does its best work where it aims to be a comprehensive social theory which carefully theorizes the linkages between culture and political economy. Without these structural understandings, cultural studies remains a sociology and aesthetics of culture, whether it is conducted under the name of objectivist New Criticism, economistic Marxism or an apolitical deconstruction. The vast majority of cultural studies works fall short, neither aspiring to be comprehensive social theory nor drawing on structural understandings of the social world in grounding their own cultural readings. This sort of work, under a variety of supposedly theoretical and political banners, has become cultic, as I argue in Chapter 9. I want to deprogram this sort of cultural studies. It exists parasitically off the varieties of cultural products and practices that bombard us around the clock, seven days a week, scripting conformist lives lived thoughtlessly through the simulacra (Baudrillard, 1983) of the culture industry.

I am not saying that a critical-postmodern cultural studies cannot or should not do close readings of popular cultural works and practices. But these readings must be connected to, and must further develop, social theory that explains the circuitries of cultural production, distribution and reception in both ideological and political-economic terms. Thus, a critical cultural studies both produces insights into the complexly interrelated social totality and fans the embers of hope that continue to glow. As such, a radical cultural studies is a totalizing expression of an insurgent cultural politics that refuses the dominant cultural and socio-political hegemony. It is an instance of what I (1991a) have called a lifeworld-grounded critical theory. In the next chapter, I turn to an overtly political application of cultural studies in my discussion of feminist cultural theory and criticism, much of which is owed to the perspective discussed in this chapter.

Chapter 7

Feminist Cultural Studies

The Feminist Critical Project

Kate Millett initiated feminist cultural studies in her (1970) book, *Sexual Politics*. Since then, the project of feminist literary and cultural criticism has been central on the feminist agenda, defining a host of interpretive and critical activities for feminist academics (e.g., see Radway, 1984; Mulvey, 1988). The feminist critical project is dedicated to exposing male hegemony in culture as well as opening a space for women to make (and evaluate) culture. Indeed, in the last section of this chapter I argue that feminist cultural studies is designed to be both feminist theory and feminist practice, auguring just the sort of engagement I advocate for cultural studies in my concluding chapter. Although there are silences and omissions in feminist cultural studies, it is clear that there has been a flourish of recent activity around the feminist critical project that bears heavily on the emerging shape of a materialist theory and critique of culture.

Some of the central issues involved in a discussion and evaluation of feminist cultural studies are whether a feminist cultural studies can stand on its own as a total or sufficient theory of culture, whether it only complements other versions of cultural studies, and whether it is wrong to separate feminist cultural studies from other radical perspectives on culture in terms of a political and critical division of labor. Most feminist cultural theorists believe that feminist criticism is somehow *sui generis* – that one of the most important features of the feminist critical project is to fend off attacks from the outside, especially from male Marxists, that indict the supposedly self-limiting, self-isolating nature of feminist criticism. The orthodox male left asks why there needs to be a separate, even if auxiliary, feminist criticism either supplanting or in addition to other versions of radical cultural criticism. The standard cultural-feminist answer is that the feminist critical project is important because one of the crucial tools of male domination is the silencing of women's voices (e.g., see Silverman, 1983). Millett begins a rich and varied tradition of feminist criticism that both subverts male cultural hegemony and empowers women to find their voices as well as to appreciate the voices of other women who have written, painted, composed and directed – either to be ignored or to go unappreciated by 'malestream' criticism (see Moi, 1988).

Within this general framework, feminist criticism has branched off in a number of directions, one of the most important of which, cinefeminism, is discussed in the next section of this chapter. Feminist criticism (e.g., Millett) originally concentrated most heavily on literary culture, exhuming forgotten or neglected women writers and challenging the representation of women in patriarchal culture. In the next two sections of this chapter I discuss these critical practices at greater length as they are applied to cultural issues in the broadest sense, not only including literature. Feminist criticism has become so central to Anglo-American humanities that there is scarcely a department in which one cannot find scholars, graduate students, courses and conferences dealing with these issues of feminist textual politics. These issues have become extremely central to the agenda of mainstream literary criticism, as one can gauge by examining the proceedings at recent MLA annual meetings in the US and noting that the current President of the MLA is Catherine Stimpson, a well-known feminist and participant in the women's studies program at Rutgers. It seems that every other MLA paper is about feminist criticism and feminist theory. It is clear that feminist theory is anchored in the feminist critical project as it is played out in English and literature programs (e.g., see Kolodny, 1975, 1980, 1984; Felman, 1985, 1987). Although feminist theorists and critics can be found across the humanities and social sciences, they are clustered in the literary disciplines not least because the feminist critical project concerns itself with issues of male cultural hegemony.

Feminist cultural studies is broader than feminist literary criticism. Nevertheless, many of the most important critical approaches in feminist cultural analysis follow from the textual-critical activities of people like Millett, Felman and Kolodny. If cultural studies treats culture as a text, the impetus for this sort of textual criticism originally came from engagements with real texts, including fiction and poetry. It was natural for Millett to begin with a discussion of women writers and the depiction of women in male literature inasmuch as literary culture, at least until the 1950s, was a primary form of public culture. Although movies have become increasingly popular since the 1920s, the Hollywoodization of film culture did not take place until after World War Two, paralleling the emerging significance of television in mass culture. Up until then, novels were one of the primary vehicles for transmitting cultural imagery about gender relations as well as appropriate gender values. The representation of women, by women and men writers, mattered greatly for the way people came to think about gender relations. Hence, as Millett demonstrates, the feminist critique of patriarchal literary culture was an extremely significant component of the development of feminist consciousness in general.

The role of feminist criticism in the nascent women's movement (see Evans, 1980) cannot be underestimated. College-age women were exposed to courses in women's studies and English on feminist literary criticism; indeed, they demanded such courses as part of the feminist New Left's demands to reform the university. Women out of college were also exposed to the political project of feminist literary criticism through a variety of outlets like *Ms* magazine, in which women writers were discussed and male writers criticized. Perhaps even more than the male New Left (which had its own sacred texts like C. Wright Mills' (1959) *The Power Elite* and Herbert Marcuse's (1964) *One-Dimensional Man*), the feminist New Left was steeped in the emerging political and critical literature of the time, much of which included feminist literary criticism. Millett's own book was extremely important in setting the agenda of feminist criticism and cultural studies for the next two decades, as were some of the works of Germaine Greer (1971). This work prepared the way for later feminists who were concerned to understand patriarchal culture through its main literary and cultural expressions.

In this sense, the emergence of feminist literary criticism as an exemplar of feminist cultural studies responded to ongoing political struggles both within and outside of the university. One could say that feminist criticism was an academic pursuit, centered in literary disciplines. In another sense, though, the academic project of feminist criticism was intensely political, both reflecting and heightening the ongoing political passions consuming the women's movement as a whole. More than any other version of cultural studies, feminist cultural criticism was a directly political project, relatively unmediated by the nuances and niceties of academic scholarship. This is not to deny that feminist criticism has developed highly technical codes impenetrable by amateurs; indeed, in my penultimate chapter I indict recent feminist criticism in much the same way I indict other types of cultural studies for the way it has lost touch with the grand passions and struggles of the 1960s and early 1970s.

Nevertheless, however much one objects to the academization of feminist criticism, it is difficult to deny that feminist literary and cultural critics are more involved politically with their topics and audiences than are most male cultural critics. Academic feminism is still involved in the struggle to legitimate itself in the university and then to change the university, burrowing from within the bastions of male privilege and male knowledge (see DuBois *et al.*, 1985). Marxists, too, fight for the right to coexist with bourgeois scholars in the academy (Agger, 1991b). And yet there is something decidedly more political, more agitational, about academic feminism in its desire to confront male privilege and female exclusion at every level of academic practice, from job search committees to undergraduate curricula. Marxists, being predominantly male, are less compromised in the university and thus they restrict their radicalism to their scholarship. They need not protect their whole beings as outsiders.

Some Marxists are exceptions to this rule, especially non-orthodox ones who ally themselves with feminists and the women's movement. And some feminists are so conciliatory that their demands turn out to be no more radical than the demands of any group yearning to ascend the various ladders of 'success' in capitalism. I do not want to overdraw this point about the engagement of university feminists. Yet it is worth noting that feminist criticism is directly engaged in struggles that never seem to quit. The difference between academic Marxism and academic feminism can be explained in theoretical terms: feminists have always been more committed to the notion that the personal is political, thus problematizing a host of discursive, literary, interpersonal and pedagogical practices that orthodox male Marxists regard as nonproblematic (e.g., the subordination of women to men). There is something about feminism itself that predisposes radical feminist academics, like feminist critics, to politicize their personal and professional lives in thoroughgoing ways, even if many of these feminists frequently do not theorize the world sufficiently in terms of totality to make a real difference.

Canonizing Women

Feminist literary criticism, like the broader feminist cultural studies that it later spawns, has two main foci. It addresses the absence of women writers, readers, voices and experiences from the largely male canon of official literature and culture. I discuss that theme here. Feminist criticism also addresses the sexist representation of women in literature and culture, a theme to which I turn in the following section. Feminist cultural criticism canonizes women by deconstructing the established canons of literary and cultural heroes, finding the fault lines along which the canon tends to collapse under its own weight. The feminist canonization of women primarily gives women a place in the otherwise male-dominated canon, insisting that women have produced important literary and cultural works and that these works should be studied.

This activity of giving women a place in the canon stresses both the positive gains to be realized by recognizing that women are good writers and have a valid and distinctive perspective on the world and the negative effects of pretending that men are the only writers and culture heroes. This is a two-sided attack. Feminists insist that women are writers, too, and should be heard. They insist that women have always written, although women have had a much more difficult time than men in gaining access to print as well as to credibility. They also argue that the canon's obliviousness to women's voices suggests that men's experience and perspective somehow *stand for* universal human experience and perspective, thus further diminishing the role of women in culture. On the one hand, feminist literary and cultural critics take the absence of women in the canon to mean that women writers have been ignored. On the other hand, these feminists view the absence of women in the canon to signify the conflation of male experience and perspective with a putatively universal experience and perspective. These are both bad, especially where women's experience and perspective have been shaped by historical forces of domination, making it even more preposterous that men should be the only writers (and the only ones to be given a hearing).

Feminist criticism opens up the canon and rewrites history. It also interprets canonization as a patriarchal practice that gives men all the available dialogue chances, in Habermas' (1979) terms. But it does something even more fundamental, from the point of view of a politicized cultural studies. Feminists insist that feminist criticism is itself a contribution to culture in the way it politicizes issues of cultural production, practice and interpretation, becoming a vital part of the culture itself. Far from being a reflection of culture or simply a means of cultivating the cultural inheritance ('... the best that people have thought ...'), feminist criticism intervenes strongly in cultural discourse as a transformative practice, virtually an oeuvre in its own right. This point is driven home where feminist critics have availed themselves of poststructural insights, notably the idea that reading is a form of writing. A poststructural feminism views itself as important cultural practice, not only retrieving forgotten literary women and challenging the male usurpation of cultural experience and perspective but also becoming a formative part of culture in its own right, notably through literary reviews and journals and in the classroom (see Weedon, 1987; Flax, 1990).

Feminist critical practice has always been involved in the politics of culture and especially of pedagogy. 1960s consciousness-raising built on the notion that the personal is political, thus requiring women to interrogate their own heretofore 'private' experience as a form of political sharing and thus mobilization. This extends to feminist pedagogy, where feminist scholars insist that teaching students from a feminist perspective is a valid and significant part of overall political change, especially for the difference it makes to awakening a feminist self-consciousness in women who wish to create culture, not only interpret it. Feminist criticism functions as a consciousness-raising tool that helps to remake the general culture, not only interpreting it in the style of canonical criticism. As such, feminist criticism is political as well as intellectual practice. Indeed, the line between feminist criticism and feminist cultural practice fades to the point of indistinguishability.

Some lament this valorization of criticism as strong writing. Not only feminist critics but everyone influenced by poststructuralism meets the objection that in raising criticism to the level of original cultural creation they are engaging in self-aggrandizement: those who cannot 'do', criticize! One can understand the sense of this critique, just as one can sympathize with the complaint that women's studies' focus on the classroom as a site of political contestation tends to lead one to lose sight of the larger political arena. Nevertheless, all radical cultural studies people believe that criticism *is* action of one kind or another, if not sufficient action. It is perhaps easiest to see this in the case of feminist cultural criticism, which was always closely tied to feminist consciousness-raising, one of the original goals of the American women's movement as it split off from the male-dominated New Left. Indeed, one might observe that feminist criticism has been academized, removing it from the political arena, at least compared to 1960s and early 1970s consciousness-raising.

The development of arcane technical languages (e.g., Lacanian poststructuralist feminism; see Kristeva, 1980; Irigaray, 1985; Cixous, 1986) in which to conduct such criticism has tended to divert this criticism from the task of consciousness-raising in the mundane sense of opening students' minds to their own participation in their self-victimization (e.g., playing out the culturally scripted roles associated with 'femininity' as depicted in literature). The Europeanization and academization of feminist criticism have muted this aspect of the pedagogical politics of feminist teaching. Nevertheless, defenders of a poststructural feminism would probably argue that there is nothing inherently obscurantist or elitist about this type of feminist criticism and that, in some respects, it helps heretofore stupefied women students come to grips with their own innate technical and rhetorical competences to read, speak and write languages heretofore forbidden to them – and reserved for men, who have typically monopolized both science and theory.

Another primary aim of feminist cultural criticism is to decenter men from their dominance of various official canons and genres. Equally as troubling as the omission of women from the canon and from criticism is the installation of men as *those who speak for women* – universal subjects of world history. A good deal of poststructural feminist criticism has focused on the issue of the voices in which culture is expressed, the standpoints from which knowledge is claimed (see Richardson, 1990b, 1990c). This involves all sorts of issues, from gender to class and race. Male standpoint is deconstructed as the necessarily partial standpoint of people with a particular interest in the ongoing hegemony of men over women. 'Man' is the particular voice of men, just as 'Truth' is the particular truths of those who hold power and create official knowledge.

Feminist criticism helps women reclaim language. Decanonization involves decentering male claims to speak for everyone – claims that are typically not expressed but implied, making them that much more difficult to deconstruct. It is not as if classical western authors or playwrights explicitly equate 'Man' with particular men; it is the fact that they do not make these claims but only imply them that provides feminists with critical ammunition. The canonization of women involves raising questions about the subtle androcentrism of culture. As often as not, feminist criticism attempts to attach a gender to language that otherwise purports to be gender-free or gender-neutral. Feminist critics in a sense respond to the secret male-centeredness of culture by interrogating the ways in which men speak for women by speaking for all of humanity.

The Representation of Women in Culture

Where a good deal of feminist cultural criticism canonizes women and decenters the male voice, feminist cultural critics also challenge the representation (and misrepresentation) of women in cultural works. Of course, cultural works like novels and films contain women, often extravagantly so. When I suggest that androcentric culture subtly conflates male perspectives with those of humanity as a whole, thus ignoring the specificity of the particular gendered standpoint of women cultural creators, I do not mean to imply that mainstream culture fails to represent women. In a sense, these are issues that are dialectically connected: the canon excludes the voices of women writers and challenges the universalization of male writers, one effect of which is to establish the legitimacy of particular representations of women by male (and some female) authors in their cultural works.

Feminist criticism in the British and American women's movements in the 1960s and 1970s concentrated on this aspect of sexism. These critics focused on the sexist representation of women as members of the 'second sex' (de Beauvoir, 1953). At issue were the ways in which women are trivialized, feminized and sentimentalized in mainstream culture. Feminist criticism today in no way recants this focus on the (mis)representation of women in culture (see Brownmiller, 1973). But it concentrates on pornography specifically (Dworkin, 1974, 1981, 1988; Lederer, 1980; MacKinnon, 1979, 1984, 1987, 1989; Soble, 1986; Thornton, 1986; Turley, 1987; see Leong, 1991). In a sense, the feminist concern with the representation of women has evolved into a focused concern with the objectification of women in pornography. This focus itself has generated a good deal of controversy in its own right, where some feminists (e.g., Steinem, 1978, 1986; Elshtain, 1984) distinguish between erotica and pornography, while others (e.g., Dworkin, 1981) reject all sexualization of women in culture as inherently pornographic. Although it is not my interest to adjudicate that debate here (see English, 1980), a poststructural feminism would probably find it difficult to distinguish between erotica and pornography. What is interesting here is the way in which questioning about the representation of women in general has narrowed into a concern with pornography, thus perhaps deemphasizing other objectifications that cannot readily be subsumed under the narrower rubric of pornography (see Lacombe, 1988).

The representation of women in cultural works is obviously important for feminists who are concerned with raising consciousness. Both men and women take their gender cues from popular culture, as well as from the family, religion and formal education. The ways in which women are portrayed matters enormously for early childhood and adolescent socialization as well as for adult learning about issues of gender. Feminist sociologists distinguish between sexuality and gender – biological and social identities as sexed beings. (Again, a poststructural feminism would challenge this clean separation, which is so frequently made by more liberal/rational feminists – a challenge in which I would join; see West and Zimmerman, 1987). The portrayal of women's and men's appropriate gender identities and sexual preferences in mass culture is a crucial feminist topic where feminists reject hard-and-fast gender-identity differentiations as well as the dominant heterosexism in our culture at large.

The feminist cultural critique of the representation of women targets a number of typical portrayals of women (and men):

1. Women's depiction as sexual objects for men.

2. Women's depiction as primarily responsible for domesticity, housework, child-rearing and caregiving.

3. Women's depiction as the weaker or secondary sex.

4. Women's depiction as normally as well as normatively heterosexual.

One of the most lasting contributions of the feminist movement has been to transvalue the ways in which women and men are represented in culture, including ways in which women and men are read in cultural texts and documents. Feminist criticism has given many of us a new way of viewing women in culture, subverting the normative ways in which they are represented as sex objects, housewives, helpmates, dim-wits and heterosexuals (or, if lesbians, then degenerate). This has begun to inform the ways in which women novelists, directors, producers and artists portray women; these cultural creators reflect on their representational gestures, interrogating taken-for-granted assumptions about the way the lens, brush and pen depict female sexuality, women's relationships to each other and women's relationships to men. Even some male cultural creators have begun to set aside traditional representations of the sexes in light of feminist criticism, although one must not exaggerate the extent to which this is taking place. Notoriously 'feminist' men writers and directors are often every bit as sexist as 'traditional' men in the way they portray women as objects of male delectation.

The feminist interrogation of the representation of women in culture is increasingly bound up with the interrogation of representation in general (e.g., the so-called crisis of representation, occasioned by poststructuralism). The crisis of representation refers to the way in which both critics and authors are questioning the extent to which any aesthetic gesture can (or should attempt to) reflect the world accurately. With Derrida, it is argued that language, in fact culture generally, transforms the represented object in a way that makes representation extremely problematic. Poststructuralism has shortened the distance between the writer and the world, between representation and that which is to be represented, in such a way that we can no longer assume that language or figural gestures, even photographs, do not leave their own mark on the world, thus ineluctably changing it. Representation is in crisis because language has lost its ability to convey meaning unproblematically (assuming it ever could). It is no longer possible for writers or directors to portray women, for example, 'as they really are' without recognizing that there is no *as-they-really-are* but only women constructed by the authorial gaze and text.

Poststructural cultural theory helps us recognize that women become texts (Baudrillard's [1983] simulations) in that they are written into existence, not found 'in reality' somewhere and then pasted into the text or glued together out of pieces of celluloid. Women do not exist in nature, as Rousseau might have imagined. They are not accessible culturally except *through* culture, and the ways in which culture imposes its own perspective on things. Feminist critics, especially poststructural ones, have revolutionized the ways in which we understand that sexuality and gender are constructed, thus drawing attention to every last detail of the aesthetic oeuvre, from opening credits through the final fade shot.

One of the central themes of poststructural feminism (e.g., Irigaray, 1985) is the way in which women are constructions of men and of male culture. This is of course not to deny that women are substantial, autonomous beings in their own right. But there is a sense in which *women are a text* on which is inscribed the sentiments and interests of men. To be a woman – wo-man – is to be not-man, an Other defined in reference to men and male culture. This fact alone is extremely relevant to feminist cultural criticism where it helps feminist critics unearth the meanings of socio-sexual domination from the ways in which men define women (and themselves in terms of their dominance of women). Women are sexual objects *for men*, just as they do housework *for men* (and men's children). Inappropriate women (e.g., see Agger, 1989c) are women who reject their definition in terms of men, especially in the case of lesbians who refuse to believe that they are failures as women because they choose not to be with men. A great deal of cultural wrath is reserved for lesbians, who are portrayed as man-haters, angry, frigid, anti-children and anti-family – all-round gender traitors and losers. Even some *soi-disant* feminist authors and filmmakers portray lesbians in these terms, deconstructing their otherwise feminist intentions where their heterosexism belies their attack on sexism (against heterosexual women).

The representation of women's sexuality and sexual identity is crucial for feminist cultural studies. Although it is clear that the critique of pornography occupies much of the attention of feminist cultural studies, the deconstruction of representations of lesbians in culture deserves equal attention for what it tells us about the deepest levels of men's derogation of women – here, those women who have chosen against men. Lesbians are typically portrayed as *dykes*, women aggressively hostile to men, too ugly to 'get' men, unresponsive to the call of romantic love, etc. These representations more than any other (perhaps even including hard-core pornographic representations of women) encode what our culture thinks about women who stray from the straight and narrow, daring to exercise their sexual and personal autonomy in defiance of norms surrounding what it means to be a woman, notably feminine (i.e., attractive to men).

Deconstructive interpretive strategies concentrate on the text's or work's marginality in order to discern the repressions and overdeterminations inhabiting the space between margin and center. One can learn a great deal about the text's center by reading its marginalia – in this case, one can learn a great deal about men and male culture by reading their representations of women, especially in pornography and in the depiction of lesbianism. One can learn very little about women as such by reading these representations inasmuch as these representations re-present men's views of women (and women's views of women where the women authors and directors are captives of male ideologies about gender relations; see Soothill and Walby, 1991). Women readers are notoriously suspicious of men's views of women, whether in novels, film or television. The male representation of women is necessarily self-serving and thus one can investigate patriarchy by examining the ways in which it portrays women – marginalia to men's center.

This is essential to deconstructive methodology: the reader lays bare the relationship between what is said and what is repressed or implied in order to show that what-is-said depends on an ensemble of textual gestures that go unreported on the surface of the argument. These gestures are *repressive* in the psychoanalytic sense in that they bury certain assumptions and experiences far beneath the surface of the work, making it extremely difficult for the casual reader to discern these deeper repressions for what they say about the text as a totality. In the case of feminist cultural criticism, the feminist deconstructor aspires to uncover the repressions that constitute the interest men have in portraying women as sluts, dykes or mommies. Men's interest is in domination – patriarchy. Although true, it is beside the point that men who portray women in derogatory or inaccurate terms harbor sexist motives. One must demonstrate the logic of textual repression that covers over the male interest in women's objectifying representation in a way that shows *how texts work* when they develop their encoded implications of a particular view of women and men. Deconstruction decodes these implications as arguments for a certain state of affairs, here a world in which women act out roles scripted for them by men. Deconstruction decodes the gender text in which women are represented as a polemical device, not simply as a mirror held up to a world in which some women participate as prostitutes, lesbians and mothers. *This decoding transforms representation into rhetoric – arguments for a certain order of things.* As such, decoded gender texts can be opposed, as feminists do when they insist that women can be different from the ways in which men portray them. After all, gender texts teach both women and men how to be gendered; they are normatively constitutional and thus must be interrogated as scripts of obedience and submission.

This is not mainly a comment on the so-called effects of pornography – whether pornography 'causes' violence against women (see Morgan, 1980). Post-structural feminist cultural critics argue that the (mis)representation of women is already an act of violence, objectifying women into effects of men's interests and needs (see Coward, 1982). This is not to identify physical brutality against flesh-and-blood women with their cultural representation; violence against women in terms of their objectification falls along a continuum. Few feminists would maintain that for men to whistle at women is as objectifying, as 'violent', as for men to beat up women. Yet a poststructural feminism would underline their common source in the male objectification of women – literally, turning women into objects, representing them as available for male reproduction, surveillance, delectation, abuse. If violence is construed narrowly as overt physical abuse, then the correlation of pornography and violence is relevant (and there is considerable evidence that pornography and violence are positively correlated – less that individual men who consume pornography engage in violence against women than that pornography in general creates a culture in which it is appropriate to do women violence). If violence is construed more broadly as the objectification of women, then one need not demonstrate these correlations; the representational objectification of women is violence itself (see Ellis, 1984; Manion, 1985).

As for the notion that erotica and pornography should be distinguished, thus giving women access to erotic excitation within a positive sentimental context, poststructuralism suggests convincingly that such distinctions are, at best, tenuous. The feminist erotica business is booming, both in response to the theoretical claim that erotica and porn can be differentiated and in response to the notion that women deserve the same 'rights' as men (i.e., to be sexually aroused by the representation of the male and female body and of men and women having sex). Women in growing numbers today attend male burlesque shows as well as 'bachelorette' pre-nuptial parties. There is a sense of turning the tables on men in these rituals, claiming for women what men have always claimed for themselves, namely the right to enjoy sexual representations and exhibitions. But poststructural feminists, who question the validity of sharp lines between (legitimate) erotica and (illegitimate) pornography, have difficulty with these practices and with the allegedly feminist theories that legitimate them, preferring to deconstruct the representation of women's sexuality as a power play by men. For women to acquiesce to these practices only reduces their ability to resist their own representation and hence degradation by men.

The defense of feminist pornography ('erotica') is paralleled by a defense, particularly among lesbians, of sado-masochistic sexual practices. Gay leather bars proliferate in major urban centers in the US, the UK and western Europe. Sado-masochism is judged acceptable if conducted in a feminist context, notably between consenting adults, especially women. But, again, it is difficult to separate feminist from misogynist sado-masochism in a clear way. The defense of feminist sado-masochism is typically conducted through a rhetoric of choice that empowers women to decide for themselves what sorts of sexual practices and representations they wish to engage in, neglecting the fact that we *learn* what we want from our culture – here, the identification of pain and sexual pleasure. A deconstructive feminist criticism would argue that we learn a great deal about gender relationships by examining the appeal of sado-masochism as well as pornography to women as well as to men. In particular, we learn how sexuality has been alienated to such an extent that we only enjoy it if we can equate it with the experience of pain, both 'giving' it and 'getting' it. Nothing is more emblematic of a society in which men and women are pitted against each other structurally, in which even the most private experiences of human intimacy have been commodified and rendered unpleasant.

I have little sympathy for the pro-porn posture of feminists, especially in light of a poststructural feminism that blurs the boundaries between erotica and pornography as well as between violence and objectification. Like Frankfurt critical theory, this Derridean feminism helps us examine the most minute details of human experience and practice in terms of their invasion by the colonizing, administering, commodifying imperatives of dominant society. Representation has become a political battleground because politics has been displaced (e.g., Habermas, 1975) from the traditional political arena into spheres of existence heretofore regarded as non-political, notably the realms of sexuality and textuality. How women are portrayed in culture matters greatly for the sexual politics transacted between men and women. To ignore this is to ignore the whole cultural politics of feminism, which forces us to examine representation as a political vehicle in the ways in which it encodes imageries of appropriate conduct and consciousness.

A society in which women are displayed only as whores, dykes or mommies is bound to reproduce these behaviors on the part of women, who normatively respond to the representations scripted for them by an androcentric culture. I am not suggesting that women mechanically enact these roles portrayed for them as appropriate, although some do. Rather, representation helps create a total culture within which both men and women conceive of themselves and their identities with reference to established conceptions of the limits of possibility. For young women and men to consume a mass culture that locks women and men into bestial, degraded, hierarchized social relations virtually ensures that *representation becomes reality*, even if we tell ourselves that the lives depicted on the screen and in the text are only simulations – that people can choose to reject the patterns screened for them by Hollywood and New York producers. Culture has an incredibly powerful momentum that cannot be undone through singular heroic gestures of defiance or resistance. Few women (especially women born after 1960, the end of the baby boom) free themselves from the representations of what it means to be a woman – to prettify oneself for men, to live for men, to aspire to marriage and children, to view other women as competition, etc. If cultural representation is not preponderant, then why do so many women wear make-up, shave their legs, get married, have children, accept primary responsibility for childcare and housework, subordinate their careers to those of their spouses?

A late twentieth-century feminism must reckon with the power of cultural representation in ways that liberal feminism typically does not. Poststructural feminism rejects the rational-choice liberalism of pro-choice ideology, particularly the notion that the point of feminism is to give women maximal 'freedom of choice' (like men, supposedly). A poststructural feminism, like critical theory, recognizes that 'choice' is not free in this society, constrained by structures of discourse and power that impose 'choices' on people, not the other way around. To suppose that women simply *choose* their lives independent of the way women's lives are represented in culture is naive; such a notion reflects the unfreedom of the general society and misleads individual women about the choices available to them. In this way, a feminist cultural studies makes an important contribution to political and social theory, particularly in the way it develops a politics of representation that unravels the disciplining functions of cultural imageries of women in a social order deceptively premised on alleged freedom of choice.

Nothing is more timely than a feminist cultural studies inasmuch as the roles of women in culture are being actively interrogated today. Since Millett, feminism has always thematized issues of the cultural representation of women. These issues have been rejoined by poststructural feminists concerned to develop feminist film and media theory in ways that give the lie to liberalisms denying the impact representation has on women's everyday lives and thus on the power structures of patriarchy. A poststructural feminism pivots around a textual politics that becomes a sexual politics; it interrogates the cultural transactions of power that take place in texts and on screens. These feminists take texts seriously inasmuch as they take popular culture seriously as a site of political contestation (e.g., Balsamo, 1990). They develop a materialist cultural studies that does not read texts and cultural practices *sui generis* but carefully contextualizes them in the material circuitries of cultural production, distribution and reception. Feminist cultural studies is on the agenda today because culture is the realm into which political contestation and crisis have been displaced, as Habermas (1975) originally argued. Habermas considers the women's movement to be a 'new social movement', in his (1981b) term. In significant respects, the women's movement has displaced the male proletariat as one of the most relevant 'collective subjects' of emancipatory practice in the late twentieth century.

For this reason alone, more traditional Marxists must address developments in feminist cultural studies for what they can tell them about ways in which to refresh a tired, sexist Marxism. Although I suspect that feminist cultural studies is still too invested in the interest-group representation of the needs and interests of women and not of all humanity, feminist readings of pornography and the depiction of women, particularly lesbians, are important for a Marxism that would address the dialectic of Master and Slave, self and other, in this post-Marxist global context. Marxists should not recant their Marxism in light of feminist cultural studies but rather redevelop Marxism along the lines of a cultural studies that moves dexterously back and forth between the concerns of public and personal politics as well as political economy and ideological critique. In significant respects, feminist cultural studies is a much more developed materialism than are the latter-day Marxisms of so-called analytical and rational-choice Marxists (see Wright, 1985; Elster, 1989; Roemer, 1986). By comparison to the feminist readings of pornography and other representations of women, these neo-Marxisms are irrelevant, as apolitical as the bourgeois social theories they purport to oppose.

Feminism and Poststructuralism

The precise relationship between feminist theory and poststructuralism has been addressed before (e.g., Balsamo, 1987; Weedon, 1987). I (Agger, 1989a) have discussed the convergence among critical theory, feminist theory and poststructuralism in terms of my analysis of the domination of reproduction. It is clear that Marxists have ignored the realm of reproduction for too long, crying out for a feminist corrective that restores the centrality of reproduction to a comprehensive critical social theory. But it is not exactly clear how feminist theory articulates with poststructuralism. I am less interested in the textual hermeneutics of Derrida and the French feminists, especially those influenced heavily by Lacan, than in the theoretical and analytical possibilities opened up by the engagement between feminist theory and poststructuralism, especially as this bears on the possibilities of a feminist cultural studies (see Fraser, 1989).

Feminist poststructuralists borrow from both Derrida and Lacan (see Felman, 1987). From Derrida they borrow his critique of phallogocentrism – the way in which male speech dominates writing, especially the writing done by women. Western thought since antiquity has tended to privilege speech over writing for the way in which speech brings the listener into what Derrida calls the 'presence' of the world, whereas writing is more mediated and thus somehow less valid. It is clear that Derrida's critique of the philosophy of presence can be used by feminists who resist the male appropriation of language; they argue that male concepts of reason and reasonable language issue in discourses that exclude women and women's writing, particularly in the realms of speculative philosophy and science (see Harding, 1986). Derrida's own poststructuralism is self-consciously feminist in his concept and critique of phallogocentrism, refracting his overall critique of western positivism that, according to him, fundamentally ignores the undecidability of language and thus the political and social ambiguities of all social engineering.

The French feminists like Irigaray (1985), Cixous (1986) and Kristeva (1980) are thoroughly Derridean in the ways in which they understand the aporetic nature of language and writing. They all agree with Derrida that texts have many levels of often contradictory meaning, typified by the hierarchy of text over subtext. As feminists, they use literary methods of deconstruction to bring to light the hidden assumptions and contradictions of male texts that purport to speak for women or about them. Inasmuch as feminist theory has focused on the politics of language, a deconstruction of phallogocentric language has been especially pertinent, showing the ways in which men usurp the dialogue chances of women and thus reinforce their own political and social power.

Lacan also energizes poststructural feminist cultural studies where theorists have utilized his basic distinctions between the realm of the Imaginary and the realm of the Symbolic to suggest expressive differences between women and men writers. This emerges most clearly in the cinefeminism discussed in the next section. Essentially, Lacan builds on Freud's psychoanalytic theory by adding poststructuralist notions about language. He argues that women have more access than men to the realm of non-linear, evocative discourse (so-called round writing). Men inhabit the realm of symbolism and language, including the activities of science and philosophy. This realm of expression is governed by linear notions of logic and discourse. Lacan (1977) develops a complex account of how men and women move between these phases of development, suggesting new ways of viewing the unconscious (which, he argues, is structured like a language).

Feminists use Lacan to suggest a distinctively feminist or womanly cultural discourse. It is a style more characteristic of Lacan's Imaginary than of his Symbolic, which is essentially male. Feminist cultural theory, especially film theory, regards the ways in which dominant culture is created from the point of view of men's desire, which in the case of film and television is achieved through *the gaze* – the way in which the camera functions as a male eye through which to behold objectified women (see de Lauretis, 1984, 1987; Mulvey, 1988). In a sense, then, cinefeminism examines the ways in which women are constructed through the male gaze of the camera as well as by men in the audience who, in the darkened privacy of the theater or television room, reappropriate aspects of experience in the realm of the Imaginary otherwise repressed in their struggle to assert themselves in the realm of the Symbolic.

Cinefeminism

Feminist film theory or *cinefeminism* (see Walters, 1992) is a particular application of a poststructural-feminist approach to cultural studies. As I said, cinefeminism likens the camera to the male gaze. It is indebted to Derridean and Lacanian notions about how the cultural work positions its subjects – who then construct the meaning of the cultural work in their own interpretive practice. Thus, *woman* is constituted in male audience members' construction of female representations in film and television. Men make women, who signify the not-male, in a two-step process: first, the male gaze of the camera presents women as sexual objects, prostitutes, lesbians and mothers; then, second, men in the audience gaze upon the film and receive/reproduce these aspects of womanness. Women, thus, are doubly constructed, according to the desire of both camera men and audience men. Women function as objects of male desire, which is expressed in terms of this two-step process of presentation/representation.

The essential poststructural thesis of cinefeminism is that *the camera is not neutral*. It represents a particular perspective and engages in editorial selectivity; it is not value-free, as positivist theorists of news and film often suggest. Not only does the camera lie; the cinematic perspective is fictive itself in the sense in which the camera both ignores a whole range of possible topics and distorts the topics it does frame. Feminist film critics focus on the ways in which the male directorial gaze constitutes women as objects for men and ignores aspects of sexual politics and power transacted both between men and women on the screen and between the film(maker) and audience off screen. Film is thoroughly political for feminist poststructuralists in the sense that filmmaking and viewing are inherently processes constituting, and constituted by, directorial, editorial and interpretive authority. This authority involves the commitment of the camera to a particular view of the world that it screens as if the camera did not exist but was merely a value-free mirror. As poststructuralism indicates, this view of presuppositionless representation is false because every representation is a commitment of sorts to a certain formulation of reality: representation conceals the fact that its own perspective and selectivity help constitute the 'reality' it presents as indubitable fact, especially in the case of the camera, which all too easily conceals itself concealing.

Although cinefeminism is phrased in the dense rhetorics of Lacan, Derrida and feminist film theory, there is nothing particularly mysterious about this approach. Essentially, feminist film critics are saying that we must understand the ways in which men involve themselves in the construction of filmic images of women in order to change these constructions, thus producing more feminist movies and feminist audiences. Cinefeminism differs markedly from liberal-feminist studies of the content of filmic images of women, rejecting this approach as overly positivist. Instead, poststructural cinefeminists argue that it is equally as important to examine ways in which women are signified or represented, thus provoking a certain reception of these imageries by an audience trained to construct 'women' out of celluloid. Where liberal feminists urge that 'more' women be depicted in popular culture, as well as women who are professional, independent and smart, poststructural cinefeminists draw attention to the processes of the signification, representation and reception of imaginary women through the male gaze. Although these two approaches are not necessarily opposed, they tend to be carried out in very different ways, by critics with radically different interests (e.g., see Stern, 1979–1980; Kuhn, 1982; McCabe, 1986; and de Lauretis, 1984, 1987).

Cinefeminists focus on the gestural and directorial ways in which film women are presented by the male director and represented by the male audience. Women make and watch films, too. The Lacanian thrust of poststructural feminist film theory focuses attention on the ways in which men present and represent women in order to satisfy their own psychoerotic desire. One almost has the impression that feminist Lacanians ignore the fact that women are not just screen images interpolated through the male gaze but also real people who sit in theaters very angry about the ways in which 'they' are represented on the screen. Walters (1992) calls for a more materialist feminist cultural studies that does not succumb to the nearly apolitical stance of Lacanian feminists who neglect the existence of real women in favor of a study of simulated filmic women. This is an important corrective to the dominant tendency of cinefeminists, like that of poststructuralists generally, to ignore the social, political and historical con-texts within which poststructural readings take place. Texts cannot be separated from their contexts, the language games within which they transact their powerful images of appropriate femininity and masculinity. Nor can we assume that the effect of these texts is always and everywhere the same, especially once we differentiate the audience along lines of gender. One could even suggest that a good deal of feminist cultural practice involves resistance against male images of women on the level of real women's everyday lives, from ordinary language to film and television.

Cinefeminism functions as feminist theory and practice where it empowers both directors and audience members to make and view film in a new way, attentive to the subtexts of gender inhabiting both the camera's gaze and the narrative unfolded on the screen. Like feminist literary criticism, cinefeminism helps viewers deconstruct the portrayal of women as well as to interpolate where the male gaze claims universality for itself. Cinefeminist viewers learn to watch male film *as women*, resisting the leering cinematic gaze by reading across the grain of the film for what is really going on – the objectification of women. As well, cinefeminist viewers learn to watch female film as the disruption of the male gaze, learning to view themselves as women in terms not beholden to the standard male objectifications of women. For their part, cinefeminist filmmakers break the male gaze by refusing the voyeuristic male directorial obsession with women *qua* objects for the delectation of men. This involves not only changing the narratives of movies (e.g., boy meets and conquers girl) but also the cinematic gaze itself, turning it away from women *qua* object and onto the whole ensemble of gendered relationships in which men and women are involved as people who transact power, albeit one-sidedly. Cinefeminist directors thematize sexuality as power, refusing to allow it to stand as a referent for hungry male desire. The abundant sexuality of contemporary cinema is demystified as the power play it usually is. Instead, cinefeminist directors refocus the camera on the ways in which men objectify women and women acquiesce fatefully to their own objectification.

Cinefeminism is feminist theory in the sense that it helps understand the subtle cinematic structures of domination encoded on celluloid and enacted in the darkened privacy of the theater. It is feminist practice in that it empowers feminist directors to make films differently. Poststructural feminists focus on film both because films are a significant screen of power (Luke, 1989) and because, unlike television, films are easier to make differently by defiant directors who buck the jumbo-movie syndrome of Hollywood. Film schools are full of feminist teachers and students who want to read and make movies that break the male gaze. These movies would elaborate new ways for women to view each other and men that do not acquiesce to objectification by pretending that the cinematic gaze is somehow value-free, devoid of the deep political, sexual and metaphysical commitments that frame all cinematic selectivity and perspective.

Feminist Cultural Studies as Feminist Theory and Practice

In this sense, cinefeminism functions as an active intervention in the cultural field itself; it is not only an academic project. It is also a contribution to theoretical and empirical knowledge about how the cultural world functions to distort the role of women in social life. Cinefeminists make new movies representing women's perspectives; cinefeminists also view movies differently, deconstructing the male gaze and learning to think and see like feminists. These activities on the part of feminist cultural critics help narrow the distance between feminist theory and practice, precisely the aim of radical cultural studies. Better than most male Marxists, feminist theorists and critics integrate their theory and practice through the general example of feminist cultural studies and the particular example of cinefeminism. To be sure, cinefeminism is an insufficient critical practice. Although it is crucial that women and men learn how to deconstruct the male gaze and become habituated to a feminist cinematic eye, it is less clear that the transvaluation of feminist filmmaking will make a significant dent in cultural hegemony. After all, movie production and distribution are highly centralized, and becoming more so. Feminist cultural theory is long on innovative textual reading but short on literary political economy (see, e.g., Agger, 1990). There is a general aversion to economic theory and analysis in feminism, perhaps stemming from an aversion to male Marxism which for so long has ignored the whole realm of reproduction as apolitical – women's work.

Although certain socialist feminists (e.g., Walby, 1990) have begun to challenge this one-sidedness from within feminism, it is hard to see that feminist cultural theorists have developed a more active interest in the political economy of culture, thus providing a materialist con-text within which cultural texts are to be read and challenged. As Walters (1992) argues, feminist cultural theory, especially cinefeminism, too often lacks a materialist foundation addressing the real historical conditions within which cultural works and practices are conducted. I agree with Walters, although I do not share her optimism that we can easily change the focus of cinefeminism in particular and feminist cultural theory in general by grafting some of the Birmingham interpretive strategies onto the feminist cultural project. As I indicated in Chapter 5, the Birmingham tradition itself lacks clear theoretical perspective, unable to ground a materialist cultural studies that functions simultaneously as critical social theory.

Of course, poststructuralists of all sorts, both feminist and otherwise, reject theoretical totalization as an intellectual and political aim. Cinefeminists who derive in one way or another from Derrida, Lacan and the French feminists share this aversion to comprehensive theoretical explanation, instead preferring more regional strategies of cultural interpretation and intervention. This is unfortunate, reflecting the pitfalls of poststructuralism. Although poststructuralism helps feminist cultural theorists ask some interesting questions about culture-as-text, it also deflects the project of empirical theoretical explanation without which it is difficult to move beyond local cultural readings to a more general account of the dialectical interpenetrations of culture, everyday life and political economy. In this sense, feminist cultural studies fails to function adequately as social theory, even though many of its practitioners intend it to serve as a version of feminist theory, which, as Cixous (1986) and others argue, must be written in a 'womanly' fashion – non-linearly, allusively, playfully.

Whether feminist theory can be composed in this way is open for debate. I do not believe that theory can dispense with discursive writing or methodological rigor at a time when the world requires totalizing perspective. Feminist 'round writing' works well as poetry but not as social theory. It does not help women locate themselves on a topographical map of the world situation and thus to begin to organize their discontent in transformative ways. A great deal of feminist cultural criticism indulges in what Barthes (1975) called the pleasure of the text, attempting to embody the Imaginary marked out by Lacan as the special preserve of essentially womanly knowledge.

This raises issues addressed differently in debates about so-called feminist methodology (e.g., Keller, 1985; Harding, 1986) and science. Feminist cultural theorists (e.g., Smith, 1987, 1990a, 1990b) argue that theory and criticism must build on the everyday experience of women – here, the women who create and consume culture. Although at some level experience is crucial in the process of social analysis and social change – after all, false consciousness is a factor in domination – theory must point beyond experience in order to formulate the structural principles according to which oppression operates. The theory and critique of the male gaze are very important contributions to understanding how cultural hegemony works in this type of patriarchal society. But the male gaze, as I understand it, is not simply a phenomenological concept; it is also a structural property of a patriarchy in which men look at, and treat, women as objects. One must theorize the functions of the male gaze as well as outline principles according to which we can transform the male gaze deconstructively. Unfortunately, few feminist cultural theorists explicitly develop a political and social theory within which one can locate the male gaze as an axial principle of what Foucault (1977) calls discipline. Indeed, as Fraser (1989) has argued, some of Foucault's work, although itself undertheorized, can offer feminist critical theory many theoretical resources. In certain respects, his *The History of Sexuality* (1978) is a formative contribution to a materialist feminist cultural studies, articulating the complex overdetermination of ideological, experiential and structural underpinnings of the discursive formulation of sexuality in a patriarchal and heterosexist world. Many feminists have little use for Foucault, discussing his rather architectonic approach to the analysis of discipline and discourse as yet another male betrayal of the project of the female Imaginary.

This begs the unavoidable question of whether feminist cultural theorists really believe that a feminist culture will be inaccessible to male experience and practice. Lacanian feminists believe that women belong more in the realm of the Imaginary and men more in the realm of the Symbolic (perhaps mediated by the so-called Mirror phase). This is a regrettably biologistic formulation, neglecting the critical philosophy of history developed by the later Freud (what Jacoby [1975] calls 'negative psychoanalysis' in contradistinction to the hegemonic medical model of psychoanalysis – adjustment therapy).

Certainly a culture dominated by the male gaze needs to be interrogated in terms of both its structural operations and the ways in which the male gaze plays out in the lived experience of men who objectify women. But feminist cultural theory has offered few alternative formulations of cultural possibility other than this resort to a Lacanian concept of the female Imaginary and a French feminist notion of womanly writing. Are men prevented from gaining access to the realm of the Imaginary in a way that does not require them to resolve the Oedipal conflict by consuming objectified simulations of vulnerable, violated women on the screen and in texts? A materialist cultural studies refuses to differentiate bio(onto)logically between the possibilities of women's experience and expression and men's experience and expression. It insists on a certain experiential and expressive universality to be developed through a rigorous deconstruction of the male gaze and male writing. But this deconstruction will not only grant men access to the female Imaginary (the use of metaphor, indirection, poetry, new ways of seeing and knowing, etc.); it will also grant women access to the realm of the Symbolic in which women do science and theorize competently and differently. Liberation is a two-way street, freeing women to 'be' men and men to 'be' women. If Freud was correct about our fundamental androgyny, then critical theory must portray emancipation in terms of reciprocal role changes and not focus only on the ways in which men should become more like women in their concourse with the world.

For men to learn to experience the world and express themselves in non-'macho' ways would go a long way toward inhibiting the aims of aggressive and competitive maleness. Feminists of all sorts recognize the male will to power in both the male gaze and male technological externalization (where nuclear weapons function as phallic symbols). But it is also true that women must liberate themselves from their nearly millennial relegation to the realm of the Imaginary, if by that we mean a realm of experience and expression dominated by intuition, metaphor and emotion, thus freeing women from their relegation to eternal nurturance. Women can learn to deal competently and productively with symbol systems heretofore regarded as the bio(onto)logical perserve of men. The radical feminist argument that women are ineluctably different from men (e.g., Daly, 1973, 1978; Gilligan, 1982) only reinforces these differences at a time when for women to be different means for them to be *less powerful*. Women must reconstruct their own gender identity, discourse and practice in a way that empowers them to become like men in terms of a range of these expressive and technical capabilities. Only by doing so will we really transvalue the meanings of sexual orientation and sexuality.

A feminist cultural studies that does not entrench itself in Lacanian biologism can lead the way in democratizing and androgynizing the expressive possibilities available to men and women. Critical theory and orthodox Marxism alike have ignored hierarchies built on gender for too long. Feminists correct this oversight, but threaten to reproduce their own hierarchy based on putative biological difference. This gets us nowhere. Instead, we must build a genuinely feminist culture in which people degender their discourse and their practice. Feminist cultural studies becomes a comprehensive social theory and practice where it intends this level of universality. Short of it, feminist cultural studies remains regrettably self-isolated, hence easily integrated.

Chapter 8

Needs, Values and Cultural Criticism

Positivist Cultural Studies: Seven Assumptions

Having surveyed the range of approaches to cultural studies in the preceding five chapters, I want to speculate further about the political opportunities and responsibilities of a radical cultural studies. In this context, I begin by indicating the extent to which the Frankfurt, Birmingham, postmodern and feminist approaches to a political cultural studies are still quite marginal with respect to mainstream approaches to the sociology of culture dominating interpretive discourse especially in the US. Most culture studies, both within and outside sociology, are positivist (see Denzin, 1986, 1990, 1991); they endorse value-freedom and they reject the leftist and feminist engagement with culture in terms of transformational interests: the point is to understand the world, not to change it (e.g., Griswold, 1986; DiMaggio, 1986; Wuthnow, 1989). A good deal of the pop-culture tradition in the US, exemplified by quantitative media studies as well as by the work of people affiliated with the cultural studies group at Bowling Green University (e.g., see Batra and Ray, 1986; Skinner, 1989; Loukides and Fuller, 1990; Lad Panek, 1990; Myers, 1990; Wells, 1990; Wright, 1990), remains apolitical, in clear contrast to the more politicized cultural studies traditions of orthodox Marxism, the Frankfurt School, the Birmingham School, feminism, poststructuralism and postmodernism. It would be a serious mistake to ignore this mainstream cultural empiricism; to do so would give the false impression that all cultural studies people are radicals of one kind or another. In fact, many are garden-variety empirical-positivist social scientists who analyze popular culture in the same way they analyze other 'social facts', as Durkheim (1950, pp. 1–13) called them. Some might view the term *radical cultural studies* as an oxymoron; I want to believe that it can be a tautology if the social analysis of culture is decoupled from its positivist tendencies.

As in the earlier discussion of Lyotard's version of postmodernism, at issue here is *relativism*. Although Lyotard calls himself a theorist of relativity but not a relativist, it is clear that his version of postmodern cultural studies rejects ideological posturing as illegitimately totalizing; as I indicated earlier, he opposes what he calls grand narratives like Marxism for their arrogant claim to understand and thus transform all social institutions and practices. The positivist popular-culture tradition shares this aversion to politics with Lyotard, although it does not theorize its own relativity/relativism in the way that Lyotard (1984) has done.

Once we dig beneath the surface of the positivist pop-culture tradition in its various formulations, we discover a number of its most important subtexts. It is necessary to keep in mind here that it is sometimes difficult to distinguish clearly between positivist and non-positivist versions of cultural studies, especially in the case of studies heavily influenced by poststructuralism. As I argue in Chapter 9, many examples of cultural studies, even though they profess a political intent, are in fact so technical in nature that they lose any purchase on issues of social change, as in the case of the most involuted versions of feminist poststructural film theory. Thus, some of the deepest assumptions of positivist cultural studies are to be found in studies that appear to deviate sharply from these positivist versions if only in the sense that they are more self-consciously and densely theorized. But the degree of a reading's apparent theoreticity does not relate directly to its political possibilities. After all, some of the relatively under-theorized works of the Birmingham CCCS tradition are much more engaged with material social reality, and with the possibilities of social change, than are more theoretically nuanced studies, even those of the Frankfurt School theorists (see Hall, 1982). Although theoreticity is important for developing cultural readings in the direction of a more total social theory (as well as for informing those readings dialectically with total social theory), theoreticity is no guarantee of one's engagement, especially where cultural theory becomes readily fetishized as a self-reproducing interpretive method applicable to all sorts of apparently disconnected cultural works and practices. Just because one appears not to be positivist does not mean that one's own cultural analyses are somehow more firmly linked to the possibility of political change.

Positivist cultural studies makes the following deep assumptions:

1. Cultural studies, like all social analysis, must be value-free. The point is not to change the world but only to understand it (even if understanding it can lead to certain social reforms to be initiated by people outside of the analytical process).

2. Popular culture is a structurally and functionally necessary feature of modern societies; it is largely healthy and necessary, even if some of its excrescences are unfortunate (e.g., heavy metal rock music; but see Frith, 1983; Orman, 1984; Grossberg, 1986). All cultural expressions are seen to fulfill certain basic needs. The cultural analyst must not impose his or her own disdain for mass culture onto the masses themselves. Instead, he or she must develop a studied empathy with populist/popular culture, attempting to understand its positive relevance for ordinary people.

3. Popular culture is treated as entertainment, diversion from the quotidian which, ironically, it celebrates. It is conceptualized as an activity comprising 'leisure time', time spent away from paid labor. Parsonian-era sociology (e.g., Parsons and Bales, 1955), still dominant in the US, does not conceptualize household labor as value-producing work, instead restricting the notion of work to paid labor. Similarly, culture is conceptualized as occurring in the private sphere, outside of paid labor.

4. There are no pre-given principles for evaluating cultural works and practices as 'better' or 'worse' than other works and practices. The cultural analyst must refrain from making these judgments, instead retreating to positivist value-freedom. High-culture preferences are to be subdued rigorously, especially where intergenerational cultural analysis is being attempted.

5. Although mass culture is a profitable business, the culture-industry thesis of the Frankfurt School is rejected out of hand. The essential structural-functionalism of a neo-Parsonian sociology of culture (e.g., see Alexander and Seidman, 1990) suggests that cultural producers and distributors serve certain important social needs. Although positivist pop-culture analysts may examine the circuitries of cultural production, distribution and consumption, they are much more likely to focus on cultural readings, given this structural-functional bias.

6. As a result, it is concluded that popular culture should be examined not mainly in terms of its encoded political messages and forms (e.g., Baudrillard's [1983] critical analysis of simulations) but in terms of the internal dynamics of its presentation, representation and consumption (e.g., see Browne and Madden, 1972). Of course, poststructural, postmodern and feminist cultural analysts also examine cultural works and practices outside of the social con-texts within which texts take on enormous political import. As I have indicated before, there is a discernible tendency for cultural studies to become a thoroughly technical exercise in internal and immanent interpretation of the production of meaning and not a broader social-theoretic exercise in tracing the connections between art/ideology, on the one hand, and social, political and economic practices, on the other (see Brenkman, 1987; Luke, 1991). In this regard, positivist pop-culture analysis is not alone. Indeed, one of the main challenges for a radicalized cultural studies is to overcome this technical, apolitical approach to culture.

7. There is a difference, however, between the immanentism and technical fetishism of positivist cultural studies and those of poststructural and postmodern cultural studies. The latter view themselves virtually as cultural interventions in their own right, reflexively gauging their own contribution to the sense of the texts and practices they examine, where the former ignore their own constitutional impact. Of course, positivists do not recognize their own intervention in the fields of what they study; positivism lives the lie that analysis does nothing to change the things being analyzed. Although both species of cultural analysis tend to be decontextualizing, treating cultural works 'in their own terms' (or rather, trying to do so but failing), poststructural and postmodern critics view themselves as cultural creators in their own right while positivist critics view culture-as-culture and criticism-as-criticism. The former are self-aggrandizing, claiming a certain virtuosity; the latter, like positivists, ignore their own constitutional impact by supposing that studying cultural phenomena in no way constitutes a cultural contribution. This is similar to the way that positivist scientists believe that their analytical interventions in the inert world somehow change it, thus distorting science, viz. Heisenberg's principle of indeterminacy as well as other developments in the post-Newtonian philosophy of physics.

These seven assumptions ground a cultural empiricism that thinks it refrains from making cultural judgments. Although some of these assumptions can be found in other species of cultural studies, especially in the more disengaged ones, they are characteristic of the quantitative media studies and apolitical popular-culture studies that dominate cultural analysis in the US. It would be a serious mistake to overstate the US influence of the European-influenced cultural studies that I have discussed so far. Although they are important in the project of reconstructing Marxist and feminist cultural analysis, they are not as influential in mainstream cultural analysis as more positivist approaches that embrace the aforementioned seven assumptions about the relationship between criticism and society.

Taken together, these assumptions ground a version of cultural analysis that treats television, movies, music, art and trade fiction as surface phenomena in a well-integrated social system (see Hoppenstand and Browne, 1987, on Stephen King novels). In the parlance of Parsonians, these cultural works and practices help integrate the social system, providing both values and diversions for people otherwise preoccupied with the workaday grind. The notion that culture is entertainment dominates nearly all journalistic treatments of cultural phenomena. Indeed, cultural coverage and analysis have become staples in newspapers and on television. The lives and shows of illustrious culture heroes are busily dissected by pundits and consumed by members of the supposed leisure class. We identify with the Magic Johnsons and Chers in order to fill our own empty lives, an analysis pursued by Debord (1970) in his important work *The Society of the Spectacle*, a founding contribution to left-postmodernist cultural studies. At the same time, we also recognize that we are somehow deprived of the same *frissons* of excitement experienced by these stars living in the fast lane or in a fish-bowl. Our own lives seem comparatively impoverished by contrast – and not only in the obvious sense of our personal wealth.

Debord's dialectical analysis of the society of the spectacle is one of the best examples of a left-oriented cultural criticism that considers both ideological and political-economic factors (also see Inglis, 1990). It is very far afield from the Parsonianism that interprets popular culture as a healthy release from the rigors of work characterized by what Durkheim called *anomie* or normlessness. Where Durkheimians like Parsons contend that culture is a realm in which people develop collective consciousness or common values with which to integrate them into the body politic, Marxists like Debord argue that culture is a region of contestation in which people struggle over definitions of the good life as well as social justice. For Marx, of course, culture was ideology – practised deception about domination. It could be transformed through social and political practices that uncover the objective interests of elites in certain shared conceptions of the social world. One day, according to early Marx (1961), people would share a common species being, as he called it – a solidarity based not on mythologies about power but on valid perception of people's true interests in nonalienated activity.

Must Cultural Studies Make Judgments?
(Or: Can It Avoid Judgments?)

This raises the question about cultural judgment posed earlier in my discussion of the Frankfurt School's mandarinism (see Jay, 1984): should cultural critics make judgments about cultural works and practices from the outside, as it were? Can we develop criteria of cultural validity that enable us to evaluate works and practices as more truthful and worthier than others? Poststructuralists and post-modernists, like positivist cultural analysts, reject the Archimedeanism of the Marxist theory of culture as arbitrary and elitist. They suggest that people like Marcuse (1964) are in no position to decide which needs are 'false' and which 'true', as he appeared to do in his *One-Dimensional Man* (and as Horkheimer and Adorno do in their [1972] *Dialectic of Enlightenment*, in which they elaborate the culture-industry thesis). Before I discuss and defend Marcuse's false-needs thesis as a linchpin of a radical cultural studies, let me briefly address the general issue of cultural evaluation as it helps differentiate positivist/postmodern from non-positivist/poststructural versions of cultural studies.

Here postmodernism (e.g., Lyotard and Foucault) and poststructuralism (Derrida) stand opposed to each other. Lyotard and Foucault join positivists in arguing that cultural critics must not pass judgments on discursive practices outside of their own discourse/practice, in Foucault's terms. Lyotard's insistence on the relativity and incommensurability of discourse/practices grounds his attack on Marxism. This is fundamentally similar to the positivist notion that cultural criticism must not attempt to impress its own values and judgments on cultural works and practices, which instead must be appraised internally, in terms of their own meanings. Derrideans, though, disagree. They challenge positivist claims to value-freedom: they argue that all analysis is simultaneously criticism – all interpretations are interventions in the sense that they engage in selectivity and embody perspective. The art critic emphasizes aspects of a particular artist's oeuvre, bending it in the direction of his or her own critical interests. The movie critic focuses criticism on genres that are of most immediate interest. The book reviewer does not simply report on the whole text (whatever that might mean) but is enormously selective in what he or she thematizes in the way of critical discussion.

Poststructural cultural criticism diverges from postmodern cultural criticism in this sense: poststructuralists deny the very possibility of disinterested cultural commentary and criticism. They emphasize the commensurability of discourse/practices, if not their ultimate decidability. After all, although Derrida despaired of finding a transcendental language for adjudicating all disputes (contending that language is always imprisoned in its own aporias: Nietzsche's prison-house), he believed that people could read and write intertextually, across the great divide of textual difference. It is essential for Derridean deconstruction to attempt to retranslate discourse/practices in a way that brings their aporetic logic to the surface. By translating one discourse/practice into another, one could recognize the impossibility of lucidity that daunts every expressive act and yet at the same time show the iterability and flexibility of language in a way that builds bridges and starts dialogues. Derridean criticism gives the lie to ordinary-language phi-losophy, which relies on reductive notions of linguistic simplification to solve irreducibly complex metaphysical problems. Unfortunately, verbal pyrotechnics do not solve problems in their own right, nor do slogans – ideologies.

All sorts of critical postures are disqualified in light of this powerful Derri-dean deconstruction of the pretense of critical neutrality. No longer can positivist or postmodern critics pretend that cultural analysis simply *describes* cultural works and practices *in their own terms*. Instead, the language of criticism is unavoidably constitutional: it cannot fail to impose the values and constructs of the critic on the critical topic, in a sense changing it. That is why we know that we can only 'trust' cultural reviewers who share our sense of cultural judgment: when we read the movie reviewer in the local newspaper we know that we are reading a review of movies and not the movies themselves. This seems obvious. But it matters enormously for the ways in which we attach differential significances to critical judgments that, at some level, reflect the interest of the reviewer and not a transcendental disinterest resonating objectivity.

This is not to deny objectivity but to recognize that every subjectivity is already objective – if not the *same* objective. Subjects construct objects, one of the central lessons of poststructuralism as well as phenomenology. Reading is a form of writing. These insights can be radicalized where we empower subjectivity to take charge of its own political life, tracing pre-theoretical object constitution back to the constitutional field of everyday life that grounds overall political and social change (viz. both Piccone [1971] and Habermas [1984, 1987b]). Derrida's claim that reading constitutes writing need not be a capitulation to relativity/relativism; the fact that readers can read things differently is less important than is the fact that reading can rewrite writing, thus transforming the whole cultural and political fabric. Ultimately, positivist cultural studies is conservative for the same reason all positivism is conservative: in reducing cognition to presuppositionless representation it loses the opportunity to extend its own ineradicable constitutionality in a political direction. Value-freedom is a ruse concealing the constitution of value – including the value of epistemological *laissez faire*. Positivism protects the present world by appearing only to reflect it in the chilling lens of social ontology. The critique of positivism historicizes the world into the molten possibility of new directions and constellations.

By allowing a positivist cultural studies merely to report on episodic cultural developments, these developments are frozen into place, experienced by readers and writers as the indubitable facticity of alleged modernity. Let me offer some examples here. Television criticism assumes that television is both good and necessary; however much television critics may sometimes carp about the lack of 'quality' in broadcasting, they rarely interrogate a society beyond or without television. It is assumed that television is here to stay. As a result, television critics criticize shows, genres and trends as well as the personalities filling the dramatis personae. But they rarely trace television *qua* object back to the constitutional literary and editorial activities of the busy scribes who compose the scripts enacted on the screen. (The same is true of movie criticism, although movie criticism tends to proceed at a somewhat slower pace than television criticism, pausing to concentrate more on particular films and genres and thus having the opportunity to engage in the sort of deconstruction I am talking about. Unfortunately, judging by the prevailing level of reportage about film, this promise is rarely fulfilled.)

Positivist television criticism rarely interrogates the overall social role of television. Even more rarely does it deconstructively trace what is seen on the screen to the original literary and editorial constitution lying behind the glossy representations that conceal literary and editorial artifice. These so-called production values conceal busy literary artifice precisely in order to present television as a piece of nature. Television is part of the social geology of our world. And this

impression is reinforced by critics who concentrate on television's surface articulations, leaving intact the concealment of its authorially constituting practices –
the really interesting ways in which cultural meaning lies at the nether level of
every text.

As such, there is no avoiding cultural judgment if by that we mean an active
engagement by criticism with its critical object. Criticism deconstructs the
seamlessness of cultural texts and practices by raising its feverish authorship to
full view, laying bare the assumptions encoded in it about the world – goodness,
truth, justice and beauty. *To criticize is already to judge,* even if criticism is
formulated in apparently non-evaluative terms. Once we realize this, we become
much less chary about making overtly evaluative judgments. Poststructuralism
liberates us from the illusion of presuppositionless representation in the realm of
cultural studies. To describe a film or novel is already to engage in evaluation,
even if one's interpretive language is shorn of evaluative adjectives. Criticism is
encoded in interpretation where we recognize that reading rewrites writing, as
much in positivist criticism as in more self-consciously poststructural readings.

If judgments are unavoidable, then we on the left should not shy away from
them as if they are somehow illegitimate. A radical cultural studies must not
refrain from intruding its radicalism into all levels of its critical analyses; nothing
goes untouched by the constitutional gaze of the reader inasmuch as meaning is
impossible without readerly intervention in the sense of the text. Radicals under
sway of positivism are themselves infected by the positivism of the general
culture. Accordingly, they are led to believe that even they can describe objectively and appraise even-handedly without somehow engaging the text under
evaluation in overtly constitutional terms. The fact that every reading writes
should not be a cause for lament but an occasion of a renewed engagement with
cultural texts and practices that create an insidious kind of hegemony in the way
they present themselves as veritable pieces of nature, as obdurate as the inert
environment.

The momentum of Lyotard's postmodernism, a secret positivism, is nearly
irresistible at a time when Bell's (1960) end-of-ideology thesis is being recycled in
the post-Reagan era of Euro-American and Asian capitalism (now threatening to
spread to eastern Europe, where sadly people confuse the oxymorons of *democracy* and *capitalism*). Although cultural studies abounds, both in academic journals
and in the popular media, there seems to be a tendency for this outpouring of
cultural analysis to be somehow less political than the more politicized traditions
of Marxist, neo-Marxist and feminist criticism with which I am concerned here.
Even these traditions have become highly technical, losing sight of the political
engagement of the CCCS group, for example. This is not a simple matter of
requiring academic and intellectual cultural critics to go to the barricades; after
all, where *are* 'the barricades' today, at a time when the Berlin Wall has come
tumbling down and the left–right polarity is being renegotiated? Indeed, Adorno was hardly an activist, although his cultural criticism (e.g., his *Aesthetic
Theory*, 1984) reeked of the political in its thoroughgoing deconstruction of the
textual politics of cultural hegemony and his subsequent advocacy of modernist
opposition in the work of Kafka, Beckett and Schoenberg. The issue here is not
so much the extramural political activities of the critic but the ways in which
criticism addresses culture in a politically critical way, attempting to subvert the

subtle cultural equations of the good with goods. As Marcuse put it so well (1968), cultural criticism, treated as a form of cultural and political intervention itself, must break the hold of *affirmative culture*.

So this is the central issue, as it is for poststructuralists: cultural criticism has 'content' of its own that constitutes and reconstitutes the cultural field. As such, then, cultural judgment in its own right changes the cultural field when it is applied to its critical topics, objects and practices. Although radical book reviews and film criticism do not substitute for radical books and films, the line between criticism and its cultural object has blurred under the influence of poststructuralism, which interrogates all dualisms. *What counts as culture* has been revalued since Derrida. Criticism is both cultural creation and political resistance, something unheard of by more positivist critics for whom the divide between criticism and culture is as vast as the Grand Canyon.

Although positivist critics sometimes make personal judgments of their cultural objects – the thumbs-up or -down posture so typical of mass-market cultural criticism – these evaluations are somehow external to the very acts of cultural analysis, the concluding embellishments of the objectivist reviewer who has prepared the way by 'objectively' describing the cultural object or practice before offering a personal judgment of it. In this sense, the critic passes off criticism as the episodic, temperamental gesture of a person who has not really engaged deconstructively with the text or practice but who is paid to give advice to cultural consumers wary about being bamboozled in the marketplace. Although some positivist critics go far toward the sort of constitutional and reconstitutional analysis made possible by deconstruction, thus blurring the line between positivist and poststructural cultural criticisms themselves, these critics are the exceptions and not the rules. They tend to be found where they do not labor under heavy editorial constraints and where they have more than a few hundred words to spend on a review.

It would be instructive to do a systematic study of the constitutional nature of reviewing. Such a study would need to examine empirically the ways in which reviewers and cultural analysts deal with the fault line between their supposedly descriptive discussions and their 'personal' evaluations. Most positivist reviewing in the US and UK tends to force the evaluation section of the review into a kind of subtext whereby it embellishes the stronger, supposedly objective part of the review. And upon deconstructive analysis, this objective body of the review would be found to be not unalloyed description but full of evaluative nuances. In a way, then, even positivist criticism manages rhetorically to engage in strong reading by interweaving evaluation with supposedly objective analysis. Thus, the concluding thumbs-up or -down posture of the reviewer is almost superfluous, suggesting that all of what went before was sturdy analysis embellished by this concluding evaluative gesture that can be taken with a grain of salt.

Such an analysis of reviewers' discourse would also have to consider the political–economic context within which reviews take place. The culture industry feeds on aesthetic judgments that substitute for advertising pure and simple. Again, a rhetorical-textual analysis of cultural advertising reveals that the work's own self-praise is subtly intermingled with epigrammatic blurbs from ecstatic reviewers ('... the best thriller of the year ...'), creating an irresistible confection not to be missed by the savvy culture patron. Clearly, value is added to these advertisements where the reviewers whose praise is excerpted (and, sometimes, taken out of context) are well-known and write for periodicals of record. One can detect a dud where the reviewers whose epigrams decorate the work's advertising write for obscure regional and local publications, suggesting a telling topography (or what Jameson [1988] has called a cognitive map) of popular culture in terms of the concentric circles of critical influence radiating outward from the cultural epicenters of New York City, Los Angeles and London.

This analysis is not meant to demean the working critic. Culture critics do important work, especially where they debunk the claims made in the name of certain mainstream cultural works. They also do important work where they support more marginal and subversive projects, some of which occasionally fall through the cracks and emerge as powerful counter-hegemonic forces in their own right. The culture industry is full of stories about how luck, timing and a few good reviews from powerful patrons helped ensure the mainstream 'success' of obscure ventures that otherwise would have been doomed from the start. Spike Lee's first feature-length film, *She's Gotta Have It*, with its grainy production values (perhaps proof positive of his film's 'authenticity'), was extremely fortunate to receive enough critical praise and sufficient mainstream distribution to catch fire, paving the way for his development as a major 'alternative' movie maker. (One could also interrogate the effects of this mainstreaming on his own oeuvre and public posture where one examines his more recent films and his participation in the Nike advertising campaign for Air Jordan basketball shoes. I am not among those who view *Do the Right Thing* as a ghetto call to arms; that is a paranoid reading of the film. Yet Lee's profitable participation in the Nike campaign as Mars Blackman, his signature character, seriously imperils his claim to be politically avant-garde. But that is another story, more fully told elsewhere.)

The cultural criticism-of-criticism is important in its own right. An empirical examination of how Lee's first film was reviewed would help explain the fate of his emerging oeuvre. The culture industry is not monolithic, as Lee's example demonstrates. And certain feminist filmmakers are shepherded and nurtured by sympathetic critics who take the project of building a feminist culture seriously. Yet there is only so much in the way of critical and political intervention that reviewers can do within the confines of the media as they are presently structured. Editors overdetermine reviewers' prose, assigning them to review schlock mainstream movies and constraining their sponsorship of alternative movies and cultural perspectives. The capitalist/positivist journalistic format does not lend itself to deconstructive criticism, preventing the boundaries between objective and subjective analysis from being creatively blurred so that reading is encouraged to become strong writing. Editors, publishers and readers come to expect the quickie reviews that name the movie's big stars, recapitulate its plot and offer a summary judgment of its watchability. Indeed, many American newspapers now use audience surveys to determine viewers' own responses to major movies, sometimes comparing audience evaluations with those of reviewers. Based on these surveys, one can 'scientifically' determine one's chances of liking a given movie, thus helping one spend one's entertainment resources carefully. Major newspapers have developed culture sections that are thinly-veiled versions of *Consumer Reports* in this sense, further subordinating the role of criticism and critics in the process.

But no matter how much cultural criticism is banalized in these terms, criticism and evaluation are inevitable – perhaps the more so the more that reviewers conceal their own evaluations underneath the objectivist accoutrements of the episodic review. The pretense of value-freedom is belied by the evidence of current cultural criticism: either reviewers encode their own constitutionally critical perspectives within the gestural nuances of the body of their reviews or else reviewing is turned over to the practitioners of survey research, who examine audience responses and thus guide the cultural choices of consumers. The appearance of flip judgments ('... Rex Reed raves ...' or '... Siskel and Ebert give two thumbs-up ...') conceals the more powerful critical judgments that they make in the portions of their reviews devoted to objectivist analysis. This is true of news reportage and journalism as a whole (see Rachlin, 1988); even a cursory deconstructive reading of *Time* and *Newsweek* and a casual viewing of national network news reporting reveal that objectivist reporters imprint their own constitutional version of things by their use of adjectives, tone, expression and rhythm. By the end of the Reagan Presidency, and in Britain since the eroding hegemony of Thatcher, mainstream reporters have ill-concealed disdain for the competence and reasonableness of these national leaders. The reportage of Reagan underwent a sea change during the eight years of his Presidency: reporters initially enthralled by his charm came to view him as an imbecile barely able to function. One did not have to read editorials or study television to detect this shift. One could see and hear it in the smirking, carping tone of daily objectivist reports filed by the White House press corps. True loyalists were the exceptions; they stood out as strangely sentimental, as they did during the collapsing Nixon Presidency. Indeed, ABC star Diane Sawyer's only career liability is her devotion to Nixon while working as a ghost writer for him in post-Watergate San Clemente; even today she finds it difficult to resist defending him ('the man') against all challenges. Sawyer's handlers put their own spin-control on this nostalgia by calling it a lapse of sentimentality on her part, a symptom of true Southern gentility.

The Problem of False Needs

The unavoidability of cultural judgment, disclosed by poststructuralism, leads either to complacency with regard to defending one's validity claims against external challenges or to a self-conscious defense of a theory of needs that helps explain why people choose to consume culture that contradicts their own objective interests. In the first case, one might conclude that the constitutionality of every reading means that every reading is as good as every other and every cultural work and practice equally worthy. Although one might have a preference for one's own reading, the indeterminacy and undecidability of readings make it fruitless to elaborate an objective theory of needs that grounds one's criticism in certain enduring standards. This is conventionally termed *relativism*, although the relativity/relativism that emerges from poststructuralism and postmodernism is decidedly different from a more self-conscious ethical relativism. Derrida and Lyotard are not explicitly deciding all values equivalent but saying instead that such decisions are impossible. One cannot be certain that one's values are superior to those of others, given the incommensurability of language games and value systems. This is how poststructural and postmodern relativity/

relativism differs from the ethical relativism inspired by a non-Eurocentric anthropology (which, confusingly, has modern roots in poststructuralism; e.g., see Marcus and Fischer, 1986).

Poststructural relativists show the undecidability of values and truth claims by demonstrating that the ground of judgment 'outside' the text proper (e.g., subtext) is not really outside at all but exists in tension with the text in an undecidably dialectical relationship. Derrida challenges the indubitability of truth claims, although his position does not strictly rule out truth. He says rather that truth is itself encoded in its own prison-house of common usages and deeper assumptions, giving it a con-text inseparable from its text proper. Applied to the realm of cultural studies, this relativity/relativism issues in a posture that ironically insists on its own evaluativeness (much as I argued in the preceding section) but, at the same time, insists that evaluations are incommensurable because they are conducted in self-referential languages which frustrate external translation and hence adjudication.

This relativity/relativism is countered by a more Archimedean posture that insists not only on the inevitability of cultural judgments (e.g., in the movie reviews I discussed above, where nuance – and thus evaluation – is omnipresent) but on the priority of certain judgments over others. Even to raise this issue in a poststructural and postmodern context is to court ridicule; by now, the Archimedeanism of Platonists and Marxists alike has been widely discredited in the frenzy of the new relativity/relativism (which we Marxists interpret as yet another formulation of liberalism). Even French feminist theorists, as I discussed in Chapter 7, have incorporated poststructural principles of textual incorrigibility into their own critical practices, making it difficult for them to devalue sexist literature effectively given their predilection for technical methodological obscurantism and relativism.

To be a Marxist and feminist means to insist on the priority of one's own truth claims, especially when faced with false consciousness. For the left, consciousness is false not only because it has been deceived by the deceptions of ideology and hegemony but because it has not been allowed to determine its own content, instead being filled from the outside. Marcuse's (1964) classic treatise on false consciousness, *One-Dimensional Man*, is controversial for the way in which he seems to arrogate to himself the ability to decide which needs are true and which are false. This is read to imply an untoward vanguardism and elitism on his part, risking all of the authoritarian consequences that have traditionally followed from these judgments. One wants to avoid these untoward consequences without renouncing the ability to make judgments about the substance of cultural expressions that contradict the best interests of their consumers.

As a way of building the case that one can find a middle way between relativity/relativism, on the one hand, and Archimedeanism, on the other, let me reconstruct Marcuse's theory of false needs, which, in many respects, resembles Horkheimer and Adorno's culture-industry thesis. His theory has been read erroneously by people opposed to the leftist project as well as by more nuanced readers who reject his claim to have found a ground for making universal truth claims about human needs. The current poststructuralisms and postmodernisms define themselves in terms of their difference from Marxism in the sense that they reject the idea that one can make absolute cultural judgments without reference to the con-texts of difference within which such judgments arise.

Marcuse says this: in advanced capitalism, people lose the ability to think critically about values, discourses, practices and commodities. The universe of discourse is so narrowed by dominant interests that people lose a critical perspective from which to gain distance from conventional wisdom about the 'goods' life. Of course, he points out that it is in the interest of capitalist domination for people not to recognize fundamental alternatives to business-as-usual. People led to define their happiness in terms of consumption tend to stimulate production as well as to lock themselves into system-serving conformity, refusing to challenge the hegemonizing inertia of the quotidian. Captive of false needs, people act against their own true interests in liberation. They run in place on the treadmill of capitalist consumption and conformity.

Marcuse argues that 'one-dimensional' thinking is, in Gramsci's (1971) terms, hegemonic in the sense that people do not learn to think beyond the sheer present – the prevailing patterns of social, economic and personal arrangements that they experience as second nature, as intractable as the tides. Where false consciousness in Marx's era took the form of substantively false textual claims about the rationality of reality (e.g., religion and bourgeois economic theory), today false consciousness is inchoate, written and read in the seemingly brute facticity of a bourgeois everyday life that people experience as unchangeable. Put differently, human experience today is characterized by the impossibility of transcendence, of social change. Since it seems impossible to 'fight city hall' – to change dominant social and economic relationships – people are induced to pursue happiness in the creature comforts and symbolic attainments defined as relevant by the prevailing order. Their conformity is thus ensured from the inside. People are, in Marcuse's (1955) terms, 'surplus repressed'; that is, they constrain themselves beyond what they would need to do in order to live peaceably in an advanced industrial order not premised on profit but rather on the global satisfaction of basic human and emotional needs.

Needs are false not simply because they have a deleterious content – violent television shows, movies that degrade women, cars that pollute the environment and lead to highway fatalities, etc. Although these things are bad in themselves, they represent consumer choices that have in effect been made *for* people, given the preponderant influences of advertising, socialization and peer-group pressure. The good life is defined in terms of present levels and styles of attainability, not in terms of qualitatively different criteria of maximal social justice as well as a benign relationship to nature. As I noted earlier in this book, *needs are false because they are imposed from the outside*. People are duped into consuming cultural commodities that both serve profit and divert attention from the bigger picture – our conformist obedience only reinforcing social and economic inequality.

Marcuse treats culture as a profitable diversion, and false consciousness as the attitude in which people conduct their everyday lives oblivious to the possibility of substantive social change. One-dimensional thinking is the foreclosing of historical imagination such that the future appears only to be a quantitative extrapolation of the present – *more*. These attitudes and behaviors reproduce the system, giving it additional forward momentum. It is incredibly difficult to formulate alternatives to the system because language itself has been robbed of transcendental, critical meaning. The universe of discourse has been nearly closed, Marcuse says, making resistance extremely difficult (he calls this resistance the Great Refusal, stressing the heroic, uphill character of any opposition that could make a significant difference to overall social change).

Not only are material needs false, according to him. The language and culture have been taken over by conformist imperatives. It is difficult to imagine a different society in ways that do not trade heavily on the present social arrangements. Hence hegemony is rationalized in everyday discourse because language is divested of critical meaning – the Derridean ability to produce difference. Social criticism amounts to ameliorating social reforms, piling one small adjustment on top of another, thus ironically improving the functioning of the larger system. In this context, social and cultural criticism becomes desperate, indefatigably resisting its own cooptation by a system that turns language upside down. An example: during the Vietnam War, the US military talked about the strategy of 'pacification', referring to the way whole villages and people were destroyed in order to make Vietnam safe for democracy. Another: the foodstore chain 7-Eleven promises 'freedom' to its customers, confusing the aspirations of democratic political theory with the promise of eating a microwaved hot dog and drinking a huge beverage.

In this context, public discourse falls by the wayside. Social critics have to shout loudly to make themselves heard, purposely exaggerating their social criticism in order to resist the cooptation and integration of their language. Marcuse (Marcuse *et al.*, 1965) talks about how the system develops 'repressive tolerance', pretending to accommodate dissenting voices but really doing so only in order to coopt them. Today, we in the west are claiming a variety of important oppositional movements in eastern Europe as our own, pretending that the assault on neo-Stalinism and bureaucratic socialism amount to ringing endorsements of capitalism. Thus, false needs are conveyed through public language, leading people to confuse the meaning of words that subsequently lose their ability to retain intellectual and critical autonomy.

Cultural studies in its more radical formulations is tantamount to Marcuse's Great Refusal. Students of cultural studies engage in the critique of the ideology and discourse of false needs, pointing to ways in which cultural works and practices enslave us to pre-given meanings that impose themselves on us thoughtlessly. For example, by watching an endless series of moronic television shows depicting regular people in various domestic and work situations, we come to believe that we are actors in sitcoms and dramas. We identify with the characters and imagine ourselves to be leading satisfying, melodramatic lives. We learn values from *The Cosby Show* and *LA Law* – definitions of the good life as well as of right and wrong. We are also led to believe that the Cosbys and the ensemble of actors on *LA Law* represent average citizens; we suppose that these shows reflect reality accurately, especially in the ways in which they resolve conflicts and epitomize morality.

Cultural studies lays bare the deceptions encoded in these dominant cultural artifacts. It criticizes the needs these cultural practices purvey through the guileful representations of a frozen second nature – reality as it 'must' be – and instead suggests alternative formulations of both human needs and social reality. For example, the unlikely example of the Cosby family can be readily deconstructed by examining the near-absence of affluent black families in which both parents are professionals. This deconstruction would also focus on the unreality of a family in which the mother is virtually never seen to be at work outside the household and in which no one is depicted doing housework or childcare.

In this respect, by demonstrating people's unfreedom to them – their inculcation by aspects of the dominant ideology, in Althusserian terms – critical theorists presume to be able to distinguish between true and false consciousness, true and false human needs. If one has trouble with this very differentiation, rejecting it for its absolutism, then one will certainly adopt something like the relativity/relativism stance of Lyotard, other postmodernists and all pluralist liberals. If, on the other hand, such a distinction makes sense, then one can follow through on the critical implications of that distinction for social theory and political practice, deconstructing the ideological claim that the cultural marketplace is like every other market in the sense that people are only being given what they want. Critical theorists believe that people 'want' what they are led to want, and that they can learn to want differently. Marcuse does not impose a definitive set of true needs from above but simply argues for social contexts in which people are free to make these choices for themselves.

The typical non-Marxist sociologist might respond that all wants are learned, making this utopian criterion of an influence-free world simply unattainable. But Marcuse as a Marxist would argue that the most basic human need is self-determination, elaborated in the variety of choices people make about how they live their lives. Marx (1961) in his early writings said that people were beings of labor, of praxis, endlessly creating themselves in the ways they externalize themselves in the world. This historicized Hegel's own concept of self-externalization, allowing for the possibility of the alienation of these self-externalizations under certain conditions of domination. Marx said that people were most human where they realize themselves in their tasks. This is possible where their tasks, and the products of their tasks, are owned and controlled by them, enabling them to reap the full value of their labor.

To be sure, this notion of a dominationless society is a utopian concept, the demonstration of which rests in the future, as well as in the struggle it takes to get there. In this respect, Marcuse and the other Frankfurt theorists are only building on Marx where they argue that people can make free choices about their needs once they are liberated from the constraints of domination, which in late capitalism are both internally and externally imposed. Where Marx talked about false consciousness as a factor in domination, Marcuse adds that false consciousness in the form of false needs is as much self-generated as imposed from without. False needs are politically efficacious precisely because they do not require cultural commissars to enforce them. Instead, people stroll about freely in the well-stocked supermarkets of desire so abundant in late capitalism (and now opening for business in erstwhile state-socialist countries, thus bringing state capitalism into the late twentieth century).

As Foucault (1977) similarly argues, discipline in modern society comes as much from within as from without. His example of Bentham's Panopticon is telling: prisoners are kept in line *by themselves* where they fear that they are continually being watched by the all-seeing eye of centralized surveillance. Similarly, the iron cage of Weber's capitalism is gilded; people experience their servitude to false needs as pleasant and meaningful, giving them a sense of productive purpose. It is virtually impossible to grow up in a capitalist society and not yearn for the goods life, thus diminishing the chances that people will become social critics and rebels. False needs are the ultimate form of cooptation in the sense that their falsehood is not experienced as such simply because they are never tested: people are not so much presented with falsifiable evidence of the superiority of the commodity society as they are subtly socialized to live effect-ively and happily in the malls of this society. Of course, this is literally untrue: false needs are a text, albeit a text (as I have argued, Agger, 1989a) that leaks out of its covers into the everyday lifeworld itself, making it that much more difficult even to discern, let alone validate or falsify, these claims as discrete propositions. No one can remember where he or she learned that freedom is bestowed by credit cards, although this is indispensable knowledge in late capitalism. Instead, credit buying appears to be a fact of life, an outcome of unalterable social nature.

A Marcusean program of cultural studies challenges this appearance of the rationality of reality, protesting its existence as second nature somehow outside of history. Critical theory historicizes the world, opening it to the possibility of being seen and lived differently. In the Frankfurt School's sense, the political function of critique is to disrupt the illusions of harmony and rationality fostered from the ground up as well as from the top down in bourgeois society. It is simply false to suppose that a ruling elite brutally imposes falsehoods on the masses, as Marx and Engels (1947) implied in *The German Ideology*. That was truer then than now, when ideology is a lived practice reproduced a billion times a day in the quotidian endeavors of people who fill shopping malls and crowd theaters in order to receive their doses of simulations as well as stimulation through which they identify themselves as favored participants in social life.

Today ideology is linked subliminally with pleasure, as Marcuse (1955) carefully outlined in *Eros and Civilization*, his Freudian reading of Marxism (see Agger, 1991a, Ch. 7). His 1955 book prepares the way for *One-Dimensional Man*, which followed almost ten years later. Through his adaptation of psychoanalytic theory to the structural principles of critical theory Marcuse explains the psychoerotic interest of people in what Baudrillard calls simulations – the various imageries and representations through which people funnel their unsated desires. Ideology is libidinalized as well as detextualized in late capitalism. People not only consume Pepsi (the beverage) but also its simulations presented in advertis-ing, including the drink's star-studded advertising for itself. People are gratified not only to drink Pepsi; they derive pleasure from acquiring jazzy cans of Pepsi-the-text and Pepsi-the-simulation – the media representations of Pepsi as Idea.

Commodities are turned into texts through this process of simulation. Yet the text of Pepsi is not the same sort of book as the Bible or *Capital*, which can be taken away and perused slowly, requiring arduous hermeneutic work both to derive meaning and signal devotion. Like all simulations, Pepsi (as a text) is read quickly, almost instantaneously. It pulsates from the television screens that serve as its dominant medium of representation, urging people to break out of their humdrum lives and flock to buy Pepsi, which promises not only to sate their thirst but to rejuvenate their social being. People live their commodities (as simulations) in the same sense that Althusser (1970), in his own Freudianism, suggests that ideology is lived practice. People do not pause carefully to decon-struct the validity claims of Pepsi advertising but they read – or drink! – the text of Pepsi quickly, uncritically. In this sense, it is difficult to talk of false needs as if these needs are deliberately inculcated by the falsifying texts of advertising (although that is certainly a factor in the simulation of Pepsi as a way of life). Rather, the needs are read off the screens of power (Luke, 1989) in such a way that they are unmediated by reflective thought and judgment. Where earlier forms of ideology had to be worked over interpretively in order for them to be acquired and actualized, needs in fast capitalism are short-circuited in such a way that they miss this process of mediation: they are printed on the screens and texts of power and thus imprinted as second nature on the oblivious subjects of late capitalism. Needs become wants in the sense that they are experienced almost as erotic impulses, not as the reflective constructions and mediations they were in an earlier stage of capitalism. The mass mediation of reality defuses critical mediation.

Against this backdrop, the Marcusean postulate of false needs appears less elitist, as does his version of ideology critique. He is not simply saying that people are taught the wrong values (although he should say that, too – values representing aggression, competition, acquisition) but rather that the process of valuing, wanting and needing has become almost primordial in a society of simulations: people do not arrive reflectively at their needs for commodities but are imprinted with these needs through the insidiously hegemonic quotidian, which conceals its own hortatory textuality. This makes it all the more difficult to challenge these patterns of needs by external critiques (see Leiss, 1976). Virtually no critique or critic can remain outside the system of reification, simulations, jargon and encoding because *there are no outsides – no worlds apart in late capitalism.* Even critique is swallowed harmlessly, notably in the form of academized writing comprehensible to narrow disciplinary specialists but not to the general public (see Agger, 1990; Brodkey, 1987; Jacoby, 1987 for critiques of academic writing as social practice).

One can certainly indict critics for hastening, even endorsing, their own obscurantist academization. Too many of us have earned our intellectual spurs through processes of acculturation somehow equating the turgidity of writing with profundity – more aptly, with tenurability. Critical theory specializes itself in order to compete in the established academic marketplace, as Habermas (1984) unironically noted in the preface to his own dense Volume One of *The Theory of Communicative Action,* which represents recent critical theory's self-jargonization at its most extravagant. Habermas laments the estrangement of Adorno's and Horkheimer's work from the mainstream of academic legitimacy when they were alive. But the price of institutional legitimation is the loss of public voice and hence political relevance. Habermas' own architectonic Parsonianization of critical theory only repeats Parsons' own obscurantism (see Mills, 1959), perhaps affording critical theory greater academic legitimacy but further depriving it of critical distance from the engulfing world.

But Habermas is no more to blame than are most other critical theorists, poststructuralists, postmodernists and feminist theorists. We have all contributed to the decline of our own discourse at a time when the scope of public discussion shrinks, thus further insulating elites from grassroots challenges. In this situation, it is no wonder that we are all programmed by simulations that flow electronically and textually out of cultural points of production in Madison Avenue and Hollywood. It is incredibly difficult to challenge these detextualized simulations, and the lives they script for us, because they are deauthorized and hence cannot be readily read as the political recommendations they really are. It is precisely the task of a radicalized deconstruction to authorize these simulations so that we can contest their usurpation of meaning by forcing them to come clean about their own deliberate ontological choices.

The Frankfurt critics, including Habermas, never arrived at a sufficiently self-conscious discourse theory to be able to unpack these detextualized codes of power. The theory of the culture industry remains incomplete without deconstructive strategies of textual subversion (e.g., a critical theory of advertising; see Harms and Kellner, 1991). In this sense, poststructuralism can play a vital role in the further development of critical theory. By the same token, though, poststructuralism fails to function effectively as critical social theory if it neglects cultural judgments with which to guide its own deconstructive activities. Without a notion that human needs and wants are produced and reproduced through mass culture, and without an accompanying regulative principle of autonomous need formation (such as early Marx's), deconstruction peters out into its own empty methodologism, as I further argue in Chapter 9. Cultural studies is poised on the brink of the political: it can function as the ideology-critical arm of a broadened critical theory, as I urge, or it can descend to the same sociologism and methodologism that have hampered the positivist sociology of culture as well as an apolitical version of deconstruction. The choice is ours – we who take culture seriously as a factor in domination and as a potential liberatory medium.

Toward a Non-Archimedean Cultural Criticism

This discussion only begins to address the dilemma of a politicized yet non-Archimedean cultural criticism. It is tempting to purvey a cultural studies that knows all the answers, prescribing values in the same way that the culture industry subliminalizes values through its nearly irresistible processes of simulation. This temptation must be resisted lest a radical cultural studies exhibit the same mandarinism that delegitimates the original Frankfurt critics' indictments of mass culture. At its best, a radical cultural studies can offer ways of helping people resist the entrapments of what passes for ideology today, notably the detextualized discourses imposing themselves on us without our own mediation of them. This cultural studies can help us detect and deconstruct claims about rationality that the world makes on its own behalf. Where these claims are formulated in falsifiable empirical statements (e.g., capitalist economic theory), they can be resisted effectively through counterfactual claims. But where these ideologizing claims are not made in discourse but rather encoded in presentations and representations (simulations), then it is much more difficult to decode cultural works and practices for the ontologies they silently recommend.

Archimedeanism is the posture of indubitability about values posited from outside of history. Platonism is the most enduring example of this stance, postulating timeless Ideas with which to orient rational practice. Marxism has been accused (e.g., Lyotard, 1984) of the same thing, fortifying an indictment of its political authoritarianism. Marx said that people need to be unencumbered by the constraints of social and economic domination in order for them to realize their true essence as creatures of self-creative praxis, a Greek concept retained by Hegel and Marx. People are what they make themselves in the way of their creative and productive externalizations in nature. Under conditions of domination, their externalizations (e.g., human labor) take on forbidding lives of their own (what Marx called alienation, Lukács reification and the Frankfurt theorists domination). Freedom lies in recouping these externalizations, including cultural products and practices, thus reversing the direction of their alienation. In this way, people will be in charge of social life and not captives of it.

For Marx, this was to happen through workers' ownership and control of the production process. Feminists correctly add that this must happen in the realm of reproductive work, suggesting a broadening of Marxism to include the ostensibly apolitical realm of housework, childcare and sexuality. Following Frankfurt cultural theory, this must also happen in the realm of cultural production and consumption, decommodifying cultural products and practices in the same way that all human labor will be decommodified. Seen in this way, a radical cultural studies inspired by both Marx and the Frankfurt School does not prescribe timeless cultural Ideas (e.g., elevating modernism over postmodernism or premodernism, certain types of classical music over rock-and-roll, European culture over non-occidental culture). Instead, a radicalized cultural studies advocates the abolition of needs imposed and self-imposed through the circuitries of cultural commodification. These needs today involve the enhancement of consumption and conformity, what Foucault (1977; see O'Neill, 1986) called discipline. True needs involve the liberation of cultural choice, reflecting a real heterogeneity of temperaments and styles. As early Marx said, the human essence is marked by a diversity of expressions and externalizations. In this sense, then, true cultural needs would involve unfettered self-expression as well as substantive political–economic autonomy.

It may seem that I am trying to have my cake and eat it, too, where I suggest that the falsehood of certain empirical human needs should be the criterion of cultural judgments. Where culture enslaves, it is to be deemed false. Where culture empowers us to create it in our own diverse ways, it is true. At least, this prevents me from having to offer a definitive list of cultural products and practices somehow worthier than other possible products and practices. The falsehood of needs is to be judged by Marcuseans less with reference to the expressive content of cultural products and practices than with reference to the con-texts in which these contents are imposed on people. Today, this happens so automatically that people are actually seen to have chosen them in a deliberate way.

Cultural studies debunks the rational-choice model of cultural consumption by showing that people are not in fact free to make these choices. This deconstruction belongs to the overall leftist attempt to demystify the supposed rationality of the marketplace as a historical ruse: people have never been free to enter and exit the marketplace under capitalism when they have only their labor power to sell in exchange for wages. The myth of cultural autonomy is part and parcel of liberalism, as well as of its latest articulation in postmodernism. People are not free to choose because we are programmed by simulations that have been detextualized, dispersed into the sense and sentience of an unreflected everyday life so that they cannot be evaluated on their own merits. It is nearly impossible to escape the present universe of discourse in order to think and speak in different ways that evade the overdetermined meanings imposed on us by the language games of cultural commodification. Our experience is deeply infiltrated by the rhetoric and content of cultural capitalism, so much so that even to conceive of alternatives trades on these deforming meanings. Marcuse asks how people can speak the truth in a society in which words like *truth* have been mangled, indeed applied to their very opposites. His answer is that we have to invent a language that drinks deeply of radical otherness, portraying a believable, attainable social order not beholden to capitalist principles of domination and the deformation of meaning. This is easier said than done: even criticism has been defanged in an era when it is almost impossible for intellectuals to survive outside the university (see Jacoby, 1987).

Clearly, Marcuse's solution is fraught with ambiguity. By calling for a Great Refusal, Marcuse recognizes that individual heroism will be Pyrrhic. At the same time, people must refuse, even if these local refusals do not constitute a metaphysically inflated Great Refusal. What people should do depends in large measure on the nature of their own lifeworlds. Intellectuals can certainly engage in a variety of ideology-critical activities that together lay bare the dominant discourse as a dangerously self-enclosing one. Repressive tolerance must not be tolerated, yet this must be achieved without inviting Stalinist intolerance. Cultural studies is a project for people who denounce the culture industry yet recognize that liberation movements must not avoid the lifeworlds of people who have been heavily saturated by invisible ideology. As Adorno (1973b) indicated in *Negative Dialectics*, 'Dialectics is the self-consciousness of the objective context of delusion; it does not mean to have escaped from that context. Its objective goal is to break out of the context from within' (p. 406).

Cultural studies constitutes the Great Refusal today – better, the numerous refusals that sometimes congeal into what Habermas (1981b) has called 'new social movements'. Cultural criticism helps foster difference as well as defiance, showing the 'objective context of delusion' in late capitalism. Cultural studies is dialectical in Adorno's sense because it recognizes that we cannot assume that we possess an unequivocal, untainted language not already inflected by the dominant contexts of cultural meaning deforming most attempts to pierce mythologies somehow purporting to make the real both reasonable and rational. It appears that only fools would attempt to reverse the evolutionary direction of history, uncoupling capitalism and progress. But modernity does not exhaust historical possibility any more than does postmodernity – the eternal present of today. History is essentially discontinuous; indeed, as Foucault told us, history is made by historians, who recoup it after the fact. Until history is written the past remains an indeterminate flow and flux of contingent activities that comprise the labors of the world's many. It is possible for history to be written differently, with a different denouement.

That is the proper task of cultural studies, which suggests the possibility of different modes of experience and existence not constrained by the self-disciplining tendencies of the culture industry. But there are different versions of cultural studies, some more political than others. I advocate a cultural studies that helps demystify the experience of postmodernity and thus contributes to the deconstruction of the postmodern, hence fulfilling the project of modernity. Other analysts of culture view cultural studies as a self-referential vocabulary that occupies academics who engage in never-ending cultural readings, surrounded as we are by an explosion of possible textual sources and topics. Clearly, cultural studies has split apart into different political articulations. In my next chapter, I explore the more affirmative tendencies of cultural studies by examining its cultic character, notably its academization. In my final chapter, I argue for a more politically invested version of cultural studies that inserts itself directly into everyday life as a mode of resistance.

Chapter 9

Deprogramming the Cult of Cultural Studies

Cultural Studies as Affirmative/Academic Culture

In the preceding chapter, I discussed some of the assumptions of positivist cultural sociology, which I raised in counterpoint to the non-positivist approaches to cultural studies discussed in the body of this book. Although I favor a variety of these non-positivist approaches, there is a real tendency for these approaches to become as ritualized and methodologized as the positivist approaches to which they are opposed. Unfortunately, cultural studies has tended to become a cult – an endlessly self-reproducing series of ungrounded readings not anchored in the framework of an overarching social theory and political practice. In this sense, cultural studies has lost the promise of its origins in the engagement of the Marxist sociology of culture. This is not universally true; indeed, my final chapter is devoted to a discussion of more political versions of cultural studies that firmly implant themselves in the political process. I am pointing to tendencies here, not inert realities. It is precisely because I want to further the project of cultural studies that I draw attention to certain regressive features within it that defeat its political purposes.

Any schematic overview like this necessarily oversimplifies. Having to paint with a broad brush risks missing nuanced differences. But not to generalize sufficiently would mire this account of cultural studies in the very particularism that causes it to become sheer technical method, devoid of theoretical and political connections. This is a major issue when we consider the gathering momentum of poststructural and postmodern approaches to cultural studies as they are positioning themselves as significant alternatives to the positivist cultural studies dominating the field in American and British popular-culture analysis. In a sense, then, I am arguing that cultural studies should return to its more political roots in the work of the Frankfurt School, the Birmingham group and some feminist cultural critics, especially those who do not drink deeply of a fatefully depoliticizing poststructuralism.

When cultural studies loses its political valence it becomes as affirmative as the affirmative culture targeted by Marcuse (1968, pp. 88–133) as the ruination of critique. The main sources of this regression on the part of cultural studies people are the academization and methodologization of cultural studies. As cultural studies becomes a specialty and even a discipline, with its conferences, journals, superstars and lingo, it degenerates into a method that can be used willy-nilly, regardless of the historical and political contexts within which cultural topics arise. Cultural studies becomes affirmatively academic where cultural studies is claimed by scholars as a distinctive body of knowledge and method that somehow subsists either within or beyond the established disciplines. This effort to academize cultural studies by giving it both an institutional housing in the university and a generally applicable critical method dooms cultural studies to the same political obscurity experienced by the mainstream academic disciplines. The effort to legitimize cultural studies as a defensible academic pursuit robs it of exactly the contextual and methodical dexterity that it needs in order to remain engaged politically.

The same tendencies threaten critical theory and feminist theory. Housing them in the university obligates them to develop a protocol of technical procedures that are fetishized for their own sake. Disciplined academics engage in self-referential discussions that legitimize their common enterprise rather than solve real empirical and political problems. I am not denying that such self-professionalization is sometimes necessary in a hostile intellectual world, where traditionalists relentlessly obstruct these interdisciplinary and counterdisciplinary endeavors. But the peril of intellectual professionalization is self-isolation, advanced by people who view their own intellectual identities in terms of the variously rising and falling fortunes of their own disciplines. This is especially the case in new disciplines that need to scramble in order to develop a sufficiently differentiated institutional posture. In the case of cultural studies, its proponents feel the need to organize themselves into an academic subculture which is both separate from and connected to the main academic disciplines. This need is objective: not to develop the intellectual and institutional legitimacy of one's topic and method spells obscurity, even unemployment.

I am not arguing against academization per se. Indeed, the academization of theory has given me and my cohorts livelihoods. I am not pretending to be made of better or purer stuff. But there is a price to be paid for academization, especially in the case of cultural studies, which, after all, addresses mass culture and not only the mandarin cultural traditions canonized in the interpretive disciplines like English and comparative literature. This price is isolation from the venues in which the most compelling and politically relevant examples of popular culture were given birth. This is where a non–positivist cultural studies tends to become as affirmative as the positivist sociology of culture from which it intends to break, no longer interrogating cultural works and practices for their hegemonic or counter-hegemonic potential but simply addressing them as almost incidental to the work at hand. In other words, the development of cultural studies threatens to justify a cultural studies for its own sake – *l'art pour l'art*. This is what I mean by the affirmative/academic tendencies of cultural studies as they are presently constituted.

An obsessively self-referential and methodological cultural studies forgets that it exists for the sake of analysis and critique, not for its own sake. It is abundantly clear that the hyperspecialization of literary theory under the rubric of poststructuralism has tended to place much more emphasis on theoretical developments than on the interpretive work that can be done using these new-fangled literary theories (see Newman, 1985). I am not arguing against this theoretical recrudescence; without it, we would still not understand how to read texts against themselves, as deconstructors capably do. But it is more than a little ironic that poststructural literary theories neglect their own literariness where they lose sight of their difference from the works they supposedly aim to interrogate. Although the boundary between theory and literature must be deconstructed to show that theory is a kind of literature and literature a kind of theory, poststructural literary theorists tend to efface this boundary altogether in the interest of aggrandizing their own intellectual efforts. This is a subtle imperialism that neglects the difference between theory and literature, utterly substituting the former for the latter and thus losing any practical con-text within which literary theory could do useful work in deconstructing the theory/literature duality as well as literary texts themselves for their imbedded meta-theoretical assumptions about the nature of class, gender, race and all the rest.

This theoretical self-aggrandizement depoliticizes theory. The Derrideans, especially Americans like Paul de Man who cluster around the Yale School, understand themselves to be political in their formidable challenge to dominant literary methodologies. But this is only literary politics, academic infighting – not the politics of ideological contestation. The Yale critics forsake politics where they obscure the difference between academic criticism and cultural works and practices available to be criticized. Although literary theory is literary in its authorial nature, it is not all literature. Derrideans too often forget this, instead standing in for literature where literature drops out of sight. In one sense, this empowers criticism to be more than mere value-free description or morally elevating acculturation (viz. Leavis-era *Scrutiny* criticism, the exemplar of canonical literary criticism in the Anglo-American world). In another sense, this obscures the non-identity of criticism and literature in a way that inflates criticism to the point of narcissistic self-absorption. The busy Derrideans in English and comparative literature departments are like children at Christmas, so enthralled with their new toys that they lose sight of the world beyond play, toys and holidays – and thus they quickly lose interest in the new toy once its aura has been degraded, the holiday over. How long will the journal *Postmodern Culture* 'printed' only on computer disk and transmitted via electronic mail subsist? Or is it an example of a democratic literary production and reception process – postmodernism at its best?

In spite of the regressive tendencies of a literary postmodernism, though, a political deconstruction (e.g., Ryan, 1982; Agger, 1989a) is the single most important contribution to the rejuvenation of Marxist and feminist theory since the Frankfurt School and de Beauvoir (1953). The critique of ideology developed in nineteenth-century slow capitalism makes little sense in late twentieth-century fast capitalism, when the boundaries between texts and material things fade to the point of virtual identity. Deconstruction helps us find, decode and then rewrite ideology that increasingly takes the form of Baudrillard's simulations and not the straightforward texts of religion and bourgeois economic theory readily debunked by Marx. For his part, Marx did not need a deconstructive methodology because his debunking of the overtly ideological texts of religion and economics could take place in an unironic way: Marx could simply show the falsehood of theological and political-economic propositions with reference to the empirical world. The absence of God and the inequity of the labor contract could be demonstrated through books like *The Holy Family* and *Capital*. This is not to say that Marx did not deconstruct these ideological texts, and the material practices underlying them. Marx was a deconstructor *avant la lettre*, laying bare the aporias of capitalist ideology by showing the self-undoing momentum of their contradictions. Yet Marx did not theorize the nature of his criticism, a point made convincingly by Habermas (1971) in *Knowlege and Human Interests*, the pivot around which Habermas' later (1984, 1987b) reconstruction of historical materialism turns.

Whether, as Habermas claims, Marx needed to reflect on his own critical method of reading and demystifying ideological texts, *we do*. We need to theorize reading in order to read politically, undoing texts' stance of value-freedom. This is especially urgent when old-fashioned books are rapidly becoming obsolete under pressure of technological developments in publishing and reception like desk-top publishing and microcomputers. This has been the direction of my own work, from *Socio(onto)logy* (1989c) and *Fast Capitalism* (1989a) to *Reading Science* (1989b) and *The Decline of Discourse* (1990). I have tried to develop a notion of textual politics that suggests a postmodern feminist critical theory capable of engaging deconstructively with the new texts of ideology that script obedience in ways simply unforeseen by Marx.

I view cultural studies as the most coherent programmatic expression of this version of critical theory, providing a focused ideology critique at a time when it is hard to distinguish between ideologizing texts *per se* and the material practices with which they are inextricably intertwined and from which they are thus nearly indistinguishable as simulations. Cultural studies in its best sense reads the politics into and out of discourse/practices in a way that raises imbedded ontological and political validity claims to clear view, both contesting these claims and proposing new ones. This version of radical cultural studies not only theorizes the culture industry as literary political economy but intervenes in culture directly, using deconstructive insight about the relative indistinguishability of criticism and culture to best political advantage.

Cultural studies is its own worst enemy where it allows its own sharp textual-political insights that dehierarchize the reading-writing relationship, and thus model dehierarchizing on all sorts of socio-sexual and political levels, to become ritualistic interpretive codes somehow ungrounded in a larger political project. This language risks Zhdanovism only if we define *larger political project* in inflexibly vanguardist terms. I want to avoid any stringent definition of that project except to say that we need to liberate people from domination in the realms of production and reproduction as well as to liberate nature from its own agony in technological society. It has become a cliché that our enemies here are capitalism, sexism and racism; like all clichés it is true, and yet we need to think beyond this catechism if we want our concepts to do real intellectual and political work and not become substitutes for analysis. Although my version of cultural studies is decidedly Marxist and feminist, to *be* Marxist and feminist today is up for grabs. Dogmatic Marxisms and feminisms abound, deciding truth with reference solely to issues of affiliation. But intellectual and political iconoclasm should not be judged traitorous out of hand. We must listen carefully to Marxism's and feminism's internal critics who rebel against the ritualization of Marxist and feminist assumptions about political and intellectual correctness.

To be Marxist and feminist involves interrogating Marxism and feminism in light of changing historical circumstances as well as the immanent needs of theoretical revisionism. True believers are found everywhere, not only on the left (see Hoffer, 1966). And the left's right (Breines, 1985) is no further left than the right itself. In some sense it is more smugly self-satisfied, having internalized political virtue simply by way of its slogans and self-importance. The left must live deconstructively in the sense that it must subject its own assumptions, discourses and practices to continual interrogation lest its repertoire of lifeworld practices, including intellectual practice, congeal into potentially authoritarian dogma. It is in this sense that deconstruction functions powerfully as political theory, valorizing dissent, deviance and distance in the midst of emotional and political commitments to the cause, whatever that might be. Like Merleau-Ponty's (1964) version of an existential-phenomenological Marxism, deconstruction teaches humility. The left needs a sense of its own fallibility, just as deconstructors require political commitment so that their irony does not become political theory in its own right – cynicism. Irony and allusion, no less than cynicism, do not constitute a progressive political theory, as the example of Nietzsche shows (but see Warren, 1988). Although Nietzsche remains one of the most powerful critics of the Enlightenment, his own irrationalism got the better of his critique of the Enlightenment's positive thinking, when, alternatively, it could have grounded a critical social theory in the fashion of Marxist Nietzscheans like Horkheimer and Adorno (1972).

Cultural studies is so important because through it we can better understand how the processes of depoliticization work, even applying these insights to our own intellectual work. The depoliticization of cultural criticism only parallels, and in its own small way reinforces, depoliticization at large, an issue treated somewhat differently by Habermas (1975) in his *Legitimation Crisis*. Today the political arena is reserved for the brokering of special interests that in no way challenge the linkage between the state and capital or the polity and patriarchy. Although as Habermas indicates, the state still needs the political arena in order to secure enough democratic legitimation to function, the amount of legitimation produced by electoral politics is relatively insignificant compared to the vast supplies of legitimacy produced by the culture industry and consumerism. People will put up with all sorts of political venality like Watergate and the Savings and Loan scandal in the US as long as they can get gas for their cars in which to drive to shopping malls in order to acquire the simulated commodities represented to them as the essence of satisfaction today. It is difficult to overestimate the system-supporting outcomes generated by the culture industry when it comes to maintaining popular legitimation of a social and economic system otherwise dangerously skewed in favor of elites. Indeed, one of the central missions of the culture industry is to defuse resentment otherwise directed at the rich and powerful. To do this, the culture industry turns celebrity into a text in its own right, simulating people like Donald Trump, Lee Iaccoca, Ronald Reagan, Michael Jordan, Michael Jackson, Prince Charles and Lady Diana in a way that makes it possible for us to identify with them without losing sight of our (meritocratic) difference from them.

A critical cultural studies debunks the screening of celebrity as a way of producing legitimation in a hierarchical society. A conformist cultural studies loses the political edge of this deconstruction and instead simply proliferates readings of these media-tions, treating them as they would any cultural text or practice. Where the outcome of both versions of cultural studies are deconstructive readings that show how the production of these simulations carefully conceals its own authorship, thus representing reality as an incontrovertible piece of nature, an affirmative cultural studies does not relate the texts it engages to the political con-texts that make use of texts in order to perpetuate power. Foucault is an important figure here because he can be read in two opposite directions, both as an author of a politicized cultural studies that locates texts in political con-text and as a representative of a more affirmative cultural studies that fails to interrogate power differences in a way that suggests either the abolition or democratization of power. Foucault argues that power is everywhere, rejecting Marxism in this. The reading of Foucault is crucial for determining the trajectory of one's own version of cultural studies. Those who learn from his archaeological readings of discourse/practices like prisons and sexuality view his political theory as uncritical, regressing behind Marxism. Those who accept not only the example of his particular readings but also his political theory view Foucault as a profound post-Marxist compared to whom even the most sophisticated neo-Marxists are judged to be living in the stone age.

Foucault has become a central figure in recent cultural studies debates (e.g., Fraser, 1989; Poster, 1989, 1990). Situating him with respect to critical theory, poststructuralism, postmodernism and feminism is seen as relevant by those who regard his cultural readings as extremely productive if insufficiently worked out in terms of their implications for the development of a general critical social theory (of the universality of Habermas' [1984, 1987b] communication theory). I tend to read Foucault more as a postmodernist than a poststructuralist, although this matters much less than does an appraisal of the relationship between his cultural readings and his political theory, such as it is. Habermas' own (1981a) response to poststructuralism and postmodernism should be read in light of the emerging scholarship on Foucault (see Dews, 1984, 1987). In many respects, I agree fully with Habermas' reflections on what he calls the philosophical discourse of modernity and postmodernity expressed in both his (1987a) book and an article (1981a) attacking postmodernism as a neoconservatism of sorts.

Part of the problem in settling scores with Foucault as the most emblematic and productive postmodern cultural reader is that his postmodernism, like Derrida's poststructuralism, remains undertheorized in political terms. One must take all sorts of interpolative liberties with Foucault's writings in order to prise out of them a coherent philosophy of history and political theory. This is a problem with many current non-positivist versions of cultural studies that are so forbiddingly technical and self-enclosed as to make their own political deconstruction difficult. For its part, Lacanian feminism strangely excludes the political from its own readings, almost taking for granted a certain devotional stance on the part of the reader that makes further explication of political implications unnecessary. This is extremely frustrating for people who want to develop feminist theory in the direction of critical social theory, refusing its confinement as a deconstructive methodology for dealing with women's texts and texts about women.

Deconstructing Deconstruction

Poststructuralism and its deconstructive interpretive method are the wild cards in the theoretical deck. Deconstruction can be used to radicalize one's cultural readings and thus implant cultural reading directly in the process of everyday resistance and organization. Or it can be used to upgrade the cultural capital (Bourdieu, 1984) of cultural analysts and theorists who lay claim to their own indigenous methodology and conceptual apparatus. It is eminently possible to read Derrida both ways, as political or as methodological, because he is not given to theorizing his own critical activity, thus giving license to the more methodological and less theoretical version of deconstruction. It is said that Derrida is readying a volume called *The Political Derrida* to respond to the charge that he forsakes politics. Derrida already claims Marxism for himself, although how this affects his deconstructive work is unclear. The future of cultural studies in large measure depends on the status of the politics of deconstruction, an issue that is far from settled.

This issue cannot be settled within literary theory itself. To identify oneself as a deconstructor already decides the issue of the politics of deconstruction in the direction of self-reproducing technical readings conducted outside of political context. Deconstruction appears to be the most political where it implants itself in existing theoretical and disciplinary traditions (e.g., Agger, 1989c) that have shielded themselves from deconstructive self-scrutiny for too long. Deconstruction in this sense is equivalent to theoretical and methodological self-consciousness – the self-reflection of writing that listens to itself write as well as listening to other writings write. This is the sense of the cultural studies that I propose: *it would reauthorize cultural works and practices as literary constructions that encode certain politics, perspectives and values.* Deconstruction offers this cultural studies a way of working backward from the objectified cultural object or practice to the constituting activities concealed in it, thus exposing authorial perspectivity to the political light of day.

Without this sort of deconstructive incorporation by cultural analysts, it is impossible to read advertisements as powerful statements of normative political theory as well as empirical social science. It is equally difficult to read science for its literary intentionality, or to view television and movies as hortatory and suppressive texts in their own right. Representation needs to be re-presented as constitutional activity that is inherently political in the way it challenges conventional readings of cultural works and practices suggested by those works and practices themselves. Deconstructive cultural studies reframes culture, blurring its text and con-text.

For example, a cultural deconstructor can read television not in terms of the rhythm and perspective suggested by mainstream television itself (accommodating commercials and adjusted to the average viewer's attention span, thus reproducing it) but in ways that disrupt television's own televisualization of itself. After all, television teaches us how to watch it: shows script their own readings in terms of their self-framing (pace, plot, previews, etc.). And shows and texts about television suggest a certain normative reading (television guides, television shows about television, critical writing about television, etc.).

It seems strange to think that we need to learn how to view television and movies or how to read trade fiction. But we do not step into childhood already understanding the strangeness of the electronic media and how we are to relate to them. Popular culture teaches us its own rule of interpretation that frames both culture and the world for us. Popular culture protects its own hegemony by teaching us how to read culture, blocking readings that disrupt culture's own self-reproduction. Cultural deconstruction helps us read against the grain of normative cultural reception dictated by culture itself. It disrupts the synchrony and one-dimensionality of cultural works by exhuming the authorial subject(s) buried deep beneath the surface of the finished, polished text. The deconstruction of culture in this sense gives culture back its original voice that has been heavily sublimated in the editorial, directorial and production gestures distancing culture from the constitutional activities comprising determinate aesthetic choices.

There is no other way to view television's subliminal impact on viewers than to disrupt the routine ways in which people receive it. This disruption comes from cultural readings that teach new ways of watching television, viewing film and reading fiction. Cultural deconstruction is not only another objectified practice as deauthorized as the cultural works and practices it interrogates deconstructively. *It deconstructs itself* where it reminds itself of its own constitutionally political nature, its existence in the lifeworlds of people who are concerned with cultural criticism. After all, cultural studies itself has an audience where it is directed not only to other academics who read and write for the cultural studies journals. Although it is difficult to imagine that *Camera Obscura* and *Cultural Critique* can be phrased accessibly, it is possible to develop a culture-critical discourse that is available to regular consumers of culture and thus that can help transform the reception of representation in fast capitalism. In my concluding chapter, I defend the transformation of the reception of representation as one of the foremost aims of a radicalized cultural studies.

Unfortunately, deconstructive methodologists do not transform the reception of representation because they do not write for the people for whom mass culture has a constitutional impact; they write for themselves, both to pad their academic curriculum vitae (see Agger, 1990, especially Chapter 6) and to legitimize cultural theory in the university. Although leftist academics have to publish in order not to perish, and although it is important to legitimate non-positivist, non-canonical modes of cultural criticism in the academy, these are not sufficient aims. Cultural studies must write for those whose gazes have been regulated by the culture industry and who thus live their lives in terms of the quotidian existences scripted for them and for the cultural heroes with whom they identify. It must aspire to a public accessibility without which one cannot say that theory has political impact or relevance.

This is to raise the issue of the politics of lucidity and opacity, an issue to which everyone who does cultural theory has been exposed in one way or another. In a positivist culture all 'difficult' writing is lambasted as the posturing of privileged intellectuals who would thus protect their own privilege. Adorno (1974a) himself defends opacity by pointing to the opaque world requiring allusive, dialectical interrogations. Indeed, difficulty is liberating where it challenges the comfortable habits of mind that lend themselves readily to the one-dimensionalization of all human experience. The culture industry exists in part to teach people extraordinarily simple-minded understandings of the social world (e.g., television melodramas in which complex problems are reduced to the exigencies of half-hour narratives punctuated by commercials). Stupidity is socially engendered through culture in order not to endanger the dominant quotidian.

Anglo-American analytic philosophy prizes simplicity in the service of verifiability. Abstract concepts that cannot be measured or tested are suspect. Obviously, critical theory must resist this conflation of difficulty with nonsense. At the same time, though, critical theory must also recognize its own problematic opacity from the point of view of the audiences to which popular culture is directed and whose interests critical cultural theory indefatigably defends. Theory must guard against its own hermetic self-isolation from the masses lest it lose its ability to engage in consciousness-raising as well as consensus formation. Ironically, the theory of the collapse of the public sphere is frequently carried out in a jargon that only facilitates the further erosion of public discourse. This depoliticizes the project of theory by reducing theory to yet another specialist code engaged in by other specialists.

It is not enough to say that theory must write simply and lucidly. As Marcuse (1964) has shown, this is extremely difficult where the universe of discourse is nearly closed and words robbed of their critical meanings, deployed against themselves. Plain talk is muddied where cultural meanings are largely determined by cultural hegemony. Sometimes the most transparent language is that which deals with the world's complexity head on. Nor can critical theorists simply invent a new language made up of neologisms. They must trade on conventional usages conventionally, using language against itself by showing where it facilitates liberation and where it obstructs it. Neither lucidity nor opacity is a sufficient political posture. They fatefully intermingle in discourse that attempts to deconstruct itself and other discourses. And this must be done *through* language, not around or beyond it.

I am concerned that deconstruction does not write for the people because it believes that such attempts are naive, given the state of generalized unconsciousness. The Frankfurt theorists urge that we unravel the dialectic of lucidity and opacity in the direction of public speech, creating the democratic polity prefiguratively in our own ideal speech practices. Admittedly, Habermas frustrates such democracy at every turn! His problem is not simply literary infelicity but rather a deeper-seated aversion to popular culture that makes it almost impossible for him to anticipate his own reception problems. One wonders whether Habermas imagines that many share his own encyclopedic grasp of European philosophy, social theory and high culture, that he simply neglects to 'write down' because he lives in a world unto himself and the few dozen people with whom he can have productive dialogue. At least Habermas recognizes that the central problem for critical theory is to develop a political theory of communication, which is much more than one can say about Derridean deconstruction.

Derrida is trapped by his own resonant claim that 'the text has no outside'. This sentiment appears to block his development of a textual-political theory that could reasonably make use of his own deconstructive insights into the nature of undecidability. Instead, Derrida inhabits a world of sheer textuality, although both he and other Derrideans protest this characterization. Certainly, his oeuvre does not indicate an engagement with material questions of general social theory. Instead, his work is made up of numerous engagements with other writers, whom he reads playfully as well as seriously but without any interpretive direction in the way of political critique and contestation. Derrida himself is a text to be written by his followers, who frantically attempt to interpolate meaning between his various books and essays in search of a coherent thread of meaning tying it all together. For their parts, the Frankfurt theorists are models of systematic, if dense, presentation. They require the devotional attention of acolytes who fill in the blanks of their heroes' symptomatic silences with elusive sense.

Deconstruction borders on being private language because it does not transcend the texts that occupy its reading. Where traditional objectivist criticism has given itself over to the sense of the text under review, emulating its every gesture, deconstructive criticism takes such liberty with texts that it fails to produce counter-readings in their own right. Barthes and Derrida use language so playfully that they do not relieve the density of other texts in the fashion of expansive exposition. But nor do they develop a discourse of systematic criticism that matches the texts that are their objects with challenging reinterpretations. Positivists gloat about the seeming refusal or inability of deconstructors to do line-by-line readings that do not peter out in endless silliness. I worry that this is less a temperamental problem than an outcome of the deconstructive method itself, which flattens out the supposedly aporetic nature of all writing into a universal destiny, a sort of prison-house of language. Surely some writing is less (and more) aporetic, and thus deconstructible, than others. The playfulness of the critical text (Barthes, 1975) would seem to vary with the contingencies and con-text of the text under review, thus suggesting that criticism can resist the temptation of its own obscurantism when it confronts *texts that already deconstruct themselves*, and thus need less deconstruction from the outside, as it were.

The aporia of lucidity and opacity can be eased by new formulations of writing conditioned by deconstructive notions of reading. Deconstructors fetishize an arid, atheoretical, apolitical version of Derridean analysis because they view deconstruction entirely as a critical or interpretive practice and not also as a more positive approach to composing texts and thus changing society. Yet deconstructive reading suggests a deconstructive writing that acknowledges its own inherent undecidability and aporetic nature and thus refuses to suppress these subtexts of authorial desire and difference/deferral. Instead, deconstructive writing embodies three interrelated principles:

1. Deconstructive writing exhumes its own foundational assumptions about the nature of the world from its subtextual netherworld. It refuses to suppress the evidence of passionate, polemical and perspectival authoriality. Traces of authoriality are in fact celebrated as the occasions of a democratic undecidability. In the case of a radical cultural studies, this might mean that cultural critics recognize that their critical texts are also constitutional in the differences they make to the overall cultural field. Although deconstructive cultural studies gives the lie to a positivist objectivism, there is a fatal tendency within deconstructive reading to suppress its own authoriality in the interest of purely technical, intratextual criticism. But all writing is intertextual, as Derrida and Kristeva understand. As such, it is political, changing the very world to which it is an address, even if it claims to be presuppositionlessly representational.

For cultural studies to confess its authoriality is not an occasion for lamenting the loss of objectivity. Inasmuch as there is no objectivity-in-itself but only intentionally constituted objects, as Husserl (1977) suggested, the supposed contamination of objectivity with authorial subjectivity is not a contamination at all but an acknowledgment of the constitutional nature of all writing. Cultural studies inevitably takes a stand on its cultural topic, as I argued in my preceding chapter on false and true needs. For writing to pretend presuppositionlessness is disingenuous, given how infected every reading is by its object as well as by the con-texts of politics and desire framing every literary act. Deconstructive writers do not pretend presuppositionlessness but intend their writing in a way that acknowledges their inevitable perspectivity and undecidability. Even critical texts written by deconstructors contain the same undecidability as the cultural works and practices under review. Every text is aporetic, including the Derridean one. This much should be obvious by now: deconstruction applies equally to itself, changing the nature of deconstructive writing as well as reading. Of course, for deconstructors writing and reading are dialectically inseparable, the one making way for the other.

2. Deconstructive writing not only admits its own political, ontological and existential foundation in a perspectival desire but celebrates this grounding as the possibility of any social and cultural change. Every text intends to change the world, science as much as science fiction, criticism as much as the oeuvre it addresses. For deconstructors to pretend an objectivist interest in texts misleads as to their real intentions: they intend to change the culture by reading and writing (about) it. In this sense, every deconstructive writing embodies advocacy for one or another state of affairs. Even if this advocacy is heavily suppressed by the gestures of the deauthored text, as in the case of science, it can be detected through a deconstructive reading that shows the contingencies of textual play and work comprising the finished writing.

Even science advocates where the world it represents causally is further entrenched by science's own ahistorical account of it. Momentum is added to supposed causality by causality's own text, precisely the political contribution of positivism. The Frankfurt theorists understood that positivism is the dominant mode of ideology in late capitalism, in a sense displacing the more substantive claims of religion and economic theory by its gestured presuppositionlessness. I have tried to advance the Frankfurt critique of positivism through a poststructural reading of science that shows the ethnographic construction of the science text as a distinctive literary practice establishing what I have called the *science aura* (see Agger, 1989b; see also Knorr-Cetina, 1981).

Cultural criticism is no different from science in this sense. An appropriately deconstructive cultural criticism would celebrate its perspectivity, its frank acknowledgment of its own authorial interests. Derrideans decenter the authorial subject, like they do all subjectivity. They argue that the subject is positioned by language, depicting a dreary iron cage within which writers have little room to move. But in exempting themselves from their own account of decentered authorial subjectivity – after all, their texts are full of literary play and perspective – they contradict themselves. Although poststructuralists deprivilege subjectivity, they do so subjectively, constructing their own deconstruction but ruling it out for others. As a result, second-order Derrideans, Lacanians and Barthesians seldom reproduce the vivacity of the original writings but attempt futilely to derive an interpretive algorithm from the exuberant example of the founders. The only Derridean is Derrida; but there can be many deconstructive writings if the example of his own passionate undecidability is taken seriously.

One would need to do a sociolinguistic study of the institutionalization of Derrideanism (e.g., Lamont, 1987) to understand the rhetorical and substantive regression from Derrida to Derrideans in terms of the exuberant advocacy of one's own undecidably foundational assumptions, perspectives and values. This is not to say that Derrida is manifestly a social critic in the fashion of neo-

Marxists like the Frankfurt theorists or members of the CCCS group. Rather, he writes in a way that advocates its own subtext, which could be understood as the ineluctable ambiguity inhabiting every writing that aspires, but fails, to become a new world populated by converted readers. But second-order Derrideans, like the Yale critics, read Derrida *for method*, losing the possibility of his own play-fully irreducible literary intervention. There is something decidedly studied about Derridean readings, belying their own affiliation to his important critique of positivist representation. Instead, they unwittingly create a new objectivism in the way that they cede their own voices to the dominant voice of the text that their own writing represents, albeit not in a presuppositionless way.

The best way to judge this issue is to compare textual readings by Derrida (e.g., 1976), Derrideans (de Man, 1979, 1984, 1986; see Fish, 1980, 1989) and objectivist close readers. Derrida's are the liveliest, the least encumbered by the pretensions of positivist representation. He gains sufficient critical distance from his topics – certain western philosophers – to acquire his own voice. But second-order Derrideans, like objectivist close readers, stare so intently at the text that they lose sight of the larger con-texts of society, history and existence that afford these texts plenitudes of meanings. Their readings are wooden and technical, conducted in a way that mutes the voice of the reader, who is thus prevented from becoming a writer, an interlocutor in the ideal speech situation. As a result, the texts read by Derrideans and positivists alike lie inertly on the page, stilling the engagements of intertextuality, hence democracy. Readers are captured in texts' gravitational force fields, losing sufficient distance from them that we can respond to them with necessary perspective.

Derrida insists on and gains a certain non-identity from his topics that allows him to develop his own voice. He rejects objectivist close reading because he does not want to be read that way himself. Derrida writes in a way that suggests he is comfortable not knowing all the answers, lacking an interpretive rule with which to solve the problems of opacity confronting him in the works of others. And because of this he is able to take on the challenge of comprehending the scribblings of others with an exemplary exuberance. Derrida is not a literary coward, as are so many technical academic readers, who allow themselves to be led around by the nose when it comes to essaying their own versions of things through their readings of others. Interpretation becomes an obsession where we disempower criticism from understanding and accepting, even celebrating, its own constitutional contribution to the texts at hand. Derrida understands that he is an originary reader of Rousseau. Although Rousseau has been read before, Derrida's Rousseau can be defended as an original version. To be sure, Derrida does not capture Rousseau as Rousseau meant to be captured. Recognizing this, Derrida does not eschew the interpretive task but uses it as an occasion to make sense of himself (making sense of Rousseau). This is deconstructive writing par excellence: it recognizes how it uses reading as a vehicle for writing, but not in an undisciplined way. It proceeds to develop its own *sens* via the meanings of others. It does so unashamedly, refusing to accept its own subordination to so-called original creation with which it is often compared as derivative or inferior textual work.

Cultural studies in an appropriately deconstructive frame will recognize its own aesthetic and political contribution to culture. In accepting the undecidabil-ity of writings, it confronts and accepts its own undecidability. This is cause for despair only where deconstructors secretly harbor objectivist aspirations, hoping to lay bare the one true Rousseau or the one true Melville. Deconstruction descends to technical methodologism, losing sight of larger historical and political context, where it believes that definitive readings, hence definitive writings, are impossible. This is not so much a sense that everything worth writing has been done before but utter futility about creating culture in the midst of enormous deconstructive ambiguity: if we cannot even get the black and white of the printed page straight, or prosaic television and movies, what business do we have writing? That is the question to which an apolitical, apathetic, academic deconstruction answers 'None'. For his part, Derrida shows the way as a reader who is unashamed of the perspectivity of his own versions, thus enabling him to write. As I explore in my concluding chapter, this allows cultural criticism to become valuably political at a time when the demystification of ideologically encoded cultural texts and practices is a crucial activity of resistance and transformation.

3. Finally, deconstructive writing solicits and promotes other writings, recognizing its own undecidable corrigibility. It achieves this by writing as if every writing needs to be corrected, embracing a deconstructive ethic that suggests that no story is ever complete. One needs unusual literary self-confidence to recognize the limitations of one's writing and then to solicit responses and open dialogues. Too much objectivist writing intends to have the last word, even if the author secretly recognizes this as folly. Embodied in scientific writing as passive voice, the hallmark of literary objectivism, a certain literary norm requires writers not to flinch before the impossible task of settling all disputes. Unfortunately, this norm hinders the development of self-confident humility allowing deconstructive writing to welcome others into the intertextual community.

To return to my earlier example, Derrida surely understands that people can and will read Rousseau differently. He writes about Rousseau in a purposely provocative way, challenging other readers of Rousseau to take their best shot. This is decidedly not a macho literary king-of-the-mountain tactic (see Fish, 1980) but a way of building a Rousseauean community of discourse in which dialogue chances are democratically distributed and people act to build consensus about Rousseau's oeuvre, even if, as deconstructors know, this is ultimately a futile effort. Writing in a deconstructive mode acts on the inherent intertexuality of every literary gesture. As such, writing contributes to the conversation of humanity, hence the creation of democracy (Oakeshott, 1962; O'Neill, 1974).

What this means practically is that writing presents itself in a way that solicits other versions of its own text, which embodies a clear recognition that one can never have the last word. This is as much a question of literary attitude as anything else. One recognizes genuinely deconstructive writing when one reads writing that embodies a combination of playful self-confidence and humility. In particular, this version of writing should combine empathy with irony – a realization that one is likely to be read, along with a recognition that one must proceed to make one's case even if one is likely to be misunderstood or opposed by others.

In the case of cultural studies, this conjunction of literary empathy and irony is crucial. The frustratingly technical approaches of apolitical Derrideans as well as objectivist close readers appear deaf to the way they will be heard by readers curious about their own intertextual engagements. They do not anticipate their own reception because they do not care about starting discussions and building community, even social change. Instead, they pretend representational readings of cultural works and practices that have the same indubitability as the sciences. A densely deconstructive reading of *Oliver Twist* attempts to grasp it definitively, freezing it against the molten threat of different interpretations. Positivist close reading is notorious for the notion that one can arrive at indubitable interpretations that then endure as vital parts of the culturally elevating canon. In this sense Derrideanism may be a secret positivism.

These versions of cultural reading do not want to start arguments but to end them. They intend monologue, not dialogue, hierarchy and not community. They are the problem, not the solution. They enforce the cultural hegemony of expert culture. There can be a version of cultural studies that does not separate itself from everyday life but lives squarely within it, attempting to transform it in the process. A more affirmative cultural studies is content to academize cultural analysis in the interest of the accumulation of expertise, citations and all the other honorifics of university existence. For people who practise cultural studies in that vein, it is possible to read cultural works and practices in ways that are not open to contention. This is especially ironic in the case of deconstructive critics, who live by the rule of undecidability. Ironically, they do not recognize that their own patois needs to be interrogated *and thus practised differently* for its aporias and blind-spots. Even a Derridean, using all the insights of Derrida's deconstructive method of literary analysis, cannot produce singular, timeless readings. Every version fraught with historicity blunts the sharp attempt to produce versions of culture that rival the hard sciences for their own indubitability.

In the last analysis, deconstructive cultural criticism must check its own tendency to become as technically ritualistic as the hard-core New Criticism and mainstream empirical communication studies to which it stands in counterpoint. The opposite ends of the continuum meet on the common ground of their representationality, their commitment to produce readings of culture outside of culture and language themselves. But every writing of Derrida, no less than of Pauline Kael and Hilton Kramer, is inflected by the contingent, fallible historicity and everydayness of all culture. One cannot stand outside of culture in order to read it, the fateful mistake of all Archimedeans. Instead, readings of culture are culture themselves, provoking new readings, hence community. One does not expect deconstructors to install themselves as transcendental subjects for deconstruction challenges all unreflective subjectivity as a ruse of reason. But a good deal of deconstructive criticism reads transcendentally, as if the voice of the critic were somehow not a factor in the overall analysis of the work or practice in question. As Derrida suggests, though, every reading is a writing strongly intervening in the cultural field to which it must belong unashamedly.

This deconstructive version of deconstruction responds to a certain readerly interest, too. We read cultural criticism not only to anticipate or decipher the books, shows, movies and paintings of the moment. As I indicated earlier, we also read criticism to know the critics, in whom we develop certain investments as arbiters of taste and aesthetic judgment. This can be a matter as pragmatic as figuring out how to spend our entertainment budget, in which case we need to be able to rely on critics who share our own taste and thus rarely guide us wrongly in what is likely to please. Or it can be a matter as significant as deriving

wide-ranging social insights from cultural criticism that accepts its own theoreticity, historicity and perspectivity without shame. Such criticism always situates
works and practices in con-text, imbuing its readings with what amount to
considerations of social theory and social criticism, not only objectivist appraisals
or analyses. Every text is a society, even if all societies are not texts (Wittgenstein, 1953; Hymes, 1974).

To get to the text one must pass through its society, its con-text in politics,
economics, gender and race. This is not a simple reductionism, as it was for the
Marxist criticism I considered in Chapter 3. It is a dialectical reckoning with the
metabolism between text and culture, between particular and general, that gives
particular aesthetic gestures their inflection by the generalities of common experience. There is no royal road to cultural texts, nor can such roads as may exist
bypass the social. Although I have counterposed 'good' and 'bad' Derrideanism
in this chapter, even Derrida is at fault where he extends the realm of the textual
too far. The difference between all-texts-being-societies (through which power is
transacted) and not-all-societies-being-texts is simply that the material social
world is comprised of elements that are not textual, even if textuality has been
widely dispersed from traditional books and writings into a variety of discourse/
practices including money, science, edifice and figure. Derrida is insufficiently
materialist, although I recognize deconstructively that to say this trades on a
notion of the fault line between material and ideal that is inherently problematic,
especially today when texts matter because they are matter – screens of power
(Luke, 1989). Perhaps Derrida is seen in the best light when he is compared to
derivative Derrideans who wrongly prise method out of him, forgetting the
originary constitutionality of his own irreducible engagements with certain civilizational thinkers and practices. But this is not to ignore Derrida's aversion to a
systematic critical social theory that could help him better address the con-texts
of texts. That is why in much of my own work I have tried to fertilize Derridean
poststructuralism with the more structural theory of the Frankfurt School, especially when it comes to their imaginative cultural analyses (e.g., Marcuse, 1964;
Horkheimer and Adorno, 1972).

I do not want to suggest that cultural studies should return to Derrida or
even Adorno for its answers. The Birmingham School has shown that one must
develop cultural criticism out of the particular social and political exigencies of
the day. Even though theory is highly relevant to the practice of these readings –
what I want to call transforming the reception of representation – it must be
forged in the particular empirical contexts within which theoretical propositions
are tested against the practical requirements of resistance and liberation. It should
go without saying that by testing theoretical propositions I am not calling for
positivist hypothesis testing; far from it. I am saying that *there is no such thing as
theory outside of the lifeworlds in which ideas are formulated as an integral part of the
social experience of political struggle.*

There is no body of knowledge and texts called theory that stands apart
from the empirical concerns of experience and research as modes of social
practice. For theory to be isolated in a remote wing of the academic division of
labor, for example in the case of cultural theory, dooms it to political irrelevance
especially where what passes for theory frequently refers to the particular oeuvres
of high-profile intellectual figures like Derrida who, in fact, have produced little
of a systematic social-theoretical nature. Deconstruction is inimical to hero

worship as well as the intellectual cult of personality; it is elementally democratizing. Too often, though, deconstruction is equivalent to the inert oeuvre of particular deconstructors who lionize themselves in order to achieve a certain cultural power. In this regard, one could cite the examples of Derrida, Foucault, Irigaray, Jameson. They are to blame less than their acolytes, who erroneously believe that these singular examples can be methodologized into contextless methods to be employed willy-nilly in the interpretation of cultural texts and practices. Nothing could be further from the spirit of deconstruction.

Postmodernism and the End of Ideology

In this chapter, I have opposed the fetishism of deconstruction as a purely technical method for reading cultural texts. In this, I have confronted deconstruction with deconstruction, albeit a self-deconstructing version willing to abandon the hard-and-fast interpretive certainties of objectivist criticism. In this final section, I want to talk about another aspect of the deconstructive cult of cultural studies that has less to do with the methodologization of Derrida's critical oeuvre than with the fad of postmodernism. In Chapter 6 I already distinguished between affirmative and critical postmodernisms. I argued that Lyotard's (1984) version of postmodernism only repeats Daniel Bell's (1960) earlier end-of-ideology thesis, used to disqualify Marxism as a will to power. And I urged a more critical, dialectical postmodernism that functions as comprehensive social theory, thus enabling us to address a host of contemporary social phenomena not anticipated or addressed sufficiently by Marx and Marxism (e.g., Baudrillard's analysis of simulations). In saying this, I developed a postmodern critical theory that in significant respects builds on Horkheimer and Adorno's own critique of the Enlightenment and of its betrayal by a mythologizing scientism and positivism. *A critical postmodernism (e.g., Huyssen, Aronowitz, Kellner, Agger) can offer the Frankfurt culture-industry thesis a foundation in a cultural studies approach owed to thinkers like Foucault.* In particular, this postmodernism argues not for the abandonment of the project of modernity, in Habermas' (1984, 1987b) terms, but for its fulfillment: postmodernity becomes the end of what Marx called prehistory – the long and bloody interregnum of domination.

I caution against an embrace of postmodernism, even though I have self-consciously affiliated myself to a critical theory that makes ample use of certain postmodern as well as feminist insights. Postmodernism in its establishment versions ignores social problems of the public sphere altogether, resolving postmodern anxiety with doses of commodities and commodified popular culture. The postmodernism hawked on every Yuppie street-corner must be rejected by those seriously concerned with transforming large-scale social structures. In fast capitalism, cultural and intellectual trends are ephemeral, the postmodernism craze included. Unfortunately, the establishment postmodernism so prevalent today blocks attempts to reformulate a radical cultural studies. In the rest of this chapter, I examine the modalities of the culture industry's own postmodernism which, as I conclude, is far removed from the radical Nietzschean transvaluation of all values that converges with what Marxists later called the critique of ideology. Instead of being a critique of ideology, which it could be in its best sense, an affirmative postmodernism lamely celebrates the end of ideology, hence hastening it.

Postmodernism is just about the hottest cultural and intellectual trend around. People across the humanities and social sciences publish articles and books and organize conferences and panels on postmodernism. 'Pomo' has become a minor cottage industry, giving bored post-leftist academics something new to do and read. Although, as I suggested in Chapter 6, there is a great deal to be said about the more theoretical versions of postmodernism that seriously engage with world-historical issues of social theory and social change, I am more concerned in this section with postmodernism as ideology – or, more precisely, with postmodernism as the end of ideology, which it intends to be. Here I am not talking mainly about the literate postmodernisms of Baudrillard (1983), Lyotard (1984) and Foucault (1976, 1977, 1980), although in this section I allude to these people in passing, but about the postmodernism of the American cultural establishment and culture industry – what I am calling a *New York Times* postmodernism (see Gitlin, 1988). This concluding discussion is designed as a political introduction to the fads and fashions of *New York Times* postmodernism. I am mostly dismissive of this version of postmodernism, although one can merge certain postmodern insights with the political and theoretical agenda of the Frankfurt School, neo-Marxism and feminism. I am increasingly convinced that the mainstream discourse of postmodernism, like those of *perestroika* and post-Marxism, is merely the latest, trendiest attack on the left. Here I suggest some ways in which postmodernism not only ignores social problems but becomes a problem in its own right.

My critique will possibly be heard as yet another attack on heterodox European theory that breaks the mold of Marxism-Leninism. But we must not be bound by the simplistic dichotomies that force us to choose between Marxism and postmodernism. One can (and must!) fashion a Marxist version of post-modernism as well as a postmodern Marxism that genuinely contributes critical insights to new social movements. Aronowitz (1990), Huyssen (1986), Kellner (Best and Kellner, 1991), Jameson (1981), Luke (1989), Fraser (1989) and I (1990) have offered examples of this convergence. Here, I criticize an establishment version of postmodernism in order to demonstrate the affinity between a peculiarly uncritical postmodernism, on the one hand, and perennial bourgeois social thought, on the other. Intellectual fads must be resisted and debunked, the hoopla surrounding postmodernism especially. This does not preclude a serious engagement with the discourse of the postmodern, which remains one of the most exciting theoretical challenges. It simply acknowledges that such engagements do not typify the celebration of postmodernism currently taking place across the university as well as in mainstream culture at large. Like all celebrations, this one must be viewed skeptically, especially from the vantage point of critical social theory.

Here I consider the tendencies of a glitzy, Manhattanized postmodernism to monopolize the terrain of cultural production and reception, as well as of the capitalist built environment. One finds postmodernism as an identifying slogan in nearly every avant-garde bookstore, magazine, television show and movie as well as in the buildings and malls housing cultural producers and consumers. A stroll through Sotto and Tribeca in New York or along Queen Street West in Toronto indicates the cultural hegemony of postmodernism, where hipsters dressed in black stroll and shop and dine under the *Zeitgeist* of the postmodern, whatever that is supposed to mean. Postmodernism does mean something in these formulations and manifestations: it represents a thoroughgoing aversion to political discussion and contestation, embodying the narcissism addressed by Lasch (1979) as early as the 1970s.

It is not strictly accurate to conflate Lyotard's (1984) nuanced, if relentless, critique of Marxist grand narratives with the pedestrian postmodernism of the New York galleries, clubs and critics. At least, Lyotard, like Daniel Bell (1976) before him, was aware of Marxism, recognizing it as a genuine subversion of capitalist pluralism. Thus, one could argue with Lyotard on his own terms, as Habermas (1981a) has done. The people who sell and live postmodernism in the US do not inflate their participation in the *Zeitgeist* with a serious ideological critique of the left: in fact, they do not view themselves in terms of a philosophy of history at all. For them, postmodernism is largely a consumer movement.

Where I (Agger, 1990) have distinguished between Lyotard's version of Bell's end-of-ideology and postindustrial-society theses, on the one hand, and a radicalized postmodernism with a political intent, on the other, here I want to discuss a third variant of postmodernism that in some respects is really a sub-category of Lyotard's neoconservative version, although without the philosophical patina of an engagement with Nietzsche and Heidegger. This *New York Times* version of postmodernism is simply not theoretical enough to warrant extended discussion as a full-fledged version of cultural and social theory, although it is prevalent as a cultural attitude today. It is the sort of postmodernism found in *Rolling Stone*, mentioned in *The New York Times*, developed in *New Yorker*, and cited in urbane Sunday supplement pieces on the cultural beat as well as in various critical and trade publications on the arts. This *NYT* postmodernism epitomizes a range of cultural attitudes and gestures encoding deeper political content. Of course, the essence of postmodernism is to conceal politics underneath the veneer of the rejection of politics, now as before a posture of value-freedom. Unlike the more self-consciously ideological approaches of Lyotard and Bell, this *NYT* postmodernism is not defined by its opposition to left-wing radicalism. Rather, it is signified by Lasch's (1979) narcissism, Macpherson's (1962) possessive individualism and Marcuse's (1955) repressive desublimation. Not that these are texts read by *NYT* postmodernists. But they help explain some of the valences of this postmodernism especially as it issues in the distinctive cultural creation and criticism typical of this perspective. In the rest of this chapter, I will itemize some of the features of this untheorized postmodernism in order to uncover its secret political affiliations.

An affirmative postmodern cultural studies includes the following four modalities:

1. *NYT* postmodernism rejects political discourse as out of date, shabby, irrelevant. Politics is not a venue of meaning because all political movements and personalities are viewed as venal to the point of Nixonian absurdity. One might periodize *NYT* postmodernism as post-Watergate, although there were stirrings of this postmodernism in the counter-culture, further demonstrating a certain

distance between *NYT* postmodernism and Bell's end-of-ideology perspective, especially as rendered in his (1976) book *The Cultural Contradictions of Capitalism*. As Gitlin (1987) indicates, one must divide the 1960s into a genuinely political rump (e.g., the Port Huron statement of the early SDS) and a depoliticized counter-culture devoted to many of the same cultural significations as *NYT* postmodernism.

The aversion to politics is more temperamental than doctrinal. Since Marxism is not a specter haunting the US, American postmodernism, unlike the French variety, does not take its bearings from a considered rejection of Marxism. Again, one is tempted to periodize this postmodern denial of the political as a particular feature of the post-baby-boom generation. But that is strictly incorrect: Yuppies, borne of the 1960s, are quintessentially postmodern in their consumerist individualism and political cynicism, and they derive whatever semblance of theoreticity they possess from periodicals like *The New York Times* and *Esquire* as well as from television shows like *thirtysomething*. The apolitical post-baby-boom cohort is no more apolitical than their Yuppie predecessors. The only difference perhaps is that Yuppies can fall back on the rhetoric of the 1960s as disingenuous proof of their social commitments – disingenuous, because the majority of baby-boomers in the 1960s were dope-smoking conformists and not serious political rebels.

2. *NYT* postmodernism endorses consumer capitalism and hence, by implication, rejects the possibility of radical social change – e.g., socialism. If issues of social change are addressed at all, they are addressed piecemeal. A more structural radicalism is regarded as hubris. Radicals themselves are branded as failed personalities somehow still mired in the adolescent passions of the 1960s. Although in other respects *NYT* postmodernism places value on retro gestures that encompass the less political manifestations of the counter-culture (like the Rolling Stones appearing in Budweiser ads and McCartney selling VISA cards), the angry radicalism of the 1960s is dismissed as both antediluvian and excessive. At best, mainstream postmodernism is liberal on social issues like abortion, the First Amendment and the environment but conservative on fiscal matters.

3. *NYT* postmodernism celebrates popular culture unashamedly, failing to make distinctions (which are rejected as modernist and mandarin). This robs postmodernism of the ability to expose and debunk the political codes of culture. Postmodern cultural criticism adds value to the popular, which is thoroughly commodified. This valorization of popular culture reinforces a common generational experience of the world, albeit mass-mediated, which substitutes for real community. Every baby-boomer understands that we are defined by common televisual events like the broadcast of the Kennedy assassinations or the first moonwalk. But what we want to remember about these collective experiences are not simply the events themselves but the text and texture of the cultural experience of identity formation watching Dan Rather break the first news from Dallas and living the event from Friday through to the funeral cortege. These experiences are focused retrospectively not on what they were and what they meant but on the ways they formed us, affording us both identity and meaning. My own adolescence, which is typical in this respect, can be reproduced

diachronically in terms of how the mass-mediated unfolding of these events and experiences paralleled and signified my own passage through successive stages of the life cycle, especially adolescence. A pedestrianized, depoliticized postmodernism helps us reexperience these mass-mediated public events for their contributions to our own ego formation, which is threatened by all of the colonizing forces threatening to turn us into what Lasch (1984), borrowing from the Frankfurt School, called minimal selves.

Although I decry this banalization of postmodern cultural criticism, especially where I contend that a radical cultural studies is the single best incarnation of the erstwhile critique of ideology, there is no denying the impact of this sort of retrospectively self-referential analysis of culture. Like most baby-boomers, I too reexperience myself in terms of my participation in these aspects of the popular, although for me most of these events take on political significance inasmuch as they help me chronicle my own formation as a social critic, not a contented Yuppie. One of the reasons why academic baby-boomers are attracted to cultural studies is because we experience our own selfhoods in terms of their constitution by the popular, refracted through the retrospective analysis of these public spectacles in which we can relocate central aspects of our ego formation.

There is nothing wrong with wanting to understand one's own constitution by the popular, especially where the popular encodes deep political meanings. For example, the television to which we were exposed in the 1950s and 1960s tried to turn us into men, women, parents, citizens and consumers. But *NYT* postmodernism prevents us from critically examining our differential experiences of the popular as well as the hierarchies of access and accumulation imbedded in it. It is far more important that the media presented a manufactured Vietnam War than that we came of age watching the coverage of the Tet offensive, which we then insert retrospectively into the reconstructed pastiche of our identity formation. In the movie *Platoon* or the television show *China Beach*, 'Vietnam' has become another relativized cultural experience that we examine self-referentially but not also in terms of the million Vietnamese who died during the war, an issue given important contemporary significance in the mass-mediated discourse of the Persian Gulf War (e.g., 'collateral damage' referring to Iraqi civilian casualties).

The reexperiencing of self formation through pop-culture analysis is less important than the critical evaluation of ways in which the popular is itself a differential field that not only constitutes us but also deceives us in fundamental respects. After all, the mass mediation of social reality proceeds apace; the lessons we learn about the spectacles of the 1960s (see Debord, 1970) can be applied today in helping us resist the most insidious aspects of cultural and personality formation, as well as the deflection of political mobilization, at the hands of popular culture. As I further develop in my concluding chapter, a radical cultural studies can help us read and resist mass culture as what Adorno (1973b, p. 406) called 'an objective context of delusion'.

4. *NYT* postmodernism purposely replaces substance with style, installing ironic detachment as the central social value. But neither cynicism nor irony is an appropriate political posture, especially where so much is going wrong. Both accelerate the venality of politics and the commodification of public discourse.

Post-baby-boomers are especially impervious to social problems, which they perceive to have little relationship to their own lives devoted to the consumption and celebration of cultural commodities. Teachers of social science confront a growing psychologism on the part of students, which inures them to larger structural understandings of what is going wrong. We cannot simply lay this at the door of the Reagan and Thatcher regimes, as some critics do. Certainly the 1980s were not an aberration in the sense that they are now over and will not reoccur. The privatization of social issues is part and parcel of capitalism. We noticed this self-aggrandizing privatization during the 1980s because it was especially pronounced in the images of the homeless huddled outside Trump Tower. Some leftist critics of this socio-political ennui blamed it on the putatively new ideology of postmodernism, failing to recognize that narcissism and possessive individualism are ways in which capitalism always defends itself against the threat of collective insurrection.

As I noted earlier, *NYT* postmodernism has a soft spot for the environment. It is easy for Yuppie and post-Yuppie possessive individualists to relate to the degradation of the built and natural environments because they relate so obsessively to commodities. Ironically, postmodern environmentalism commodifies environmentalism while indicting the commodification of the environment. Witness the numerous corporate tie-ins to the environmental movement: companies sell environmental awareness as proof of their own social concern. This is not to deny the possibility of a radicalized environmentalism but only to note the self-contradictory postmodernization of environmentalism in the context of capitalist consumerism.

These four features of an affirmative postmodernism contribute to the blockage of a genuine radical cultural critique that can intervene in the cultural field as a counter-hegemonic force of its own, which is the central purpose of my version of critical cultural studies presented in this book. The postmodernization of everyday life is a thin veneer for its further depoliticization, which has been gathering momentum since the collapse of the First International and the dream of an international socialist revolution. The postmodernism of shopping malls and *Miami Vice* ends ideology yet again, defusing political disputation in the name of the so-called end of history – a warmed-over version of Bell's (1973) postindustrialism. Of course, neither ideology nor capitalism has ended, in spite of the spectacularization of the 'end of communism', which, in fact, only signals the failure of Stalinist command economies denounced by western Marxists for the past seventy years. Postmodernism does not best Marxism any more than *perestroika* does; it simply transmogrifies anti-Marxism into another cultural commodity, readily gobbled up by the cultural and political establishment.

Indeed, the end-of-ideology thesis, captured figurally and gesturally in the lived experience of postmodernity (see Harvey, 1989), props up capitalism by diverting attention from substantive social, economic and cultural alternatives. As Horkheimer and Adorno (1972) noted in the 1940s, the cultural industry exists in large measure to represent capitalism as a rational social order, hence perpetuating the very commodification of all experience that gives the lie to the postulate of substantive rationality.

Horkheimer and Adorno were first exposed to Hollywood culture and

American mass media in the 1940s, from which they developed the theory of the culture industry. Where half a century ago ideology could be more readily debunked as egregious falsification, today ideology has gone underground, encoded in the Baudrillardian simulations of fast capitalism, in which the boundary between the textual and material has virtually disappeared, disabling social criticism as a result. Today, texts commanding experience are not found between covers but dispersed in the imagery, infrastructure and discourse of a postmodernized everyday life – what Baudrillard (1983) calls hyperreality – in which people believe that we live at the edge of the end of history, in the eternal present posited by Nietzsche as the fateful destination of the Enlightenment gone wrong.

Nietzsche despised the linear liberalism and rationalism that enthroned itself mythologically as a new religion of positive thinking. But *NYT* postmodernists do not read Nietzsche. Thus, they cannot appreciate the ways Nietzsche grounds both the Frankfurt School's Marxism, on the one hand, and the postmodernism of Lyotard and Foucault, on the other. The closest they get to Nietzsche is Ayn Rand, a central possessive-individualist culture hero. The *NYT* postmodernism that dominates our urban environment and its urbane cultural discourse celebrates what Nietzsche viewed as the antithesis of reason. Meaninglessness is erected as a monument to capitalism, which is now neologistically called postmodernity. But capitalism is thoroughly modernist in its essential logic; as I indicated above, postmodern architecture only embellishes a modernist public space with trivial borrowings from premodern epochs (see Gottdiener, 1991), producing the trivially different buildings that dominate our skylines. We have not yet entered a genuine postmodernity, which would have to be post-capitalist. We can make a halting step toward that genuine postmodernity by reversing the momentum of the postmodernizing culture industry that eschews ideology while perpetuating it at every turn.

The establishment postmodernism that I decry threatens to engulf postmodern tendencies in social science and the humanities. Although I and others have tried to borrow the more critical insights of postmodernism and poststructuralism in our own theorizing (e.g., see Fraser, 1989; Best and Kellner, 1991), I hesitate to endorse the postmodernization of sociology when postmodernism segues into post-Marxism. This is not to say that Marxism is a monolith; the critical feminist-Marxism that I advocate gave up on state socialism long before it was fashionable on the American left to do so. The attempt to pit Marxism against postmodernism obscures their possible interpenetration and dialogue. Nevertheless, we who care about the structural roots of social problems should be on guard against an affirmative version of postmodernism at a time when the celebration of the so-called end of Marxism becomes what Hegel (1966, p. 70) called a 'bacchanalian whirl in which no member is not drunken'.

As this discussion demonstrates, certain versions of postmodernism function ideologically where they oppose the very radicalism giving rise to my proposed version of cultural studies. This demonstrates again that subversive ideas can be deployed against themselves when they are reduced to clichés. Notwithstanding that, I am hopeful that postmodernism, like feminism, poses a fundamental challenge to Marxism that can only be met by rethinking some basic Marxist positions on the relationship between discourse and social change. Like feminism, postmodernism helps Marxism strengthen itself at a time when the nineteenth-century prophesy of class struggle seems extremely remote from the passions and problematics of the day. I have attempted to preserve Marx's vision of a better society by formulating it in discourse-theoretic terms, with the aid of postmodernism and feminist theory. Against the commodified postmodernism discussed in this chapter, I believe that we can revivify the public sphere and transform our political agenda, but only if we rethink aspects of Marxist cultural theory that have lost their vitality and relevance today (see Zaret, 1992).

Chapter 10

Cultural Studies as Everyday Life in the Society of the Spectacle

Metabolizing Cultural Studies

In the preceding chapter I began to talk about a version of postmodern cultural studies that does not inhabit the university but exists in the streets, stores, malls, theaters, magazines, newspapers and advertising agencies. What I call a *New York Times* postmodernism is the phenomenologized postmodernism of everyday lives led by Yuppies and post-baby-boomers who distrust ideology and cultivate their own mass-mediated generational experience. It is not the postmodernism of Lyotard; it is not bookish, although it has its favorite culture heroes (some of them writers) – Jay McInerney, Tama Janowitz, David Letterman, Arsenio Hall. It is worth considering the political and cultural impact of this sort of postmodernism because in many ways it is the most relevant postmodernism. After all, who reads Lyotard or his predecessor Daniel Bell? Not even neoconservative political essayists and critics like George Will and William Buckley appear to do. Postmodern theoretical texts are largely confined to esoteric graduate courses in English, comparative literature, social and cultural theory.

This is not to deny the role of cultural theory in Europe, where figures like Habermas, Sartre, de Beauvoir, Camus and Baudrillard inhabit public discourse in ways unimaginable in the US. Intellectual culture in Europe is vastly different from its counterparts in the US and Britain. European intellectuals are better integrated into a mandarinized popular culture and thus do not only write academic treatises but also publish newspaper and magazine essays and engage closely with the popular press, which solicits their opinions. A Habermas essay on the reunification of the two Germanys in a West German magazine has far greater credibility than would a similar essay by Galbraith (let alone Jameson) in an American magazine. Even Habermas' recondite two-volume *Theory of Communicative Action* (1984, 1987b) sold out almost immediately in West Germany. My critique of the unfortunate academization of cultural studies is more applicable to intellectual life in the US and UK than in Europe, where cultural studies has been better metabolized into the everyday lives of middlebrow and highbrow cultural consumers.

A minimalist agenda for American and British cultural studies might be simply to replicate the European integration of intellectuals into public discourse. This would definitely be a two-way street: not only would readers have to make a greater effort to understand political and cultural essays that are not served up in the moronic style and length of *USA Today* or Fleet Street. Writers would have to deacademize their work in a way that affords greater access to interested, intelligent but uncredentialed readers. My argument in *Decline of Discourse* (1990) about the turgidity of theoretical writing is especially relevant in the context of this discussion of non-positivist cultural studies, which is frequently composed in terms that are simply out of reach of the people who read *Le Monde* and *New Statesman*. Although I do not want to single out Jameson (e.g., 1981), the example of his own highly technical writing (which we all attempt to replicate, admiring the profundity of his ideas as well as his academic luminosity!) does not bode well for the mainstreaming of a critical cultural studies. Surely Jameson can compose himself in terms accessible to a few hundred thousand, not only a few hundred. On his behalf one might note that it is difficult for people like him to have their work published in major American or British newspapers and magazines.

But that is not the main point here. I note the relative accessibility of European cultural criticism as compared to the American and British variety largely to suggest one of the unfortunate symptoms of the academization of cultural studies. Although Derrida, Barthes and Foucault do not write public discourse, their integration into French public life is simply unequalled in the US and UK. This is doubly ironic in that European higher education has always been more elitist than in the US. The academizing obscurantism of American academic critics is surprising in light of our relatively populist attitude toward university education, which is available to a much higher percentage of people than in Europe and the UK. Somehow this does not affect the ways in which academic criticism is composed, probably because the commitment to populist higher education in the US is not a real commitment to democratize all cultural life but rather to produce a larger portion of economically relevant human capital – skilled workers.

This is borne out if one examines the relatively non-humanistic nature of the curriculum in American universities, currently under siege by neoconservatives who want to turn the clock back and do away with the more political aspects of the liberal arts. Allan Bloom (1987) and E.D. Hirsch (1987) argue for greater canonical cultural literacy among the college-age cohort in the US largely as a way of retrenching what they believe is the progressive political climate among the American professoriate (who, studies show, are not raving radicals but only mildly left-of-center; see Ladd and Lipset, 1975).

Although I disagree with much of the substance of Bloom's and Hirsch's critique of the putative left-wing dominance of the American college curriculum that has supposedly resulted in falling academic standards as well as declining cultural literacy, they raise important questions about the technocratic nature of the American university and American intellectual life generally. At a time when faculty productivity is increasingly measured in terms of grant money and not ideas it is difficult to be optimistic about American replication of European intellectuals' engagement with popular culture and public issues. It is highly unlikely that American intellectuals will find a toehold in popular experience and discourse that can propel them into important discussion of the largest issues of the day. It is just such an engagement that I urge in this chapter, notably around issues of cultural criticism. Although academic and intellectual life in this country is dominated by a narrowly technocratic productivism that puts the needs of the state and elites ahead of democratic social change, I want to argue for a cultural studies that is firmly implanted in the everyday lives of citizens otherwise bombarded with ideologizing simulations that entice them into consumerism and conformity.

This cultural studies breaks out of the academy and technical academic jargon, even though it refuses to deny its own erudition and theoretical formation. The Birmingham School offers the single best example of a theoretically sophisticated cultural studies that manages to address popular cultural works and practices using structural understandings afforded by comprehensive social theories. Although I do not find the Birmingham theoretical synthesis of Gramsci and Foucault to be particularly compelling as an alternative to Frankfurt critical theory, the CCCS group sets the agenda for a cultural studies that is intimately involved in the public processes of cultural life. I aim at a deacademized cultural studies metabolized into the lifeworlds of people who make use of cultural studies in order to resist dominant culture and create new culture.

The metabolization of cultural studies into a critical everyday life includes the following elements:

1. Cultural studies becomes directly engaged with the political functions of popular culture.

2. Cultural studies helps transform the ways in which we experience the cultural world, changing the ways we read, see, hear and write.

3. Cultural studies is shorn of its technical academic jargon and instead develops a broader, more public vernacular.

4. Cultural studies finds ways to retain its theoreticity while at the same time initiating public discourse.

5. Cultural studies redefines the realm of the popular, especially with regard to the fault line between popular and mandarin cultures, thus breaking down the experiences and practices of institutional differentiation fragmenting human activity.

In the next five sections I elaborate these aims and practices, attempting to provide a legitimate alternative to the highly academized cultural studies that proliferates in non-positivist academia. In developing this conception of a more public and political cultural studies metabolized into everyday life itself I necessarily build on the five major non-positivist versions of cultural analysis that I have discussed in this book, including Marxist theories of culture, the Frankfurt School's cultural theory, the work of the Birmingham School, poststructural and postmodern perspectives on culture and feminist cultural studies. I conceive of this concluding chapter less as synthesis than as a sympathetic transcendence of the limitations of each of these perspectives, drawing most clearly from the perspective of the Frankfurt School but without ignoring the limitations of Adorno, Marcuse and Horkheimer.

At the risk of reacademizing my argument precisely when I say that I want to turn away from a ponderously technical cultural studies, let me address the fact that the Frankfurt School's cultural theory has been the object of criticism by students of popular culture who believe that the Frankfurt theorists were completely disdainful of the popular, so much so that Frankfurt theory is read as the quintessence of the mandarinism rejected by popular-culture analysts. Although, as I indicated in Chapter 4, there is some truth to this characterization of the Frankfurt work, it misses the central preoccupation with mass culture that conditioned the Frankfurt School's revision of Marxism. The original Frankfurt thinkers understood clearly how the region of the popular was a site of both administration, commodification and contestation in post-World War Two capitalism, giving capitalism a new lease of life but also posing emancipatory alternatives. The culture-industry thesis reflects this insight, as do a good many of the particular cultural readings offered by the Frankfurt group since World War Two. The culture-industry thesis is the single most important theoretical development equipping a latter-day cultural studies, enabling it to keep its theoretical wits about it instead of descending to the unfocused, untheorized cultural readings abounding today.

It is hard to imagine a politicized cultural studies that does not trade on the culture-industry thesis. Without understanding the structural role of popular culture, a metabolized cultural studies will offer no significant resistance to the celebratory cultural readings practised by both positivist cultural analysts and the *New York Times* postmodernists I talked about in the preceding chapter. This is not to say that the Frankfurt cultural theory should be uncritically accepted; I would not be writing this book if that were true. A great deal of the non-positivist cultural analyses done since Adorno's, Horkheimer's and Marcuse's deaths have added tremendously to the project of a radical cultural studies. This is particularly true of poststructuralism and feminism. For his part, Habermas has done little to help update the original Frankfurt cultural theory in a way that would obviate my effort at retrieval and rejuvenation, especially given his (1981a, 1987a) hostility to poststructuralism and postmodernism.

Practising the Political

For cultural studies to become directly engaged with the political functions of culture continues a long tradition of radical cultural analysis, beginning with orthodox Marxism. Although I reject the mechanical and reductionist quality of much of the Lukács-Goldmann tradition, I support the notion that culture is a political factor, especially in late capitalism, where culture is in some senses the most politicized region in the public sphere. But it is not enough for radical cultural studies simply to offer analyses of the political forms and functions of popular culture, explaining the various circuitries of production, distribution and reception conditioning the ideological nature of our lived experience in capitalism. Radical cultural studies must also conceive of itself in a way that underlines its own direct contribution to counter-hegemonic political practice.

Where orthodox Marxists, Frankfurt theorists, poststructuralists, postmodernists and feminists conceive of cultural analysis as an analytical activity the results of which are collected in critical publications, presumably to be read by the public, I draw here on the CCCS tradition of cultural analysis that does not separate itself out from the ebb and flow of the politics of everyday life. Only the Birmingham School has managed to politicize cultural analysis in a way that repairs the fracture between academic and intellectual criticism, on the one hand, and the ongoing politics of everyday culture, on the other. Although the Birmingham practice of cultural politics is insufficiently worked out, it nonetheless offers valuable hints about how a future cultural studies can *directly intervene in cultural politics*.

This radicalized cultural studies not only deconstructs the enmeshing texts of popular culture but affords cultural consumers a way of seeing through, and thus reversing the momentum of, the duplicities propagated by the culture industry. Cultural theorists have not yet theorized clearly enough their own relations to the culture industry, both in regard to popular culture and academia. It is not clear how people who do cultural studies under one banner or another theorize their own political contribution, except by implication. The link between cultural analysis and action needs to be made much clearer, especially by those who are chagrined about the self-reproducing nature of the culture industry and wish to change it. Interestingly, the political reception of cultural criticism has never been high on the agenda of cultural critics, who instead spend their time either theorizing about how to do cultural studies or engaging in the particular readings occupying much of cultural analysis, both positivist and non-positivist.

A radical cultural studies needs to consider how it is received culturally and politically, especially where the reception of culture (e.g., Iser, 1978) is a central issue for cultural studies, determining the political impact that cultural practices have in the everyday life of late capitalism. At some level the reception of culture is every bit as important as its production and distribution; indeed, the original Frankfurt culture-industry thesis suggests their inseparability. Regrettably, though, the reception of popular culture has remained a topic more for quantitative empiricists who study audience responses than for critical theorists who want to change cultural reception as well as production. In this context, it is difficult to imagine that cultural studies radicals will ably address the reception of their own critique as a significant political intervention when they have not sufficiently theorized reception in general.

The most obvious exception to this indictment are the poststructuralists, especially feminist Derrideans. Shortly, I discuss how this poststructural tendency can inform a new cultural studies that focuses on the transformation of the reception and production of representation as an active political contribution in its own right. Here suffice it to say that cultural studies needs to find a way to theorize and then actualize its own cultural interventions in transcending objectivism. It is well and good for cultural critics to churn out close readings of cultural works and practices. But that does little to change the reception process if it bears little direct relation to the political project of cultural transformation – that is, if radical cultural analysis does not also *theorize itself theorizing*, making a political contribution by challenging and disrupting central modalities of reception in late capitalism.

After all, the culture industry produces representations of the world that are both inaccurate and self-serving. That is the nature of all ideology, as Marx

(Marx and Engels, 1947) understood it. These representations are encoded in a culturally constituted everyday life in which people receive and thus enact these simulations as if they are ontologically inescapable. Popular culture reproduces a certain view of the world through its representations of commodities. A radical cultural studies needs to find a way to disrupt these patterns of representation, and of the production of representation, in order to suggest substantively new modes of our interaction with other people, social institutions, commodities and nature. This cultural studies portrays utopia, and practicable ways of working toward it, by breaking the hold of deutopianizing imageries, deconstructing them against themselves by showing the secret advocacy of constitutional authorship suppressed deep beneath the surface of the quotidian. It does so by understanding itself to be an active player in the politics of cultural production and reception, challenging these dominant processes and thus implicitly and explicitly suggesting new modes of public life.

This agenda is far afield from most cultural studies projects, even those done by self-professed radicals, who are otherwise preoccupied with theorizations of the possibility of cultural reading in the first place and then with close cultural readings in the second place. The balance between theory and interpretation certainly shifts from paradigm to paradigm (e.g., the Frankfurt and CCCS traditions are more theoretically circumspect than are most cultural deconstructors, who offer what theory they profess heavily encoded in actual readings themselves, as in the notable case of Derrida). But it is difficult to escape the impression that a great deal of even the densest cultural studies manages to avoid the issue of its own possible political impact, instead reveling in the texture of its own and others' texts as if it just discovered the thick textuality of our world. Politics seems quite remote from the critical practices of most leftist cultural analysts, even, ironically, the European feminists who drink deeply of deconstruction (as Walters, 1992, indicates). All of these people avoid the possibility of their own political intervention into the cultural processes of representation that constitute ideology for almost everybody in industrialized societies.

This depoliticization of cultural studies is extremely curious. Many cultural neoconservatives (Newman, 1985) lament that too much criticism is driven by political concerns, wrecking the traditional acculturating mission of humanities disciplines in a Hobbesian society. Yet most leftist cultural analysts neglect their own relationship to the political, even if the text of their criticism, and their meta-theorizing about their criticism, expresses patent political postures and problematics. For the most part, this apparent politicization, which represents the growing hegemony of European theoretical discourse, is pseudopolitics. There is little political substance in the ways that these rhetorics inform the relationship between criticism and politics.

This is not the usual lament about the ivory-tower existence of radical intellectuals. I seriously doubt that a radicalized cultural studies will change the world overnight (although it could certainly have positive impact on a host of political and social movements). Radical cultural analysts have failed to articulate their own constitutional and agitational roles in mass culture, ironically bracketing out their own involvement in creating as well as deconstructing culture even where they interrogate every other mode of cultural practice for its imbedded ontologies. This is not to say that 'radical' cultural analysts are imposter radicals

– that their affiliations to radical politics are bogus. Surely that is true for some but not all. And it has nothing to do with the project of cultural studies, which should be inherently political. In fact, cultural studies is much more politicizing than a good many of the other intellectual practices carried out under the banner of one or another radical sect, which is one of the reasons I wrote this book. I believe that cultural studies is the last, best hope of an otherwise ossified Marxism and feminism, both of which threaten to become dogmatic discourses of affiliation.

A genuinely radical cultural studies will acknowledge its own constitutional and agitational roles in popular culture as a force of demystification. It will attempt to change the ways we see, hear, read and write, especially with reference to the dominant imageries of the social world that inundate us from cradle to grave, morning until night. Cultural studies disrupts the quotidian by debunking the representations and simulations of the quotidian proffered from all sides: fiction, movies, television, journalism, advertising, academia. This version of cultural studies recognizes its own inherence in everyday life and tries to transform the texture and texts of everyday life from within, not from the outside. I am not recanting the one-dimensionality thesis of Marcuse (1964) for I agree with him that the universe of discourse has been nearly closed to edifying, electrifying critique. But such critique must be staged immanently, in terms of the dominant rhetorics and language games of the moment, and not imported from the outside, as Frankfurt critical theory in its high modernism has too often tried to do.

It is not enough for mandarin criticism simply to disdain popular culture as an enormous manipulation. True, it is by and large a manipulation, concealing its own artifice as one possible text among many others. But we must read into and out of particular simulations of popular culture, engaging with them on the quotidian level of their production and reception, which we theorize in terms of larger structural principles of social and economic reproduction. People watch television shows like *Miami Vice* and *thirtysomething*. They browse through *People* magazine as well as *Time* and *The New York Times*. They line up to view *Fatal Attraction* and *When Harry Met Sally*. They devour blockbuster romance fiction. They read scientist textbooks in high school and college. None of us is immune, unless we live on a desert island! Perhaps the best way to begin a serious and systematic cultural deconstruction, aspiring to be a political practice for its strong intervention into culture, is to begin *on ourselves*, reflecting on all the ways in which we as radical Others have nonetheless been constituted by the dominant culture.

Only fools would pretend otherwise. We are products of our time and place – men, women, the middle class, Anglo-Americans, academics. For me as a man fully to comprehend the political possibilities of a feminist deconstruction I must position myself in terms of the fields of difference constituted hierarchically around the issue of gender. I must reflect on my own conditioning as a man and on what I actualize in the way of manly behavior in order to understand how our culture positions women subordinately with respect to men. Similarly, for me to engage in cultural criticism and media analysis I have to reflect on the ways in which I have been constituted by cultural works and practices that are typical of my generation, social class, gender and national heritage. Surely, the fact that I watched the infamous family sitcoms of the 1950s and 1960s affected the ways in which I understood my own family dynamics as well as formed my relations with women, which I have had to redo in the meantime.

At some level, then, a politically motivated cultural criticism is also self-criticism, situating one in the complex cultural fields out of which we cannot pretend to abstract ourselves. We are culture, just as we oppose the culture. Our self-understanding as acculturated beings informs the ways in which we read and criticize culture, exemplifying the liberatory self-reflection that needs to be inculcated in order for people to live the culture differently. One might think of cultural studies as a sensitizing agent, problematizing the taken-for-granted images, simulations and representations that have become second nature for most of us – the McDonald's' imagery of food as family, the filmic denigration of women, the positivist news media freezing the present into Being. In this process of cultural problematization we problematize ourselves, understanding and thus changing ourselves as the cultural conduits we have become. This empowers us to experience and then create the world in ways that do not conform to the patterns of reception encoded in the simulations insidiously dictating their own reception.

A radical cultural studies intervenes politically where it challenges representation to theorize itself, understanding how the repertoire of interpretive activities in which we habitually and thoughtlessly engage is, in fact, a careful political construction – call it ideology. The detextualized ideology of fast capitalism does not for the most part rely on old-fashioned texts to impart its worldview and thus reproduce its own world. Textuality oozes out of the covers of books and into the streets via the built environment and into homes and minds via media that dictate their own careless, spontaneous reception. This dispersed textuality must be put into words of advocacy and interest. By so doing, we can better recognize the texts counseling our conformity and consumerism for what they are and challenge them, instead of living our lives differently from the lives suggested by these increasingly inescapable imageries. In this way, cultural studies becomes a political practice engaged in by all cultural consumers and would-be cultural creators: it is a lens through which we suddenly recognize the authorship of cultural oeuvres and decode the arguments they make for hamburgers, automobiles, a certain view of women, the American Way of Life.

This reading of culture as secret advocacy is the most radicalizing contribution of a theoretical and political cultural studies. Instead of consuming popular culture uncritically, as if these works and practices simply fell from the sky and mysteriously appeared in supermarket checkout lines, bookstores, theaters, newspapers and television, we learn to interrogate the encoded arguments of these cultural forms for what they are – arguments for capitalist, sexist, racist Being. In doing so, we challenge conventional wisdom about what is good, just, true and beautiful. This interrogation forces us to strip away the levels of suppression surrounding cultural works and practices in the deceptive appearance of their own nature-like existence as inevitable, unquestioned features of the landscape of *la vie quotidienne*. Cultural studies can make culture come alive, for better or worse; it energizes culture, restoring to it the secret intentions of its artisans in a way that suggests the possibilities of new cultures not dominated by the self-reproducing logic of capital accumulation and commodification. If nothing else, cultural studies can seek and destroy ideologies wherever they may lurk, usually in the least likely places – in the female body as depicted visually in advertising, in the narrative structure of macho detective fiction, in the layout and pace of journalistic reportage that disassembles the world's totality into an unconnected jumble of bits and bytes obscuring reality, not clarifying it.

Transforming the Reception and Production of Representation

Where this radical cultural studies will politicize reception in general, showing that cultural works and practices encode ontological and political arguments that can be challenged, in particular it addresses the reception and production of hegemonic representation – the simulations that reproduce the body politic as well as political bodies (see O'Neill, 1989). Cultural studies aims to transform these representations and thus to suggest the possibility of new images and texts: its deconstructive and utopian aims are fundamentally inseparable. This version of cultural studies contests the positivist model of representation by showing convincingly that all representation is already a presentation, a strong argument for one world over another. To be sure, the dispersed texts of fast capitalism like advertising, television and journalism do not rely on positivism per se. Instead, they dispense with all truth claims because they do not present themselves as texts whose truth content must be vouchsafed epistemologically. This is precisely their strength: by avoiding claims to positivist representation, positivist representations represent all the more effectively, making it extremely difficult to deconstruct them as corrigible texts that could have been composed differently.

Representation is a political practice where it encodes its content in the illusion of an authorless stancelessness. Where the camera depicts women via the male gaze, as poststructural cinefeminism demonstrates, it suggests a universality that disqualifies alternative modes of representation, notably feminist ones. Where television reflects the satisfaction of particular material human needs in terms of commodity acquisition it suggests the universality of these needs and of the means of satisfying them. Where journalists compose themselves in terse, untheorized stories they suggest a disconnected formlessness to the world fundamentally inimical to stronger totalizing readings. In deconstructing these representations as the corrigible, interested, perspectival and passionate commitments of a certain mode of authorial subjectivity – *that of hegemony* – cultural studies transforms the way in which these representations are received and, beyond that, suggests new presentations and representations that already acknowledge their own immanent undecidability.

Transforming the reception of representation is the strongest contribution of a radical cultural studies to the modification of an everyday life characterized by uncritical reading. Conformist reception issues in conformist political practices, ever the role of ideology in reproducing domination. For cultural studies to show the possibility of alternative readings of culture helps generalize those readings into the concatenated practices comprising an overdetermined everyday life. Think how different life would be if we could all decode the world's self-advertising as a plenitude of Being. So much of what is represented as an unchangeable social life is simply the product of the various standpoints of power from which particularistic claims are inflated into general ones, e.g., white male experience standing for all possible experience.

These representations are broken where they are shown to be products of power and interest. One of the key ways in which cultural studies deconstructs representation is to show how its inflated universality is achieved at the expense of difference, the myriad ways in which people do not behave according to the norms established for them by the supposedly universal subjects of representation. Of course, simulators are one step ahead of the game, and have been for a long time: simulating their commodified lives, commodity producers position consumers in terms of their group affiliations. Thus, a hamburger chain runs a campaign targeting black people, where cigarette and automobile manufacturers target various class and gender fractions in terms of imageries that best present them to themselves. Where these simulations disclaim universality they are all the more universal. What their prospective consumers have in common is commodity desire. Instead of subverting universality, these simulations enhance it by pluralizing experience around common themes of average and desirable life in the late twentieth century. We can all recognize ourselves in these cultural representations because we have been positioned to see ourselves as players in the quotidian. Over time this creates a real universal in the sense in which white people identify the black people targeted strategically by advertising campaigns as *like them*, as in effect white. These representations block the production and reception of real difference by assimilating a plurality of subject positions to a single normative model of subjectivity – mainstream America.

Representation breaks out from texts into practice where it models a normative subjectivity and intersubjectivity (e.g., the patriarchal family) that is reproduced in the numerous everyday ways in which people enact their social scripts and roles. These Durkheimian and Parsonian roles are simulated by hegemonists, the copywriters of the culture industry. They do not magically emerge from the structural-functional requirements of civilized group life, as Parsonians contend (e.g., Alexander, 1982, 1985). Normative concepts and practices of modern life emerge from the language games of ideology, scripted by ideologists who reproduce the given via its fatalizing representation.

Representation is political in two senses. First, representation suggests a standard of the normative, for which it silently claims universality (e.g., the male gaze). Second, it provokes conformity with these norms, even (no, *especially*) if this conformity is not openly advocated but only implied. In the first case, we exchange the general for the particular, mistaking a historically specific and politically invested representation of reality with all possible realities. In the second case, we respond to representation as a frozen piece of history to which conformity is the only reasonable response.

The culture industry commodifies representation both to sell cultural products and to enforce a certain conformity. These representations are found in the encoded texts of popular culture that derive their singular force from the fact that they are not presented as discursive arguments but rather are strewn around an everyday life conducted in what phenomenologists call the natural attitude. In this attitude people accept appearances unproblematically, refusing to distinguish between social and natural objects. Popular culture is phenomenologized, implanted in everyday lives conducted in the natural attitude according to which television and movies are as indubitably invariant as the edifice of physical nature. Thus, the lives scripted in these popular representations of the popular are lived by people duped into believing that the people who appear on the screens and in the texts of power *are them*.

Cultural studies thaws the frozen landscape of popular culture by showing that representation constitutes, not only reflecting a glacial social world but in fact constructing a certain world to be experienced in the attitude of fatalistic conformity. By showing that entertainment is advocacy as much as reflection or diversion, we challenge culture to lay its cards on the table. This is politically crucial where so much of mass culture reflects us back to ourselves, depicting particular social con-texts from the point of view of postured universality. Popular culture instructs us in a certain philosophy of history, albeit silently, in the sense that it depicts social possibilities in terms that seem to relate to our own lives. In this sense, popular culture affords us our identities within social fields of difference that appear to deny us meaning on their face. Culture constructs meaning for people who no longer possess definitive texts with which to orient their existence. Even religion is represented today as the homely, friendly experience of a flexible doctrine, having been routinized as lifestyle if not transcendent experience (see Bellah *et al.*, 1985).

There is nothing wrong with learning meaning from cultural representation to which we bear the relationship of identification. In this postmodern world, identification intends to replace affiliation as the fundamental experience of social sameness and difference. Affiliation (see Bell, 1976) is represented as the archaic posture of people who derived meaning from their participation in social movements. Today meaning lies in the recognition of oneself in the frozen frames of cultural representation abounding with busy, happy, familied people *like us*. Cultural studies shows that these representational frames distort reality and thus do not provide stable, sufficient meanings. This is a radicalizing posture where they help us deposition our own subjectivities, reclaiming them from a culture that writes us, not the other way around. By deconstructing representation as silent political advocacy, we liberate experience from the simulations that increasingly live our lives for us.

Cultural Studies as Public Discourse

It is imperative that cultural studies drops its dense academic jargon and instead develops a broader, more public vernacular; without doing so, it will be impossible to implant cultural studies in the ebb and flow of everyday life as a potent, politicizing mode of ideology critique. For cultural studies to remain entombed in the theoretical libraries of rarefied intellectual critics denies it political efficacy, which is one of the hallmarks of an engaged, relevant version of cultural studies. This is not an argument for plain language, whatever that is supposed to mean (see Gellner, 1959). After all, the languages that people speak in everyday life are often incredibly distorting, scripted for them by the variety of mass media that represent ordinary discourse as idiotically shallow and atheoretical. Adolescents and their parents speak the patois of the representational figures with whom they identify on television and in the movies, reproducing the banalities of Heathcliffe Huxtable and Rambo. Thus, they are denied access to more recondite, elevated and intellectually penetrating discourses with which to make sense of the complicated jumble of experiences and practices comprising late capitalism.

My aim in deacademizing the jargon of cultural studies is not to pedestrianize it; that would completely defeat my purpose, which is public enlightenment and the initiation of broadly based social change movements. The rectification of discourse in late capitalism requires a democratization of specialist languages as much as a despecialization of codes that have become forbiddingly technical and thus exclusionary. We need a public language of critique that helps build the democratic polity composed of intelligent but non-specialist readers and writers capable of talking publicly about the big issues of the day. The creation of such a polity is impeded by literary political economies of popular culture and academic writing which force writers to write formulaic writing targeted to particular audience segments. Public discourse suffers at the hands of a commodified cultural world in which cultural texts derive significance from their exchange value, preventing people from reading and writing across disciplines and specialties and thus participating more fully in the democratic process.

Literary hierarchy supports political and economic hierarchies, which in turn provoke more literary hierarchy. This argument is central to the Habermas-generation critical theory of communication and suggests a crucial theme for a cultural studies that reflects on its own discursive contributions to culture. Although it is understandable and perhaps necessary that cultural studies first develop in the university, bringing together otherwise isolated scholars in journals, books and conferences where the level of discourse is increasingly clubbish, there is a point beyond which the academization of cultural studies discourse ironically blocks its own engagement with the popular, thus defeating it. We are in trouble when cultural theory becomes all theory, just as we have difficulties when cultural readings endlessly proliferate without congealing around a coherent thematic and theoretic center.

When I call for the dehierarchization of critical discourse I am also urging the upgrading of so-called ordinary language. It is not enough (although it is necessary) for cultural studies to conduct itself in the public vernacular lest it lose all political efficacy, particularly with regard to affording readable deconstructive analyses of cultural texts and practices. The public vernacular itself must change to accommodate new levels of insight and complexity necessary to grasp the social world fully. Indeed, the one prepares the way for the other, as Gramsci (1971) foresaw in his imaginative writings about the relationship between intellectuals and publics. In fast capitalism it is more crucial than ever to conceive of the reconstruction of the public vernacular in empowering, elevating terms so as to challenge not only the concentration of wealth but also the concentration of expertise and cultural meaning on which it rests.

It is facile to excuse the academization of cultural studies as the necessary growth phase of a budding intellectual discipline. Similarly, it is wrong to ignore the technical fetishism of many deconstructive studies, which virtually reinvent language from the ground up. Neologisms cannot do our thinking for us, even though they can be useful (e.g., I used the term *deposition* above, playing on the poststructural notion of our positioning by language). Nor does the establishment of a new academic discipline or interdiscipline signal the maturity or validity of thought. More often than not academization and the accompanying development of technical discourse reflect the retreat of thought from engaging public tasks, a real temptation in these dismal political times of the Reagan/Bush/Thatcher/Major world order.

The academization of cultural studies dooms cultural readings to be recondite, conducted in the pages of scholarly journals and not in more accessible outlets. Of course, this leaves aside the crucial issue of whether, and how, a democratized cultural criticism is going to find its way into the public forum: writing publicly and accessibly mean nothing if one cannot attain publicity. But that is a question that I will consider below, in my discussion of cultural studies' relation to the popular. Writing accessibly is necessary but not sufficient for the establishment of a public discourse of cultural criticism, without which the politicizing role of cultural readings is lost. It is simply unimaginable that cultural studies could have significant political impact when it is imprisoned in journals, monographs, conferences and classes that address a homogeneous community of people who speak the same tongue, especially fellow academics. Although cultural studies is riven by precisely this debate about accessibility, it is clear that the academizing, depoliticizing version of cultural studies, whether feminist, post-structural or Birmingham, is in the saddle and will likely remain so.

This is mainly because the academics who do cultural studies are academics first and foremost. They learn literary norms from other academic writings and colleagues during their apprenticeships in graduate school. It is not that we cannot write with felicity, simplicity and grace; most of us can if we try. But as academics we replicate academizing, obscurantist norms of literary presentation that bear the hallmark of academic legitimacy. Academic humanists perish without publications by university presses that sport numerous appurtenances of the scholarly apparatus like notes, narrow focus and an obscure, self-referential writing style. But that is not the only reason why cultural studies has been so heavily academized, like every other budding and established intellectual specialty in the Anglo-American world. It is also because cultural studies, especially in its non-positivist variants, is devoted to theory, which, it is assumed, must be a highly specialized language in its own right. The dense theoreticity of non-positivist cultural studies as much as its inveterate academicism, which it shares with every other academic specialty, dooms it to obscurantism.

Reading Lacan or Derrida competently requires an arduous apprenticeship. Graduate students in theory toil away for years working through these difficult, sometimes untranslated, texts in order to claim theory as their own world. Perhaps one has to be a theorist, as I am, really to appreciate the self-isolating, self-elevating tendencies of theory! This involves not only learning how to read and write technically (the better to claim profundity) but also how to live a theoretical life defined by one's affiliation to certain sacred texts and subcultures clearly set apart from intellectual business-as-usual. One can always spot the theory crowd, at its various levels of hierarchy: they carry themselves differently from the positivist rabble, many of whom are of humble origins and come to science as a leveling pursuit. Their dress, manner and tastes set them apart, even if they earn little money – just enough to support the illusion, the simulation, of their difference.

Whether this involves adorning oneself in black clothes and carrying a well-thumbed copy of Lacan's *Écrits* or, if one is less impecunious, wearing a leather jacket and Italian loafers while networking at conferences, the effect is the same: the theory world is elitist, even where it postures egalitarianism. This is very much the cultural studies world, too, especially where cultural studies involves a great deal of theoretical dedication en route to the sort of close cultural readings that fill the relevant journals and academic monographs. At issue here is the politics of style. Theoretically-oriented cultural studies tends to be a cult excluding lesser souls. On the evidence, of course, theory people must have value if they are intelligent enough to understand the serpentine works of Derrida and his ilk as well as the cultural *objets* claiming the critical attention of cultural readers. All such claims are suspect, however, at a time when hierarchy, as well as its ideological defense, is encoded in the surreptitious social text of the quotidian.

The leftist politics of style are well known to the rigorous right as well as to the left's own persistent gadflies who have never been reluctant to expose left fashion as fashion. Eric Hoffer's (1966) tale about true believers tells some of the story, although, as do most on the right, he neglects the fact that market capitalism produces hierarchy through its own competitive machinery. The theory business is as much a culture industry as the mainline culture industry of New York and Los Angeles. Of course, the stakes are much lower: the trendy theorist is lucky to sell 10,000 copies of a book published by a university press and to earn $100,000 a year as an academic luminary. But although the star stature of theoretical academics is relatively devalued compared to the mega-stakes of the Streeps and Redfords, this is our world and we must live in it!

A brief excursus on the cultural status of theory is in order here. The self-consciously theoretical orientations of many cultural studies people, as well as of those who do social and literary theory in general, reflect a certain hauteur on the part of theorists who imagine themselves to be superior to the number-crunchers dominating the fields of Anglo-American social science. Theory is seen to be a calling, a genuine craft, and its practitioners view themselves as savants set apart from the workaday professoriate. Although this vanguard mandarinism clearly has untoward political implications, it is intended less as a political stance than as a cultural positioning: theorists accumulate cultural capital, especially in the university (see Bourdieu, 1988). They portray themselves as different from and better than the hoi polloi, who pursue their own delimited, often quantitative researches.

One can find this hauteur throughout the academic humanities disciplines. Although empirical social and natural scientists are not without their own conceits, notably about the superiority of positivist method and its grantworthy technical applications, the cultural positioning of people in theory blatantly contradicts their own interests in *the popular*, which they dissect from the Apollonian heights of high theory. But cultural theorists for the most part purvey the study of the popular not because they genuinely wish to foster oppositional tendencies within it (whose momentum could be accelerated by a radicalized cultural studies that breaks the hold of hegemony and nurtures real difference) but because they feel superior to the masses, whose cultural works and practices are methodically dissected using the Euro-rhetoric of cultural interpretation.

The secret elitism of cultural theory subverts the emancipatory intentions of leftist cultural theorists, who profess allegiance to one form of radical social change or another. But it is difficult to detect the political energy in most examples of cultural studies, which are composed in recondite ways simply inaccessible to everyday cultural consumers. Examples of this energy are few and far between, judging by recent examples of cultural readings abetted by the high Euro-theory I have been talking about. And inaccessibility is defended on the grounds of theoretical necessity: supposedly one needs a background in European philosophy and social thought in order to do cultural analyses that explode hegemonizing cultural simulations and practices, thus entrapping their quotidian readers in the sticky ontological amber preventing them from living differently. Although I would agree that such a background in high cultural theory is indispensable in order to understand the range of interpretive possibilities available to critics as well as to ground cultural readings sufficiently in larger theories of social structure, one can use theory in a way that does not block public discourse but, indeed, enhances it. This is perhaps the most fundamental challenge posed to cultural theorists who view themselves as both acculturated intellectuals and political critics.

Unsparing opponents of the theorization of cultural studies suggest that cultural analysts theorize obsessively and densely in order to add value to their own tribal stature. Barthes argues that the boundary between literary criticism and cultural creation fades upon deconstructive inspection. This insight is a valuable component of the critique of positivism's notion of presuppositionless representation. But this insight can also get out of hand where critics arrogate cultural creation to themselves, instead of pointing out that the hierarchy of creation over criticism (writing over reading) needs to be leveled in revaluing the constitutional role of criticism. More than a few cultural critics, especially those of a non–positivist bent, position themselves as important cultural figures not in order to subvert cultural and political hierarchy but merely to add luster to their own names, however cheap the coin of academic status might be in the larger world.

The ability to shape one's criticism in public prose is an essential requirement of the political democracy that radical critics prefigure in the example of their own work on the popular. The New Left (see Marcuse, 1969) clearly recognized that cultural process and product cannot be cleanly separated. Instead, the politics of everyday life have enormous constitutional impact on societies of the future, making our choices in the moment extremely important for what will necessarily emerge out of them. Cultural criticism joins the politics of everyday life where it positions itself politically and rhetorically. Critics who want democracy act democratically, addressing themselves not only to fellow intellectuals but to the whole range of people affected by the gigantic web of popular culture and mass media. Although establishing public discourse is as much a process of raising stupefied cultural consumers to a higher level of discernment and critique as it is of democratizing critical discourse, it is imperative that theorists do not define the problem self-servingly. It is easy to bemoan the condition of public culture as if the only problem is the lamentable public ignorance about culture, letters, politics. This easily earns points for the erudite critic. But it is also important to recognize that theory's own politics of style matters significantly for the ways in which people are taught to receive culture, penetrating the mass cultural criticism of the daily newspapers, magazines and television. I am not freighting cultural criticism with too much cosmic responsibility here but only suggesting that cultural studies must be done in accessibly public vernacular if it is to avoid reproducing the very hierarchies it professes to oppose.

Nothing will be easy about edifying public taste while democratizing the rhetoric of cultural theory and analysis. All the manifestos in the world will not change the fact that the culture industry is highly centralized and concentrated, beating back most challenges to it. But one of the essential theses of cultural studies is that culture is an ongoing set of works and practices that are somehow non-identical to the cultural hegemony imposed from above and reproduced from below. Ideas, experience, taste, oeuvres fall through the cracks; they make a difference. As well, resistance is provoked by the very hegemony obscuring it. Although seemingly impenetrable from the outside, the culture industry is not a *deus ex machina* and never was.. It can be changed through a combination of indefatigable political and critical work, auguring a future prefiguratively in the way we try to change the culture as well as our own lives. People are already at work making culture that challenges the quotidian: *this* is the central hope of critical theory and one that must be exemplified in cultural studies work conducted beyond the self-perpetuating language games of the elitist university.

Theorizing Reading, Reading Theory or Reading Theoretically?

Given all of this, what will a radical cultural studies actually do in the way of analytical work? Assuming that cultural studies can manage to position itself in the midst of everyday life, helping transform the reception of representations, how will the texts of these studies be written? The answer to these questions is suggested in the distinction I am trying to draw between a cultic cultural studies that revels in its own theoreticity but does not engage in public discourse, on the one hand, and a cultural studies that enters the cultural and political fray unashamedly, using pragmatic tools at hand in order to be understood, on the other. The challenge for a critical cultural studies is to help people read culture theoretically and politically without allowing cultural studies to become a formulaic exercise in reading theory or theorizing reading: rather, a radical cultural studies must teach people how to read, and thus live, theoretically, beyond the imperatives of the culture industry which are so readily reproduced in the society of the spectacle.

The challenge for cultural studies is to retain its theoreticity while at the same time initiating public discourse, teaching people how to read deconstructively. Students of non-positivist cultural studies tend to make two mistakes: either they allow their justifiable interest in theory, particularly in the issue of how to theorize the politics of reading and writing, to get the better of them, obsessively debating what it means to read, instead of doing actual readings; or they only read, failing to connect their theoretical preliminaries with the particular readings proliferating in the cultural studies journals and monographs. Part of the problem here is that theory does not adequately do its job: it fails to infuse the everyday activity of reading with enough theoreticity to slow it down at a time when texts are rapidly dispersed into the media-ted, figural and built environments. Either theory is viewed as preliminary to close cultural readings, which lose touch with larger theoretical concerns relating texts to their enveloping social con-texts, or else theory is viewed as a text itself, which is read over and over again in the mandarin world of letters. Instead of actually helping everyday readings to become theoretical, thus liberating people from the sedating, stupefying texts scripting conformist, consumerist existences, theorists either theorize reading without reading (or before reading closely, which loses its ground in prior theorizations of the politics of reading) or they only read theory, losing the political force of cultural deconstructions conducted squarely in the midst of everyday life.

Admittedly, it is crucially necessary to theorize reading, and its relationship to writing, in terms of the imbedded politics of all hierarchized language games; otherwise, reading is modeled on the positivist reception of representation, hence disempowering readers who are structurally positioned to read but not write the texts of power. Without theorizing reading, we read atheoretically, as so many cultural studies people do, proliferating specific interpretations of cultural oeuvres that do not congeal into a larger theoretical and political totality. As well, it is necessary to read theory as well as to theorize reading. Only thus can we develop a sufficient resiliency with which to defend ourselves against positivist habits of mind that subtly infiltrate themselves into the ways we read and live culture, thus losing our own critical distance from the enmeshing, encoding forces of fast capitalism. But we must also develop the capacity to read everyday cultural texts and practices theoretically, that is, in terms of their contribution to overall hegemony, which we understand in thoroughly structural terms. This is the real practical work of a radical cultural studies: it frees us from the thrall of cultural encoding and suggests alternative lives practicable in the here and now, not only in the distant future to which most millennial modernists have postponed the promise of liberation.

Reading theoretically means that we ground cultural texts and practices in their overall political, economic and existential con-texts. We must refute their recommendation of lives inimical to our own real interests (which we have already vouchsafed, in terms of my analysis of true and false needs in Chapter 8). This sort of reading requires clarity about our needs, as well as a large-scale structural understanding of the social world that allows us to evaluate the concealed validity claims of cultural works pretending to represent reality faithfully. For example, a theoretical reader might focus on the discourse/practice of 'women's magazines' (e.g., *Working Woman*, *Vogue*, *Cosmopolitan*) that script womanly lives in ways supporting patriarchy. Of course, this has been a central preoccupation of a feminist cultural studies that wants to undo the subtle, self-reproducing force of patriarchal culture in which gender texts are cleverly disguised in the irrefutable imagery of wives and mommies who reproduce everyone but themselves.

It is not enough for this kind of reading to attend to the semiotic dynamics of literary and figural presentation, the sort of technical reading that so often emerges from the pen of deconstructors. Nor is it adequate for cultural theorists to theorize the possibility of this type of reading without actually getting around to doing it. Nor is it acceptable for feminist cultural theorists to do these readings in the mandarin world of academic journals and publishers without demonstrating that regular women's-magazine readers can do these readings themselves, thus crucially liberating themselves from an important discourse/practice of patriarchal society. The dehegemonizing practices advocated by Gramsci follow from a radical cultural studies that is clear about what he called its organic relationship to the masses. Cultural theorists must demonstrate the possibility of dehierarchizing readings by dehierarchizing their own relationship to readers, who are certainly ill-prepared to read Derrida. This is one of the essential requirements of public discourse.

Ultimately, cultural studies will engage in important political work by showing that it is possible to decode powerful cultural texts and practices for the hidden persuasion they really are. Cultural studies shows the way by example, never by fiat. The Birmingham group, with its roots in Gramsci, have always understood this better than the Frankfurt School as well as poststructuralists and postmodernists. Although German critical theory and new French theory are both anti-Stalinist, their cultural politics tend to take on the worst features of elitism in spite of themselves. They are unable to phenomenologize their critical activities into the lifeworld relevancies (see O'Neill, 1972) that must ground political activity. Culture does its hegemonic damage on the level of lived experience: that was Gramsci's point. It must be addressed there, no matter how stupefied late-capitalist cultural readers are; indeed, stupefaction urgently requires a lifeworld-relevant cultural studies that avoids mandarinism at every turn.

The usual complaint about the elitism of the Frankfurt School misses the point: they were elitists in order to create democracy. But Adorno, Horkheimer and Marcuse never fully understood the blockages to comprehension created by the moronizing culture industry they attacked. Thus, they have been unable to develop lifeworld-relevant strategies of cultural reading and resistance, even though Habermas (1981b) heads in the right direction where he recognizes the importance of new social movements that spring up from the ground of people's lived experience. As I said above, it is impossible to conduct a radical cultural studies outside the framework of the Frankfurt School's culture-industry thesis. At the same time, it is equally impossible to practise a radicalizing cultural studies without greater attention to the political and rhetorical problematics of a lifeworld-based cultural studies that takes its cue from the examples of non-mandarin cultural readings conducted in public vernacular. This is not to say that cultural studies must speak the argot of the day but simply that it must recognize the ironies of using the discourse of high theory in order to suggest the possibility of rhetorical and interpretive democracy.

Deconstructing the Popular

Finally, a radical cultural studies must redefine the realm of the popular in helping transform it. It must detect and help fracture the fault line between popular and mandarin cultures, thus breaking down all experiences and practices of institutional differentiation in late capitalism. Cultural studies can use the example of its own articulation with the lifeworld contingencies of citizens to suggest the possibility of all sorts of institutional dedifferentiations that subvert the hierarchical divisions of labor and culture. In particular, a non-mandarin cultural studies can establish the undecidability of the division between popular and elite cultures, at once elevating and edifying, hence politicizing, popular culture and dehierarchizing elite culture which, now as before, serves to protect elites. Here, postmodernism can do its best work, especially where it opposes all institutions as reifications.

Postmodernism shares the Weberian mistrust of bureaucratic formal organizations, as did Lukács and the original Frankfurt theorists. Most non-Marxist postmodernists lamentably agree with Weber that the 'iron cage' of bureaucracy is unavoidable in industrial-capitalist societies. Gerth and Mills (1948) describe Weber as a 'nostalgic liberal', yearning for the high-cultural values and human meanings of pre-bureaucratic society but recognizing that the goal of politics in an age of institutional gigantism is to create optimal space for the individual, notably beyond the realm of necessary labor time. This has become a hallmark of subsequent postindustrial-society theory (e.g., Blauner, 1968; Bell, 1973) as well as non-Marxist postmodernism (e.g., Lyotard, 1984). I have tried to develop a more Marxist postmodernism (Agger, 1990, 1991a, 1991b) that criticizes bureaucratic institutionalization within a historical materialism that prepares the way for the abolition of bureaucratic capitalism as well as bureaucratic socialism. As I see it, this is precisely the agenda of critical theory and should remain so.

Postmodernists go much further than Weber where they interrogate all institutional differentiations and hierarchies as essentially spurious, merely products of human construction and convention. In this context, they argue correctly that the fault line between so-called popular and mandarin culture can be deconstructed, one of the goals of a radical cultural studies squarely implanted in the lifeworld. But unlike many cultural studies people who define themselves negatively with reference to the Frankfurt School's cultural mandarinism and who thus valorize the realm of the popular, I believe that the deconstructive relationship between popular and mandarin cultures is dialectical as well as hierarchical. That is, I envisage a redemption and rectification of the popular just as I urge the democratization and dehierarchization of elite culture. These things are inseparable: it is politically irresponsible to advocate the popular at a time when popular culture is incredibly hegemonized on both the levels of lived experience and the culture industry.

I agree with non-mandarin cultural studies that we should dehierarchize mandarin culture, a goal that I have just articulated in the specific case of the phenomenologization of cultural studies itself – the point of this book. But I also recognize that elite culture protects critique and otherness, as the Frankfurt theorists have argued. Distance and difference liberate where they afford people the space to reflect critically on their own acculturation by a tentacular culture industry, what Habermas (1984, 1987b) following Parsons has called *system*. For cultural studies simply to advocate the popular subverts the real populism of a modernist cultural theory that recognizes the colonization of popular culture by elitist imperatives of control and consumption.

This is to raise real questions about the feasibility of lifeworld metaphors in critical theory (see Agger, 1991a). Although a phenomenological Marxism (e.g., Paci, 1972) usefully traces all theoretical abstractions back to their pre-theoretical constitution in lived experience, thus dereifying their postured objectivism, I disagree with Habermas, phenomenologists and feminists that there is something intrinsically validating about lifeworld experience that makes it superior to what Schutz (1967) called theoretical or expert knowledge. Phenomenology risks dehistoricizing system-lifeworld relationships, turning everyday life into a veritable garden of Eden in which people roam free unencumbered by the social contract as well as by theoretical and scientific abstractions. Although a phenomenological Marxism offers a powerful corrective to structural Marxism (see Piccone, 1971; O'Neill, 1972), the temptation to freeze the constitutionality of the so-called lifeworld is almost irresistible to people committed to populism. Although populism is a useful American signifier of democracy, there are real problems with inflating the popular into a political program without carefully addressing its own historicity in late capitalism. After all, the realm of the popular today is incredibly administered by elites who have both an economic and ideological stake in the perpetuation of false needs experienced viscerally in the malls and movie-houses in which people are taught to decode and enact the disguised texts of cultural conformity.

This is not to deny that all social change must proceed through, not around, lived experience. It is, however, to question the inviolability of the so-called lifeworld as a state of nature unsullied by structural constraints, especially in a society based on total administration. Virtually no private space goes untouched by the imperatives of control, coordination and commodification, as Marcuse (1955, 1964) demonstrated. Although there is always what he (1964) calls 'the chance of the alternatives' – why else write and resist? – he, like his first-generation Frankfurt cohorts, cautions against romanticizing populist spontan-eism in light of the extent to which both psychic and physical degrees of freedom have been whittled down almost to zero. The Frankfurt theorists are less smug mandarins than simply skeptics: they contend that can-do pragmatism almost inevitably succumbs to the disciplining imposed on virtually every human pro-ject. They deeply mistrust American entrepreneurialism, even on the left. Their Marxism has a tragic foreboding, a maturity, absent in lifeworld radicalisms that, like liberalism and postmodernism, invest the individual with self-determination far beyond what is available to most people in administered society.

In any case, Adorno, Marcuse and Horkheimer would have regarded post-structuralism and postmodernism as flattened, dehistoricized versions of their own critical theory (e.g., the Adorno-Derrida filiation has already been noted; see Ryan, 1982; Jay, 1984). They would have applauded Derrida's stress on un-decidability and difference. But they would have viewed the relativity/relativism of Derrida and Lyotard as self-contradictorily absolute, preferring instead to differentiate what Habermas calls lifeworld-system relationships. The original Frankfurt theorists mistrusted lifeworld metaphors (e.g., see Adorno's book on existentialism, *The Jargon of Authenticity* [1973a]) for exaggerating the autonomy of subjectivity. By the same token, they would have rejected the ontological suspicion of autonomy found in poststructuralism and postmodernism, wherein administration proceeds through inevitably positioning discourse/practices that block the possibility of genuine enlightenment and thus social change. Although they would have been closer to the pessimistic portrayal of positioned subjectiv-ity found in Derrida and Foucault than to the cheery individualism of phe-nomenology, they would have recognized that both theoretical stances make the common mistake of freezing subject-object relations into social fate. As historical materialists, the Frankfurt theorists recognized that history is essentially indeter-minate. (As Merleau-Ponty [1964, p. 81] wrote, 'The date of the revolution is written on no wall nor inscribed in any metaphysical heaven' – a sentiment that was shared by the Frankfurt theorists). There is no univocal subject position, lifeworld or everyday life, whether the self-determining world of liberalism or the poststructural prison-house of language. There is only history and the mul-tiple possibilities it makes available to people and groups.

In the last analysis, a radical cultural studies would make the historicity of cultural practice and experience its central watchword. As such, it would decon-structively interrogate all categorical divisions between popular and mandarin culture as problematic. Moreover, it would position itself as a cultural practice squarely in the midst of everyday life in the society of the spectacle. Although the odds are long against successful populist agitation, social change cannot bypass the popular, even as it transvalues it. Similarly, cultural studies cannot shed its own theoretical skin, pretending to be something it is not. It must teach people how to read and live theoretically, debunking the simulations bombarding them from every direction and instead seek a more stable ground of value from which to engage in dehierarchizing cultural and political practices. This is the only way in which the culture industry can be derailed and culture reconstructed. I can think of few more promising political avenues in late capitalism.

For this reason alone, the future of critical theory lies in its articulation as cultural studies with a practical intent (see Kellner, 1989a). Avoiding grandiose and empty claims, we can phrase the political agenda of this cultural studies negatively: it wants to help people avoid domination – self-defeating, self-reproducing practices that violate their own best interests. Today, most such practices are scripted in the sphere of popular culture but concealed in the dispersed discourses or simulations so devilishly difficult to read (and hence resist) as authorial acts. Critical theory authorizes these cultural works and practices as a way of contesting their secret advocacy of the quotidian.

Bibliography

ADORNO, T. (1945) 'A Social Critique of Radio Music', *Kenyon Review*, 8, pp. 208–17.

ADORNO, T. (1954) 'How to Look at Television', *Quarterly of Film, Radio and Television*, 3, pp. 213–35.

ADORNO, T. (1973a) *The Jargon of Authenticity*, Evanston, Ill., Northwestern University Press.

ADORNO, T. (1973b) *Negative Dialectics*, New York, Seabury Press.

ADORNO, T. (1973c) *Philosophy of Modern Music*, New York, Seabury Press.

ADORNO, T. (1974a) *Minima Moralia*, London, New Left Books.

ADORNO, T. (1974b) 'The Stars Down to Earth: The Los Angeles Times Astrology Column: A Study in Secondary Superstition', *Telos*, 19, pp. 13–90.

ADORNO, T. (1984) *Aesthetic Theory*, London, Routledge and Kegan Paul.

AGGER, B. (1976) 'Marcuse and Habermas on New Science', *Polity*, 9, pp. 151–81.

AGGER, B. (1979) *Western Marxism: An Introduction*, Santa Monica, Goodyear.

AGGER, B. (1989a) *Fast Capitalism: A Critical Theory of Significance*, Urbana, Ill., University of Illinois Press.

AGGER, B. (1989b) *Reading Science: A Literary, Political and Sociological Analysis*, Dix Hills, NY, General Hall.

AGGER, B. (1989c) *Socio(onto)logy: A Disciplinary Reading*, Urbana, Ill., University of Illinois Press.

AGGER, B. (1990) *The Decline of Discourse: Reading, Writing and Resistance in Postmodern Capitalism*, London/New York, Falmer Press.

AGGER, B. (1991a) *The Discourse of Domination: From the Frankfurt School to Postmodernism*, Evanston, Ill., Northwestern University Press.

AGGER, B. (1991b) *A Critical Theory of Public Life: Knowledge, Discourse and Politics in an Age of Decline*, London/New York, Falmer Press.

ALEXANDER, J. (1982) *Theoretical Logic in Sociology*, 4 vols, Berkeley, University of California Press.

ALEXANDER, J. (Ed.) (1985) *Neofunctionalism*, Beverly Hills, Sage.

ALEXANDER, J. and SEIDMAN, S. (Eds) (1990) *Culture and Society: Contemporary Debates*, New York, Cambridge University Press.

ALTHEIDE, D. (1985) *Media Power*, Beverly Hills, Sage.

ALTHEIDE, D. and SNOW, R. (1979) *Media Logic*, Beverly Hills, Sage.

ALTHUSSER, L. (1970) *For Marx*, London, Allen Lane.

ALTHUSSER, L. (1971) *Lenin and Philosophy and Other Essays*, New York, Monthly Review Press.

ALTHUSSER, L. and BALIBAR, E. (1970) *Reading Capital*, New York, Pantheon.

ARATO, A. and BREINES, P. (1979) *The Young Lukács and the Origins of Western Marxism*, New York, Seabury.

ARATO, A. and GEBHARDT, E. (Eds) (1978) *The Essential Frankfurt School Reader*, New York, Urizen.

ARONOWITZ, S. (1990) *The Crisis in Historical Materialism*, 2nd ed., Minneapolis, University of Minnesota Press.

BALSAMO, A. (1987) 'Un-Wrapping the Postmodern: A Feminist Glance', *Journal of Communication Inquiry*, 11, 1, pp. 64–72.

BALSAMO, A. (1990) 'Reading the Gender Body in Contemporary Culture, 1980–1990', manuscript.

BARTHES, R. (1975) *The Pleasure of the Text*, New York, Hill and Wang.

BATRA, R. and RAY, M.L. (1986) 'Affective Responses Mediating Acceptance of Advertising', *Journal of Consumer Research*, 13, pp. 234–49.

BAUDRILLARD, J. (1975) *The Mirror of Production*, St Louis, Telos Press.

BAUDRILLARD, J. (1981) *For a Critique of the Political Economy of the Sign*, St Louis, Telos Press.

BAUDRILLARD, J. (1983) *Simulations*, New York, Semiotext(e).

BEAUVOIR, S. DE (1953) *The Second Sex*, New York, Knopf.

BELL, D. (1960) *The End of Ideology*, Glencoe, Ill., Free Press.

BELL, D. (1973) *The Coming of Post-Industrial Society*, New York, Basic Books.

BELL, D. (1976) *The Cultural Contradictions of Capitalism*, New York, Basic Books.

BELLAH, R., MADSEN, R., SULLIVAN, W.M., SWIDLER, A. and TIPTON, S.M. (1985) *Habits of the Heart: Individualism and Commitment in American Life*, Berkeley, University of California Press.

BENJAMIN, W. (1969) *Illuminations*, New York, Schocken.

BERMAN, A. (1988) *From the New Criticism to Deconstruction: The Reception of Structuralism and Post-structuralism*, Urbana, Ill., University of Illinois Press.

BEST, S. and KELLNER, D. (1991) *Postmodern Theorizing*, London, Macmillan.

BLAUNER, R. (1968) *Alienation and Freedom*, Chicago, University of Chicago Press.

BLOCK, F. (1990) *Postindustrial Possibilities: A Critique of Economic Discourse*, Berkeley, University of California Press.

BLOOM, A. (1987) *The Closing of the American Mind*, New York, Simon and Schuster.

BOGGS, C. (1976) *Gramsci's Marxism*, London, Pluto Press.

BOURDIEU, P. (1984) *Distinction: A Social Critique of the Judgment of Taste*, Cambridge, Mass., Harvard University Press.

BOURDIEU, P. (1988) *Homo Academicus*, Oxford, Polity Press.

BRAKE, M. (1980) *The Sociology of Youth Culture and Youth Subcultures: Sex, Drugs and Rock 'n' Roll*, New York, Routledge.

BREINES, P. (1985) 'Redeeming Redemption', *Telos*, 65, pp. 152–8.

BRENKMAN, J. (1987) *Culture and Domination*, Ithaca, NY, Cornell University Press.

BRODKEY, L. (1987) *Academic Writing as Social Practice*, Philadelphia, Temple University Press.

BROWN, B. (1973) *Marx, Freud and the Critique of Everyday Life*, New York, Monthly Review Press.

BROWN, R.H. (1987) *Society as Text*, Chicago, University of Chicago Press.

BROWN, R.H. (1989) *Social Science as Civic Discourse*, Chicago, University of Chicago Press.

BROWNE, R.B. (Ed.) (1980) *Rituals and Ceremonies in Popular Culture*, Bowling Green, Ohio, Bowling Green University Press.

BROWNE, R.B. (1989) *Against Academia: The History of the Popular Culture Association, 1967–1988*, Bowling Green, Ohio, Bowling Green University Press.

BROWNE, R.B. and MADDEN, D. (1972) *The Popular Culture Explosion*, Dubuque, Iowa, William C. Brown.

BROWNMILLER, S. (1973) *Against Our Will: Men, Women and Rape*, New York, Bantam Books.

CIXOUS, H. (1986) *Inside*, New York, Schocken.

CLARKE, G. (1990) 'Defending Ski-Jumpers: A Critique of Theories of Youth Subcultures', in FRITH, S. and GOODWIN, A. (Eds) *On Record*, New York, Pantheon.

CLEAVER, H. (1979) *Reading Capital Politically*, Austin, Tex., University of Texas Press.

COHEN, P. (1972) 'Subcultural Conflict and Working Class Community', *Working Papers in Cultural Studies*, 2 (Spring), pp. 5–51.

CONNELL, R.W. (1987) *Gender and Power: Society, the Person and Sexual Politics*, Oxford, Polity Press.

CONNER, S. (1989) *Postmodernist Culture: An Introduction to Theories of the Contemporary*, New York, Basil Blackwell.

COSER, L., KADUSHIN, C. and POWELL, W. (1982) *Books: The Culture and Commerce of Publishing*, New York, Basic Books.

COWARD, R. (1982) 'Sexual Violence and Sexuality', *Feminist Review*, 11, pp. 9–22.

CULLER, J. (1982) *On Deconstruction: Theory and Criticism in the 1970s*, Ithaca, NY, Cornell University Press.

CURTIS, R. (1989) *Beyond the Bestseller: A Literary Agent Takes You Inside the Book Business*, New York, New American Library.

DALY, M. (1973) *Beyond God the Father: Toward a Philosophy of Women's Liberation*, Boston, Beacon Press.

DALY, M. (1978) *Gyn/Ecology: The Metaethics of Radical Feminism*, Boston, Beacon Press.

DANDANEAU, S. (1992) 'Post-Marxism', *Current Perspectives in Social Theory*, 12, forthcoming.

DEBORD, G. (1970) *The Society of the Spectacle*, Detroit, Black and Red Press.

DENZIN, N. (1986) 'Postmodern Social Theory', *Sociological Theory*, 4, pp. 194–204.

DENZIN, N. (1990) 'Reading Cultural Texts', *American Journal of Sociology*, 95, pp. 1577–80.

DENZIN, N. (1991) 'Empiricist Cultural Studies in America', *Current Perspectives in Social Theory*, 11, pp. 17–39.

DERRIDA, J. (1976) *Of Grammatology*, Baltimore, Johns Hopkins University Press.

DERRIDA, J. (1978) *Writing and Difference*, Chicago, University of Chicago Press.

DERRIDA, J. (1981) *Positions*, Chicago, University of Chicago Press.

DERRIDA, J. (1987) *Glas*, Lincoln, Nebr., University of Nebraska Press.

DEWS, P. (1984) 'Power and Subjectivity in Foucault', *New Left Review*, 144, pp. 72–95.

DEWS, P. (1987) *Logics of Disintegration: Post-Structuralist Thought and the Claims of Critical Theory*, London, Verso.

DiMAGGIO, P. (Ed.) (1986) *Nonprofit Enterprise in the Arts*, New York, Oxford University Press.

DUBOIS, E., KELLY, G., KENNEDY, E., KORSMEYER, C. and ROBINSON, L. (1985) *Feminist Scholarship: Kindling in the Groves of Academe*, Urbana, Ill., University of Illinois Press.

DURKHEIM, E. (1950) *The Rules of Sociological Method*, Glencoe, Ill., Free Press.

DWORKIN, A. (1974) *Woman Hating*, New York, Dutton.

DWORKIN, A. (1981) *Pornography: Men Possessing Women*, New York, Perigee Books.

DWORKIN, A. (1988) *Letters from a War Zone*, London, Secker and Warburg.

EAGLETON, T. (1976) *Criticism and Ideology*, London, New Left Books.

EAGLETON, T. (1983) *Literary Theory: An Introduction*, Minneapolis, University of Minnesota Press.

EAGLETON, T. (1984) *The Function of Criticism*, London, Verso.

EAGLETON, T. (1986) *Against the Grain*, London, Verso.

EAGLETON, T. (1990a) *The Ideology of the Aesthetic*, Cambridge, Mass., Basil Blackwell.

EAGLETON, T. (1990b) *The Significance of Theory*, Cambridge, Mass., Basil Blackwell.

ELLIS, K. (1984) 'I'm Black and Blue from the Rolling Stones and I'm not Sure How I Feel about it: Pornography and the Feminist Imagination', *Socialist Review*, 14, 2–4, pp. 103–25.

ELLUL, J. (1964) *The Technological Society*, New York, Knopf.

ELSHTAIN, J. (1984) 'The New Porn Wars', *The New Republic*, June 25, pp. 15–20.

ELSTER, J. (1989) *The Cement of Society: A Study of Social Order*, New York, Cambridge University Press.

ENGLISH, D. (1980) 'The Politics of Porn', *Mother Jones*, 5, 3, pp. 20–43.

EVANS, S. (1973) *Personal Politics: The Roots of Women's Liberation in the Civil Rights Movement and the New Left*, New York, Vintage Books.

EWEN, S. (1976) *Captains of Consciousness: Advertising and the Social Roots of the Consumer Culture*, New York, McGraw-Hill.

EWEN, S. (1988) *All Consuming Images: The Politics of Style in Contemporary Culture*, New York, Basic Books.

FAURSCHOU, G. (1987) 'Fashion and the Cultural Logic of Postmodernity', *Canadian Journal of Political and Social Theory*, 11, 1–2, pp. 68–82.

FEKETE, J. (1978) *The Critical Twilight: Explorations in the Ideology of Anglo-American Literary Theory from Eliot to McLuhan*, London, Routledge and Kegan Paul.

FELMAN, S. (1985) *Writing and Madness*, Ithaca, NY, Cornell University Press.

FELMAN, S. (1987) *Jacques Lacan and the Adventure of Insight*, Cambridge, Mass., Harvard University Press.

FISCHER, E. (1963) *The Necessity of Art: A Marxist Approach*, Harmondsworth, Penguin.

FISCHER, E. (1969) *Art Against Ideology*, London, Allen Lane.

FISH, S. (1980) *Is There a Text in this Class?: The Authority of Interpretive Communities*, Cambridge, Mass., Harvard University Press.

FISH, S. (1989) *Doing What Comes Naturally*, Durham, NC, Duke University Press.

FISKE, J. (1987) *Television Culture*, New York, Methuen.

FISKE, J. (1989a) *Reading the Popular*, Boston, Unwin Hyman.

FISKE, J. (1989b) *Understanding Popular Culture*, Boston, Unwin Hyman.

FISKE, J. (1990) *Introduction to Communication Studies*, 2nd ed., London, Routledge and Kegan Paul.

FISKE, J. and HARTLEY, J. (1978) *Reading Television*, London, Methuen.

FLAX, J. (1990) *Thinking Fragments: Psychoanalysis, Feminism and Postmodernism in the Contemporary West*, Berkeley, University of California Press.

FOUCAULT, M. (1976) *The Archaeology of Knowledge*, New York, Harper and Row.

FOUCAULT, M. (1977) *Discipline and Punish*, New York, Pantheon.

FOUCAULT, M. (1978) *The History of Sexuality*, Harmondsworth, Penguin.

FOUCAULT, M. (1980) *Power/Knowledge*, New York, Pantheon.

FRASER, N. (1989) *Unruly Practices: Power, Discourse and Gender in Contemporary Social Theory*, Minneapolis, University of Minnesota Press.

FRIEDRICHS, R. (1970) *A Sociology of Sociology*, New York, Free Press.

FRITH, S. (1983) *Sound Effects*, London, Constable.

GARFINKEL, H. (1967) *Studies in Ethnomethodology*, Englewood Cliffs, NJ, Prentice-Hall.

GELLNER, E. (1959) *Words and Things*, London, Gollancz.

GERAS, N. (1987) 'Post-Marxism?', *New Left Review*, 163, pp. 40–82.

GILLIGAN, C. (1982) *In a Different Voice*, Cambridge, Mass., Harvard University Press.

GITLIN, T. (1980) *The Whole World is Watching: Mass Media in the Making and Unmaking of the New Left*, Berkeley, University of California Press.

GITLIN, T. (1987) *The Sixties: Years of Hope, Days of Rage*, New York, Bantam Books.

GITLIN, T. (1988) 'Hip-Deep in Postmodernism', *The New York Times Book Review*, November 6, pp. 1, 35–6.

GOLDMAN, R. and PAPSON, S. (1991) 'Levi's and the Knowing Wink', *Current Perspectives in Social Theory*, 11, pp. 69–95.

GOLDMANN, L. (1964) *The Hidden God: A Study of the Tragic Vision in the Pensees of Pascal and the Tragedies of Racine*, New York, Humanities Press.

GOLDMANN, L. (1972) *Racine*, Cambridge, Rivers Press.

GOLDMANN, L. (1975) *Towards a Sociology of the Novel*, London, Tavistock Press.

GOLDMANN, L. (1976) *Cultural Creation in Modern Society*, St Louis, Telos Press.

GOLDMANN, L. (1981) *Method in the Sociology of Literature*, Oxford, Basil Blackwell.

GOTTDIENER, M. (1991) 'Space, Social Theory and the Urban Metaphor', *Current Perspectives in Social Theory*, 11, pp. 295–311.

GOULDNER, A. (1970) *The Coming Crisis of Western Sociology*, New York, Basic Books.

GRAMSCI, A. (1971) *Selections from the Prison Notebooks*, London, Lawrence and Wishart.

GREENBLATT, S. (1980) *Renaissance Self-Fashioning: From More to Shakespeare*, Chicago, University of Chicago Press.

GREENBLATT, S. (Ed.) (1981) *Allegory and Representation*, Baltimore, Johns Hopkins University Press.

GREENBLATT, S. (Ed.) (1982) *The Power of Forms in the English Renaissance*, Norman, Ohio, Pilgrim Books.

GREENBLATT, S. (1990) *Learning to Curse: Essays in Early Modern Culture*, New York, Routledge.

GREER, G. (1971) *The Female Eunuch*, New York, McGraw-Hill.

GRISWOLD, W. (1986) *Renaissance Revivals: City Comedy and Revenge Tragedy in the London Theatre*, Chicago, University of Chicago Press.

GROSSBERG, L. (1986) 'Teaching the Popular', in NELSON, C. (Ed.) *Theory in the Classroom*, Urbana, Ill., University of Illinois Press.

HABERMAS, J. (1970) 'Technology and Science as "Ideology"', in HABERMAS, J. *Toward a Rational Society*, Boston, Beacon Press.

HABERMAS, J. (1971) *Knowledge and Human Interests*, Boston, Beacon Press.

HABERMAS, J. (1975) *Legitimation Crisis*, Boston, Beacon Press.

HABERMAS, J. (1979) *Communication and the Evolution of Society*, Boston, Beacon Press.

HABERMAS, J. (1981a) 'Modernity versus Postmodernity', *New German Critique*, 22, pp. 3–14.

HABERMAS, J. (1981b) 'New Social Movements', *Telos*, 49, pp. 33–7.

HABERMAS, J. (1984) *The Theory of Communicative Action*, Vol. 1, Boston, Beacon Press.

HABERMAS, J. (1987a) *The Philosophical Discourse of Modernity*, Cambridge, Mass., MIT Press.

HABERMAS, J. (1987b) *The Theory of Communicative Action*, Vol. 2, Boston, Beacon Press.

HALL, S. (1978) *Policing the Crisis: Muggery, the State and Law and Order*, London, Macmillan.

HALL, S. (Ed.) (1980a) *Culture, Media and Language: Working Papers in Cultural Studies, 1972–1979*, London, Hutchinson.

HALL, S. (1980b) 'Cultural Studies: Two Paradigms', *Media, Culture and Society*, 2, pp. 57–72.

HALL, S. (1982) 'The Rediscovery of 'Ideology': Return of the Repressed in Media

Studies', in GUREVITCH, M., BENNETT, T., CURRAN, J. and WOOLACOTT, J. (Eds) *Culture, Society and the Media*, London, Methuen.

HALL, S. (1985) 'Signification, Representation, Ideology: Althusser and the Post-Structuralist Debates', *Critical Studies in Mass Communication*, 2, 2, pp. 91–114.

HALL, S. (1986) 'On Postmodernism and Articulation', *Journal of Communication Inquiry*, Summer, pp. 45–60.

HALL, S. (1988) *The Hard Road to Renewal: Thatcherism and the Crisis of the Left*, London, Verso.

HALL, S. and JACQUES, M. (Eds) (1989) *New Times: The Shape of Politics in the 1990s*, London, Lawrence and Wishart.

HALL, S. and JEFFERSON, T. (1976) *Resistance Through Rituals: Youth Subcultures in Post-War Britain*, London, Hutchinson.

HALL, S. and WHANNEL, P. (Eds) (1965) *The Popular Arts*, New York, Pantheon.

HALLIN, D. (1985) 'The American News Media: A Critical Theory Perspective', in FORESTER, J. (Ed.) *Critical Theory and Public Life*, Cambridge, Mass., MIT Press.

HARDING, S. (1986) *The Science Question in Feminism*, Ithaca, NY, Cornell University Press.

HARMS, J. and KELLNER, D. (1991) 'Critical Theory and Advertising', *Current Perspectives in Social Theory*, 11, pp. 41–67.

HARVEY, D. (1989) *The Condition of Postmodernity*, Oxford, Basil Blackwell.

HASSAN, I. (1987) *The Postmodern Turn: Essays in Postmodern Theory and Culture*, Columbus, Ohio, Ohio State University Press.

HAUSER, A. (1982) *The Sociology of Art*, London, Routledge and Kegan Paul.

HAWKINS, R.P., YOUNG-HO, K. and PINGREE, S. (1991) 'The Ups and Downs of Attention to Television', *Communication Research*, 18, 1, pp. 53–76.

HEBDIGE, D. (1979) *Subculture: The Meaning of Style*, London, Methuen.

HEBDIGE, D. (1988) *Hiding in the Light: On Images and Things*, New York, Routledge.

HELD, D. (1980) *Introduction to Critical Theory*, Berkeley, University of California Press.

HEGEL, G.W.F. (1966) 'Preface to *Phenomenology of Mind*', in KAUFMAN, W. (Ed.) *Hegel: Texts and Commentary*, Garden City, NY, Anchor Books.

HIRSCH, E.D. (1987) *Cultural Literacy*, Boston, Houghton Mifflin.

HOFFER, E. (1966) *The True Believer: Thoughts on the Nature of Mass Movements*, New York, Harper and Row.

HOGGART, R. (1957) *The Uses of Literacy*, London, Chatto and Windus.

HOPPENSTAND, G. and BROWNE, R. (Eds) (1987) *The Gothic World of Stephen King: Landscape of Nightmares*, Bowling Green, Ohio, Bowling Green University Press.

HORKHEIMER, M. (1972) 'Traditional and Critical Theory' in HORKHEIMER, M. *Critical Theory*, New York, Herder and Herder.

HORKHEIMER, M. (1973) 'The Authoritarian State', *Telos*, 15, pp. 3–20.

HORKHEIMER, M. and ADORNO, T.W. (1972) *Dialectic of Enlightenment*, New York, Herder and Herder.

HUSSERL, E. (1977) *Cartesian Meditations: An Introduction to Phenomenology*, The Hague, Martinus Nijhoff.

HUYSSEN, A. (1986) *After the Great Divide: Modernism, Mass Culture, Postmodernism*, Bloomington, Ind., Indiana University Press.

HYMES, D. (1974) *Foundations in Sociolinguistics: An Ethnographic Approach*, Philadelphia, University of Pennsylvania Press.

INGLIS, F. (1990) *Media Theory: An Introduction*, Oxford, Basil Blackwell.

IRIGARAY, L. (1985) *This Sex Which is Not One*, Ithaca, NY, Cornell University Press.

ISER, W. (1978) *The Act of Reading: A Theory of Aesthetic Response*, Baltimore, Johns Hopkins University Press.

JACOBY, R. (1975) *Social Amnesia*, Boston, Beacon Press.

JACOBY, R. (1981) *Dialectic of Defeat: Contours of Western Marxism*, New York, Cambridge University Press.

JACOBY, R. (1987) *The Last Intellectuals: American Culture in the Age of Academe*, New York, Basic Books.

JAMESON, F. (1972) *The Prison-House of Language*, Princeton, Princeton University Press.

JAMESON, F. (1976–1977) 'Ideology of the Text', *Salmagundi*, 31, pp. 204–46.

JAMESON, F. (1981) *The Political Unconscious: Narrative as a Socially Symbolic Act*, Ithaca, NY, Cornell University Press.

JAMESON, F. (1984a) 'The Politics of Theory: Ideological Positions in the Postmodernism Debate', *New German Critique*, 33, pp. 53–65.

JAMESON, F. (1984b) 'Postmodernism, or the Cultural Logic of Late Capitalism', *New Left Review*, 146, pp. 53–93.

JAMESON, F. (1988) 'Cognitive Mapping', in NELSON, C. and GROSSBERG, L. (Eds) *Marxism and the Interpretation of Culture*, Urbana, Ill., University of Illinois Press.

JAMESON, F. (1991) *Postmodernism, or the Cultural Logic of Late Capitalism*, Durham, NC, Duke University Press.

JAY, M. (1973) *The Dialectical Imagination*, Boston, Little, Brown.

JAY, M. (1984) *Adorno*, Cambridge, Mass., Harvard University Press.

JENCKS, C. (1987) *Post-Modernism: The New Classicism in Art and Architecture*, New York, Rizzoli.

JOHNSON, R. (1986–1987) 'What is Cultural Studies Anyway?', *Social Text*, 12, pp. 38–79.

KEANE, J. (1984) *Public Life and Late Capitalism*, New York, Cambridge University Press.

KELLER, E.F. (1985) *Reflections on Gender and Science*, New Haven, Yale University Press.

KELLNER, D. (1984) *Herbert Marcuse and the Crisis of Marxism*, Berkeley, University of California Press.

KELLNER, D. (1989a) *Critical Theory, Marxism and Modernity*, Cambridge, Polity Press.

KELLNER, D. (1989b) *Jean Baudrillard: From Marxism to Postmodernism and Beyond*, Stanford, Stanford University Press.

KELLNER, D. (1990) *Television and the Crisis of Democracy*, Boulder, Colo., Westview.

KIMBALL, R. (1990) *Tenured Radicals: How Politics Has Corrupted our Higher Education*, New York, Harper-Collins.

KLEIN, J. (1990) *Interdisciplinarity: History, Theory and Practice*, Detroit, Wayne State University Press.

KLINKOWITZ, J. (1988) *Rosenberg/Barthes/Hassan: The Postmodern Habit of Thought*, Athens, Ga., University of Georgia Press.

KNORR-CETINA, K. (1981) *The Manufacture of Knowledge: An Essay on the Constructivist and Contextual Nature of Science*, New York, Pergamon.

KOLODNY, A. (1975) 'Some Notes on Defining a "Feminist Literary Criticism"', *Critical Inquiry*, 2, pp. 75–92.

KOLODNY, A. (1980) 'Dancing through the Minefields: Some Observations on the Theory, Practice and Politics of a Feminist Literary Criticism', *Feminist Studies*, 6, 1, pp. 1–25.

KOLODNY, A. (1984) *The Land Before Her: Fantasy and Experience of the American Frontiers, 1630–1860*, Chapel Hill, NC, University of North Carolina Press.

KRAMER, H. (1985) *The Revenge of the Philistines*, New York, Free Press.

KRISTEVA, J. (1980) *Desire in Language*, New York, Columbia University Press.

KROKER, A. and COOK, D. (1986) *The Postmodern Scene*, New York, St Martin's.

KUHN, A. (1982) *Women's Pictures: Feminism and Cinema*, London, Routledge and Kegan Paul.

LACAN, J. (1977) *Écrits: A Selection*, New York, Norton.

LACLAU, E. and MOUFFE, C. (1985) *Hegemony and Socialist Strategy*, London, Verso.

LACLAU, E. and MOUFFE, C. (1987) 'Post-Marxism without Apologies', *New Left Review*, 166, pp. 79–104.

LACOMBE, D. (1988) *Ideology and Public Policy: The Case Against Pornography*, Toronto, Garamond Press.

LAD PANEK, L. (1990) *Probable Cause: Crime Fiction in America*, Bowling Green, Ohio, Bowling Green University Press.

LADD, E. and LIPSET, S.M. (1975) *The Divided Academy: Professors and Politics*, New York, McGraw-Hill.

LAMONT, M. (1987) 'How to become a Dominant French Philosopher: The Case of Jacques Derrida', *American Journal of Sociology*, 93, pp. 584–622.

LAMONT, M. and LARREAU, A. (1988) 'Cultural Capital: Allusions, Gaps and Glissandos in Recent Theoretical Developments', *Sociological Theory*, 6, 2, pp. 153–68.

LASCH, C. (1979) *The Culture of Narcissism*, New York, Norton.

LASCH, C. (1984) *The Minimal Self*, New York, Norton.

LAURETIS, T. DE (1984) *Alice Doesn't: Feminism, Semiotics, Cinema*, Bloomington, Indiana University Press.

LAURETIS, T. DE (1987) *Technologies of Gender: Essays on Theory, Film and Fiction*, Bloomington, Indiana University Press.

LEDERER, L. (1980) *Take Back the Night: Women on Pornography*, New York, Morrow.

LEFEBVRE, H. (1971) *Everyday Life in the Modern World*, New York, Harper and Row.

LEISS, W. (1976) *The Limits to Satisfaction: An Essay on the Problem of Needs and Commodities*, Toronto, University of Toronto Press.

LEISS, W., KLINE, S. and JHALLY, S. (1986) *Social Communication in Advertising: Persons, Products and Images of Well-Being*, Toronto, Methuen.

LEMERT, C. (1979) *Sociology and the Twilight of Man*, Carbondale, Ill., Southern Illinois University Press.

LENTRICCHIA, F. (1980) *After the New Criticism*, Chicago, University of Chicago Press.

LEONG, W-T. (1991) 'The Pornography "Problem": Disciplining Women and Young Girls', *Media, Culture and Society*, forthcoming.

LEONG, W-T. (1992) 'Cultural Resistance: Cultural Agents or Cultural Terrorists?', *Current Perspectives in Social Theory*, 12, forthcoming.

LEVI-STRAUSS, C. (1963) *Totemism*, Boston, Beacon Press.

LEVI-STRAUSS, C. (1966) *The Savage Mind*, Chicago, University of Chicago Press.

LEVINE, L.W. (1988) *Highbrow/Lowbrow: The Emergence of Cultural Hierarchy in America*, Cambridge, Mass., Harvard University Press.

LICHTHEIM, G. (1961) *Marxism: An Historical and Critical Study*, London, RKP.

LINTON, R. (1936) *The Study of Man: An Introduction*, New York, Appleton-Century.

LODGE, D. (1982) *Souls and Bodies*, New York, Morrow.

LODGE, D. (1984) *Small World: An Academic Romance*, London, Secker and Warburg.

LOUKIDES, P. and FULLER, L.K. (1990) *Beyond the Stars: Stock Characters in American Popular Culture*, Bowling Green, Ohio, Bowling Green University Press.

LOWENTHAL, L. (1961) *Literature, Popular Culture and Society*, Englewood Cliffs, NJ, Prentice-Hall.

LOWENTHAL, L. (1975) *Notizen zur Literatursoziologie*, Stuttgart, Enke.

LOWENTHAL, L. (1984) *Communication in Society*, New Brunswick, NJ, Transaction.

LOWENTHAL, L. (1986) *Literature and the Image of Man*, New Brunswick, NJ, Transaction.

LUKÁCS, G. (1962) *The Historical Novel*, London, Merlin.

LUKÁCS, G. (1963) *The Meaning of Contemporary Realism*, London, Merlin.

LUKÁCS, G. (1964) *Essays on Thomas Mann*, London, Merlin.

LUKÁCS, G. (1971) *History and Class Consciousness*, London, Merlin.

LUKÁCS, G. (1974) *Soul and Form*, Cambridge, Mass., MIT Press.

LUKÁCS, G. (1980) *Essays on Realism*, London, Lawrence and Wishart.

LUKE, T. (1989) *Screens of Power: Ideology, Domination and Resistance in the Informational Society*, Urbana, Ill., University of Illinois Press.

LUKE, T. (1991) *Shows of Force: Aesthetic Texts in Political Contexts*, Durham, NC, Duke University Press.

LYOTARD, J-F. (1984) *The Postmodern Condition: A Report on Knowledge*, Minneapolis, University of Minnesota Press.

MacINTYRE, A. (1970) *Herbert Marcuse: An Exposition and a Polemic*, New York, Viking Press.

MacKINNON, C. (1979) *Sexual Harassment of Working Women*, New Haven, Yale University Press.

MacKINNON, C. (1984) 'Not a Moral Issue', *Yale Law and Policy Review*, 20, 2, pp. 321–45.

MacKINNON, C. (1987) *Feminism Unmodified: Discourses on Life and Law*, Cambridge, Mass., Harvard University Press.

MacKINNON, C. (1989) *Toward a Feminist Theory of the State*, Cambridge, Mass., Harvard University Press.

MACPHERSON, C.B. (1962) *The Political Theory of Possessive Individualism*, Oxford, The Clarendon Press.

MAN, P. DE (1979) *Allegories of Reading: Figural Language in Rousseau, Nietzsche, Rilke and Proust*, New Haven, Yale University Press.

MAN, P. DE (1984) *The Rhetoric of Romanticism*, New York, Columbia University Press.

MAN, P. DE (1986) *The Resistance to Theory*, Minneapolis, University of Minnesota Press.

MANDEL, E. (1975) *Late Capitalism*, London, NLB.

MANION, E. (1985) 'We Objects Object: Pornography and the Women's Movement', *Canadian Journal of Political and Social Theory*, 9, 1–2, pp. 65–80.

MARCUS, G. (1988) *The Predicament of Culture: Twentieth-Century Ethnography, Literature and Art*, Cambridge, Mass., Harvard University Press.

MARCUS, G. and FISCHER, M. (Eds) (1986) *Anthropology as Cultural Critique: An Experimental Moment in the Human Sciences*, Chicago, University of Chicago Press.

MARCUSE, H. (1955) *Eros and Civilization*, Boston, Beacon Press.

MARCUSE, H. (1964) *One-Dimensional Man*, Boston, Beacon Press.

MARCUSE, H. (1968) *Negations*, Boston, Beacon Press.

MARCUSE, H. (1969) *An Essay on Liberation*, Boston, Beacon Press.

MARCUSE, H. (1972) *Counterrevolution and Revolt*, Boston, Beacon Press.

MARCUSE, H. (1978) *The Aesthetic Dimension*, Boston, Beacon Press.

MARCUSE, H., WOLFF, R.P., MOORE JR., B. (1965) *A Critique of Pure Tolerance*, Boston, Beacon Press.

MARX, K. (1961) *Economic and Philosophic Manuscripts of 1844*, Moscow, Foreign Languages Publishing House.

MARX, K. (1977) *Capital: A Critique of Political Economy*, New York, Vintage.

MARX, K. and ENGELS, F. (1947) *The German Ideology*, New York, International Publishers.

McCABE, C. (Ed.) (1986) *High Theory/Low Culture: Studying Popular Television and Film*, New York, St Martin's.

McCLOSKEY, D. (1985) *The Rhetoric of Economics*, Madison, University of Wisconsin Press.

McLUHAN, M. (1967) *The Medium is the Message*, Harmondsworth, Penguin.

McLUHAN, M. (1968) *The Gutenberg Galaxy*, Toronto, University of Toronto Press.

McLUHAN, M. (1989) *The Global Village*, New York, Oxford University Press.

McRobbie, A. (1981) 'Settling Accounts with Subcultures: A Feminist Critique', in Bennett, T. *et al.* (Eds) *Culture, Ideology and Social Process*, London, Batsford, pp. 111–124.

Mehan, H. and Wood, H. (1975) *The Reality of Ethnomethodology*, New York, Wiley.

Merleau-Ponty, M. (1964) *Sense and Non-Sense*, Evanston, Ill., Northwestern University Press.

Miller, M. (1988) *Boxed In: The Culture of TV*, Evanston, Ill., Northwestern University Press.

Millett, K. (1970) *Sexual Politics*, New York, Doubleday.

Mills, C.W. (1959) *The Power Elite*, New York, Oxford University Press.

Moi, T. (1988) *Sexual/Textual Politics: Feminist Literary Theory*, New York, Routledge.

Morgan, R. (1980) 'Theory and Practice: Pornography and Rape', in Lederer, L. (Ed.) *Take Back the Night: Women on Pornography*, New York, Morrow.

Morrow, R. (1991) 'Critical Theory, Gramsci and Cultural Studies: From Structuralism to Poststructuralism', in Wexler, P. (Ed.) *Critical Theory Now*, London/New York, Falmer Press.

Mulvey, L. (1988) *Visual and Other Pleasures*, Basingstoke, Macmillan.

Murdock, G. and McCron, R. (1976) 'Youth and Class: The Career of a Confusion', in Mungham, G. and Pearson, G. (Eds) *Working Class Youth Culture*, London, RKP, pp. 10–26.

Myers, D. (1990) 'Chris Crawford and Computer Game Aesthetics', *Journal of Popular Culture*, 24, 2, pp. 17–32.

Nelson, C. and Grossberg, C. (Eds) (1988) *Marxism and the Interpretation of Culture*, Urbana, Ill., University of Illinois Press.

Newman, C. (1985) *The Post-Modern Aura: The Act of Fiction in an Age of Inflation*, Evanston, Ill., Northwestern University Press.

Nietzsche, F. (1956) *The Birth of Tragedy and the Genealogy of Morals*, Garden City, NY, Doubleday.

Oakeshott, M. (1962) *Rationalism in Politics*, New York, Basic Books.

O'Neill, J. (1972) *Sociology as a Skin Trade*, New York, Harper and Row.

O'Neill, J. (1974) *Making Sense Together: An Introduction to Wild Sociology*, New York, Harper and Row.

O'Neill, J. (1986) 'The Disciplinary Society: From Weber to Foucault', *British Journal of Sociology*, 37, pp. 42–60.

O'Neill, J. (1989) *The Communicative Body*, Evanston, Ill., Northwestern University Press.

Orman, J. (1984) *The Politics of Rock Music*, Chicago, Nelson Hall.

Paci, E. (1972) *The Function of the Sciences and the Meaning of Man*, Evanston, Ill., Northwestern University Press.

Parsons, T. (1951) *The Social System*, Glencoe, Ill., Free Press.

Parsons, T. and Bales, R. (1955) *Family, Socialization and Interaction Process*, Glencoe, Ill., Free Press.

Piccone, P. (1971) 'Phenomenological Marxism', *Telos*, 9, pp. 3–31.

Piccone, P. (1983) *Italian Marxism*, Berkeley, University of California Press.

Portoghesi, P. (1983) *Postmodern, the Architecture of the Postindustrial Society*, New York, Rizzoli.

Poster, M. (1975) *Existential Marxism in Postwar France*, Princeton, Princeton University Press.

Poster, M. (1989) *Critical Theory and Poststructuralism*, Ithaca, NY, Cornell University Press.

Poster, M. (1990) *The Mode of Information: Poststructuralism and Social Context*, Oxford, Polity Press.

RACHLIN, A. (1988) *News as Hegemonic Reality*, New York, Praeger.

RADWAY, J. (1984) *Reading the Romance: Women, Patriarchy and Popular Literature*, Chapel Hill, NC, University of North Carolina Press.

RANSOM, J.C. (1941) *The New Criticism*, Norfolk, Conn., New Directions.

RAULET, G. (1984) 'From Modernity as a One-Way Street to Postmodernity as a Dead End', *New German Critique*, 30, pp. 155–77.

RICHARDSON, L. (1988) 'The Collective Story: Postmodernism and the Writing of Sociology', *Sociological Focus*, 21, pp. 199–208.

RICHARDSON, L. (1990a) 'Narrative and Sociology', *Journal of Contemporary Ethnography*, 19, pp. 116–35.

RICHARDSON, L. (1990b) 'Speakers Whose Voices Matter: Toward a Feminist Postmodernist Sociological Praxis', *Studies in Symbolic Interactionism*, in press.

RICHARDSON, L. (1990c) *Writing Strategies: Reaching Diverse Audiences*, Newbury Park, Cal., Sage.

RICHARDSON, L. (1991) 'Value Constituting Practices, Rhetoric and Metaphor in Sociology: A Reflexive Analysis', *Current Perspectives in Social Theory*, 11, pp. 1–15.

ROEMER, J. (Ed.) (1986) *Analytical Marxism*, New York, Cambridge University Press.

ROEMER, J. and HYLLAND, A. (Eds) (1986) *Foundations of Social Choice Theory*, New York, Cambridge University Press.

ROMAN, L. and CHRISTIAN-SMITH, L. (1988) *Becoming Feminine: The Politics of Popular Culture*, London/New York, Falmer Press.

RORTY, R. (1979) *Philosophy and the Mirror of Nature*, Princeton, Princeton University Press.

RORTY, R. (1989) *Critique, Irony and Solidarity*, New York, Cambridge University Press.

ROSENAU, P. (1992) *Postmodernism and Poststructuralism in the Social Sciences*, Princeton, Princeton University Press.

ROSS, A. (Ed.) (1988) *Universal Abandon?: The Politics of Postmodernism*, Minneapolis, University of Minnesota Press.

ROSS, A. (1989) *No Respect: Intellectuals and Popular Culture*, New York, Routledge.

RYAN, M. (1982) *Marxism and Deconstruction*, Baltimore, Johns Hopkins University Press.

RYAN, M. (1989) *Politics and Culture*, Basingstoke, Macmillan.

RYAN, M. and KELLNER, D. (1988) *Camera Politica: The Politics and Ideology of Contemporary Hollywood Film*, Bloomington, IN, Indiana University Press.

SARTRE, J.-P. (1965) *What is Literature?*, New York, Harper and Row.

SARTRE, J.-P. (1976) *Critique of Dialectical Reason*, London, New Left Books.

SARTRE, J.-P. (1981) *The Family Idiot: Gustave Flaubert 1821–1857*, Chicago, University of Chicago Press.

SCHILLER, D. (1981) *Objectivity and the News*, Philadelphia, University of Pennsylvania Press.

SCHILLER, H. (1989) *Culture, Inc.: The Corporate Takeover of Public Expression*, New York, Oxford University Press.

SCHORSKE, C. (1981) *Fin-de-Siècle Vienna: Politics and Culture*, New York, Vintage Press.

SCHUTZ, A. (1967) *The Phenomenology of the Social World*, Evanston, Ill., Northwestern University Press.

SHELTON, B.A. and AGGER, B. (1991) 'Shotgun Wedding, Unhappy Marriage, No-Fault Divorce?: Rethinking the Feminism-Marxism Relationship', in ENGLAND, P. (Ed.) *Sociology on Gender/Feminism on Theory*, Boston, Aldine.

SHIACH, M. (1991) *Discourse on Popular Culture: Class, Gender and History in Cultural Analysis, 1730 to the Present*, Stanford, Stanford University Press.

SILVERMAN, K. (1983) *The Subject of Semiotics*, New York, Oxford University Press.

SILVERMAN, K. (1988) *The Acoustic Mirror: The Female Voice in Psychoanalysis and Cinema*, Bloomington, Ind., Indiana University Press.

SKINNER, R.E. (1989) *Two Guns from Harlem: The Detective Fiction of Chester Himes*, Bowling Green, Ohio, Bowling Green University Press.

SLATER, P. (1977) *Origin and Significance of the Frankfurt School*, London, Routledge and Kegan Paul.

SMART, B. (1983) *Foucault, Marxism and Critique*, London, Routledge and Kegan Paul.

SMITH, D. (1987) *The Everyday World as Problematic: A Feminist Sociology*, Boston, Northeastern University Press.

SMITH, D. (1990a) *The Conceptual Practices of Power: A Feminist Sociology of Knowledge*, Boston, Northeastern University Press.

SMITH, D. (1990b) *Texts, Facts and Femininity: Exploring the Relations of Ruling*, New York, Routledge.

SOBLE, A. (1986) *Pornography: Marxism, Feminism and the Future of Sexuality*, New Haven, Yale University Press.

SOJA, E. (1989) *Postmodern Geographies: The Reassertion of Space in Critical Social Theory*, London, Verso.

SOOTHILL, K. and WALBY, S. (1991) *Sex Crimes in the News*, New York, Routledge.

STEINEM, G. (1978) 'Erotica and Pornography: A Clear and Present Difference', *Ms*, 7, 5, pp. 53–76.

STEINEM, G. (1986) *Outrageous Acts and Everyday Rebellions*, New York, New American Library.

STERN, L. (1979–1980) 'Feminism and Cinema: Exchanges', *Screen*, 20, 3/4, pp. 89–90.

THOMPSON, E.P. (1963) *The Making of the English Working Class*, New York, Vintage.

THOMPSON, E.P. (1978) *The Poverty of Theory and other Essays*, New York, Monthly Review Press.

THORNTON, N. (1986) 'The Politics of Pornography: A Critique of Liberalism and Radical Feminism', *Australian and New Zealand Journal of Sociology*, 22, 1, pp. 25–45.

TORRES, S. (1989) 'Melodrama, Masculinity and Family: *thirtysomething*', *Camera Obscura*, 19, p. 87.

TOURAINE, A. (1971) *The Post-Industrial Society*, New York, Random House.

TURLEY, D. (1987) 'The Feminist Debate on Pornography: An Unorthodox Interpretation', *Socialist Review*, 87/88, pp. 81–96.

WALBY, S. (1990) *Theorizing Patriarchy*, Oxford, Basil Blackwell.

WALTERS, S. (1992) 'Material Girls: Toward a Feminist Cultural Studies', *Current Perspectives in Social Theory*, 12, forthcoming.

WARREN, M. (1988) *Nietzsche and Political Thought*, Cambridge, Mass., MIT Press.

WEEDON, C. (1987) *Feminist Practice and Poststructuralist Theory*, Oxford, Basil Blackwell.

WELLS, A. (1990) 'Popular Music: Emotional Use and Management', *Journal of Popular Culture*, 24, 1, pp. 105–17.

WERNICK, A. (1983) 'Advertising and Ideology: An Interpretive Framework', *Theory, Culture and Society*, 2, pp. 16–33.

WEST, C. and ZIMMERMAN, D.H. (1987) 'Doing Gender', *Gender and Society*, 1, 2, pp. 125–51.

WILLIAMS, R. (1950) *Reading and Criticism*, London, Muller.

WILLIAMS, R. (1958) *Culture and Society*, New York, Columbia University Press.

WILLIAMS, R. (1961) *The Long Revolution*, New York, Columbia University Press.

WILLIAMS, R. (1966) *Communications*, London, Chatto and Windus.

WILLIAMS, R. (1975) *Television: Technology and Cultural Form*, New York, Schocken.

WILLIAMS, R. (1977) *Marxism and Literature*, Oxford, Oxford University Press.

WILLIAMS, R. (1980) *Problems in Materialism and Culture*, London, Verso.

WILLIAMS, R. (1981) *Culture*, Cambridge, Fontana.

WILLIAMS, R. (1983) *Writing in Society*, London, Verso.

WILLIAMS, R. (1989) *Resources of Hope: Culture, Democracy, Socialism*, London, Verso.

WILLIAMSON, J. (1978) *Decoding Advertisements*, London, Boyars.

WILLIS, P. (1977) *Learning to Labour*, Farnborough, Saxon House.

WILLIS, P. (1978) *Profane Culture*, London, RKP.

WITHEFORD, N. and GRUNEAU, R. (forthcoming) 'Between the Politics of Production and the Politics of the Sign: Post-Marxism, Hegemony Theory and "New Times"'.

WITTGENSTEIN, L. (1953) *Philosophical Investigations*, Oxford, Basil Blackwell.

WRIGHT, E.O. (1985) *Classes*, London, Verso.

WRIGHT, J.W. III, (1990) 'Deregulation and Public Perceptions of Television: A Longitudinal Study', *Communication Studies*, 41, 3, pp. 266–77.

WUTHNOW, R. (1976) *The Consciousness Reformation*, Berkeley, University of California Press.

WUTHNOW, R. (1987) *Meaning and Moral Order: Explorations in Cultural Analysis*, Berkeley, University of California Press.

WUTHNOW, R. (1989) *Communities of Discourse*, Cambridge, Mass., Harvard University Press.

WUTHNOW, R., HUNTER, J.D., BERGESEN, A. and KURZWEIL, E. (1984) *Cultural Analysis: The Work of Peter L. Berger, Mary Douglas, Michel Foucault and Jurgen Habermas*, London, Routledge and Kegan Paul.

ZARET, D. (1992) 'Critical Theory and the Sociology of Culture', *Current Perspectives in Social Theory*, 12, forthcoming.

Index